PENGUIN BOOKS

CHANGING MY MIND

Zadie Smith is the author of the novels *White Teeth*, *The Autograph Man*, *On Beauty*, *NW*, and *Swing Time*, as well as a novella, *The Embassy of Cambodia*, three collections of essays, *Intimations*, *Changing My Mind*, and *Feel Free*, and a short story collection, *Grand Union*. She is currently a tenured professor of fiction at New York University and a member of the American Academy of Arts and Letters. She is a regular contributor to *The Guardian*, *The New Yorker*, and *The New York Review of Books*.

Praise for *Changing My Mind*

Time magazine's Top 10 Nonfiction 2009
Publishers Weekly Best Books of 2009
Los Angeles Times Best Books of 2009

"It doesn't seem to matter what she's writing about—Kafka, her father, Liberia, George Clooney. Just placing anything within the magnetic field of her restlessly intelligent brain is enough to make it fascinating. Smith (*White Teeth*) has the gift—the late David Foster Wallace, who haunts her book's pages, had it too—of showing you how she reads and thinks; watching her do it makes you feel smarter and more observant just by osmosis. Her account of her struggles as an author ('That Crafty Feeling') may be the most authentic, unglamorous description of novel writing ever put on paper." —*Time*

"Taken together, [these essays] reflect a lively, unself-conscious, rigorous, erudite, and earnestly open mind that's busy refining its view of life, literature, and a great deal in between. . . . Smith shows herself in more ways than one to be a very old, empathetic head on ridiculously young shoulders. . . . It's in her impassioned, compulsively dialectical and endearingly wonkish inquiry into literature that Smith really takes off." —Ella Taylor, *Los Angeles Times*

"Smith writes with a beguiling mix of assurance and solemnity, borrowing her vocabulary from many intellectual and cultural sources. . . . Smith's native intelligence, however, seems so formidable that you can't help hoping she'll change her mind yet again."

New York Times Book Review

"*Changing My Mind* is the best thing yet from this still young writer with so much promise."   —Mike Fischer, *Milwaukee Journal Sentinel*

"Possessed of both imaginative empathy and an astringent wit, rigorously non-judgmental yet armed with a state-of-the-art bullshit detector, Zadie Smith's nonfiction glimmers with the same cultural and emotional acuity that illuminated her novels *White Teeth* and *On Beauty*. In *Changing My Mind*, a collection of criticism, essays, and reviews for outlets such as *The New Yorker* and the U.K.'s *Guardian*, her instincts are expansive, inclusive, democratic, yet fiercely personal. . . . Idea by idea and sentence by sentence, *Changing My Mind* is a dazzling endorsement of reading as play, in both the theatrical and recreational senses of the word."   —Jessica Winter, *TimeOut New York*

"With *Changing My Mind*, Smith has given the art of the essay its most interesting and educational revival in years."   —Michael Lee, *BookPage*

"[W]armly insightful pieces that tease apart knotty strands of human experience . . . She has an uncanny eye for detail, on the streets of Liberia or at an Oscar gala in Los Angeles."   —O, *The Oprah Magazine*

"A wonderful essay collection for those who have read everything from Zora Neale Hurston to Vladimir Nabokov. Zadie Smith's essays contain stimulating and cranky observations about writing, politics, high culture, pop culture, and even Katharine Hepburn."   —St. *Louis Post-Dispatch*

"As the title implies, Smith's thinking evolves before our eyes as she articulates her responses to art and life. . . . Smith is a superb essayist of skill, candor, and caring."   —Donna Seman, *Booklist*

"The best of these essays are as concerned with the essence of reading well as writing well. And they are written so incisively, and with so much empathy and warmhearted humor, that they show how reading has made Smith the writer that she is. Rather than a critic advancing an argument or an academic analyzing in code, she's a writer who understands the reader's perspective, a reader who understands the writer's. . . . [E]ven when delving into politics, Smith brings a novelist's attention to language, style, and tone. If she'd never written a novel, this collection alone would make me eager to read more of her work."   —*Kirkus Reviews*

zadie smith

CHANGING MY MIND

OCCASIONAL ESSAYS

·

PENGUIN BOOKS

PENGUIN BOOKS
Published by the Penguin Group
Penguin Group (USA) Inc., 375 Hudson Street, New York, New York 10014, U.S.A.
• Penguin Group (Canada), 90 Eglinton Avenue East, Suite 700, Toronto, Ontario,
Canada M4P 2Y3 (a division of Pearson Penguin Canada Inc.) • Penguin Books Ltd,
80 Strand, London WC2R 0RL, England • Penguin Ireland, 25 St Stephen's Green,
Dublin 2, Ireland (a division of Penguin Books Ltd) • Penguin Group (Australia),
250 Camberwell Road, Camberwell, Victoria 3124, Australia (a division of Pearson Australia
Group Pty Ltd) • Penguin Books India Pvt Ltd, 11 Community Centre, Panchsheel Park,
New Delhi – 110 017, India • Penguin Group (NZ), 67 Apollo Drive, Rosedale,
North Shore 0632, New Zealand (a division of Pearson New Zealand Ltd) • Penguin Books
(South Africa) (Pty) Ltd, 24 Sturdee Avenue, Rosebank, Johannesburg 2196, South Africa

Penguin Books Ltd, Registered Offices:
80 Strand, London WC2R 0RL, England

First published in the United States of America by The Penguin Press,
a member of Penguin Group (USA) Inc. 2009
Published in Penguin Books 2010

13th Printing

"Smith Family Christmas" was published as "Scenes from the Smith Family Christmas" in
The New York Times, December 24, 2003. Copyright © 2003 The New York Times Company.
Reprinted by arrangement with The New York Times Company.
Excerpts from "High Windows," "The Literary World," "Self's the Man," and "Water"
from Collected Poems by Philip Larkin. Copyright © 1988, 2003 by the Estate of Philip Larkin.
Reprinted by permission of Farrar, Straus and Giroux, LLC and The Society of Authors.
Excerpt from "The End and the Beginning" from Miracle Fair by Wisława Szymborska,
translated by Joanna Trzeciak. Copyright © 2001 by Joanna Trzeciak. Used by permission of
W. W. Norton & Company, Inc.

Pages 298–99 constitute an extension of this copyright page.

THE LIBRARY OF CONGRESS HAS CATALOGED THE HARDCOVER EDITION AS FOLLOWS:
Smith, Zadie.
Changing my mind : occasional essays / Zadie Smith.
p. cm.
Includes bibliographical references and index.
ISBN 978-1-59420-237-7 (hc.)
ISBN 978-0-14-311795-7 (pbk.)
I. Title.
PR6069.M59C43 2009
824'.914—dc22   2009023419

Printed in India
DESIGNED BY AMANDA DEWEY

In Memory of My Father

The time to make your mind up about people is never!

—TRACY LORD, *The Philadelphia Story*

You get to decide what to worship.

—DAVID FOSTER WALLACE

CONTENTS

SEEING

FEELING

REMEMBERING

FOREWORD

This book was written without my knowledge. That is, I didn't realize I'd written it until someone pointed it out to me. I had thought I was writing a novel. Then a solemn, theoretical book about writing: *Fail Better*. The deadlines for these came and went. In the meantime, I replied to the requests that came in now and then. Two thousand words about Christmas? About Katharine Hepburn? Kafka? Liberia? A hundred thousand words piled up that way.

These are "occasional essays" in that they were written for particular occasions, particular editors. I am especially grateful to Bob Silvers, David Remnick, Deborah Treisman, Cressida Leyshon, Lisa Allardice and Sarah Sands for suggesting I stray into film reviewing, obituaries, cub reporting, literary criticism and memoir. "Without whom this book would not have been written." In this case the cliché is empirically true.

When you are first published at a young age, your writing grows with you—and in public. *Changing My Mind* seemed an apt, confessional title to describe this process. Reading through these pieces, though, I'm forced to recognize that ideological inconsistency is, for me, practically an article of faith. As is a cautious, optimistic creed, best expressed by Saul Bellow: "There may be truths on the side of life." I keep on waiting, but I don't think I'm going to grow out of it.

—Zadie Smith
New York, 2009

READING

One

THEIR EYES WERE WATCHING GOD: WHAT DOES *SOULFUL* MEAN?

When I was fourteen I was given *Their Eyes Were Watching God* by my mother. I was reluctant to read it. I knew what she meant by giving it to me, and I resented the inference. In the same spirit she had introduced me to *Wide Sargasso Sea* and *The Bluest Eye*, and I had not liked either of them (better to say, I had not *allowed* myself to like either of them). I preferred my own freely chosen, heterogeneous reading list. I flattered myself I ranged widely in my reading, never choosing books for genetic or sociocultural reasons. Spotting *Their Eyes Were Watching God* unopened on my bedside table, my mother persisted:

"But you'll like it."

"Why, because she's *black*?"

"No—because it's really good writing."

I had my own ideas of "good writing." It was a category that did not include aphoristic or overtly "lyrical" language, mythic imagery, accurately rendered "folk speech" or the love tribulations of women. My literary defenses were up in preparation for *Their Eyes Were Watching God*. Then I read the first page:

Ships at a distance have every man's wish on board. For some they come in with the tide. For others they sail forever on the horizon, never out of sight, never landing until the Watcher turns his eyes away in resignation, his dreams mocked to death by Time. That is the life of men.

Now, women forget all those things they don't want to remember, and remember everything they don't want to forget. The dream is the truth. Then they act and do things accordingly.

It was an aphorism, yet it had me pinned to the ground, unable to deny its strength. It capitalized *Time* (I was against the capitalization of abstract nouns), but still I found myself melancholy for these nameless men and their inevitable losses. The second part, about women, struck home. It remains as accurate a description of my mother and me as I have ever read: *Then they act and do things accordingly.* Well, all right then. I relaxed in my chair a little and laid down my pencil. I inhaled that book. Three hours later I was finished and crying a lot, for reasons that both were, and were not, to do with the tragic finale.

I lost many literary battles the day I read *Their Eyes Were Watching God.* I had to concede that occasionally aphorisms have their power. I had to give up the idea that Keats had a monopoly on the lyrical:

She was stretched on her back beneath the pear tree soaking in the alto chant of the visiting bees, the gold of the sun and the panting breath of the breeze when the inaudible voice of it all came to her. She saw a dust-nearing bee sink into the sanctum of a bloom; the thousand sister-calyxes arch to meet the love embrace and the ecstatic shiver of the tree from root to tiniest branch creaming in every blossom and frothing with delight. So this was a marriage! She had been summoned to behold a revelation. Then Janie felt a pain remorseless sweet that left her limp and languid.[1]

---

1. But I still resist "limp and languid."

I had to admit that mythic language is startling when it's good:

Death, that strange being with the huge square toes who lived way in the West. The great one who lived in the straight house like a platform without sides to it, and without a roof. What need has Death for a cover, and what winds can blow against him?

My resistance to dialogue (encouraged by Nabokov, whom I idolized) struggled and then tumbled before Hurston's ear for black colloquial speech. In the mouths of unlettered people she finds the bliss of quotidian metaphor:

"If God don't think no mo' 'bout 'em than Ah do, they's a lost ball in de high grass."

Of wisdom lightly worn:

"To my thinkin' mourning oughtn't tuh last no longer'n grief."

Her conversations reveal individual personalities, accurately, swiftly, as if they had no author at all:

"Where y'all come from in sich uh big haste?" Lee Coker asked. "Middle Georgy," Starks answered briskly. "Joe Starks is mah name, from in and through Georgy."

"You and yo' daughter goin' tuh join wid us in fellowship?" the other reclining figure asked. "Mighty glad to have yuh. Hicks is the name. Guv'nor Amos Hicks from Buford, South Carolina. Free, single, disengaged."

"I god, Ah ain't nowhere near old enough to have no grown daughter. This here is mah wife."

Hicks sank back and lost interest at once.

"Where is de Mayor?" Starks persisted. "Ah wants tuh talk wid *him*."

"Youse uh mite too previous for dat," Coker told him. "Us ain't got none yit."

Above all, I had to let go of my objection to the love tribulations of women. The story of Janie's progress through three marriages confronts the reader with the significant idea that the choice one makes between partners, between one man and another (or one woman and another) stretches beyond romance. It is, in the end, the choice between values, possibilities, futures, hopes, arguments (shared concepts that fit the world as you experience it), languages (shared words that fit the world as you believe it to be) and lives. A world you share with Logan Killicks is evidently not the same world you would share with Vergible "Tea Cake" Woods. In these two discrete worlds, you will not even think the same way; a mind trapped with Logan is freed with Tea Cake. But who, in this context, dare speak of freedoms? In practical terms, a black woman in turn-of-the-century America, a woman like Janie, or like Hurston herself, had approximately the same civil liberties as a farm animal: "De nigger woman is de mule uh de world." So goes Janie's grandmother's famous line—it hurt my pride to read it. It hurts Janie, too; she rejects the realpolitik of her grandmother, embarking on an existential revenge that is of the imagination and impossible to restrict:

> She knew that God tore down the old world every evening and built a new one by sun-up. It was wonderful to see it take form with the sun and emerge from the gray dust of its making. The familiar people and things had failed her so she hung over the gate and looked up the road towards way off.

That part of Janie that is looking for someone (or something) that "spoke for far horizon" has its proud ancestors in Elizabeth Bennet, in Dorothea Brooke, in Jane Eyre, even—in a very debased form—in Emma Bovary. Since the beginning of fiction concerning the love tribulations of women (which is to say, since the beginning of fiction), the "romantic quest" aspect of these fictions has been too often casually ridiculed: not long ago I sat down to dinner with an American woman who told me how disappointed she had been to finally read *Middlemarch* and find that it was "Just this long, whiny, trawling search for a man!" Those who read *Middlemarch* in that way will find little in *Their Eyes Were Watching God* to please them. It's about a girl who takes some time to find the man she really loves. It is about the discovery of self in and through another. It implies that even the dark and terrible banality of racism can recede to a vanishing point when you understand, and are understood by, another human being. Goddammit if it doesn't claim that love sets you free. These days "self-actualization" is the aim, and if you can't do it alone you are admitting a weakness. The potential rapture of human relationships to which Hurston gives unabashed expression, the profound "self-crushing love" that Janie feels for Tea Cake, may, I suppose, look like the dull finale of a "long, whiny, trawling search for a man." For Tea Cake and Janie, though, the choice of each other is experienced not as desperation, but as discovery, and the need felt on both sides causes them joy, not shame. That Tea Cake would not be *our* choice, that we disapprove of him often, and despair of him occasionally, only lends power to the portrait. He seems to act with freedom, and Janie to choose him freely. We have no power; we only watch. Despite the novel's fairy-tale structure (as far as husbands go, third time's the charm), it is not a novel of wish fulfillment, least of all the fulfillment of *our* wishes.[2] It is odd to diagnose weakness where lovers themselves do not feel it.

After that first reading of the novel, I wept, and not only for Tea Cake, and not simply for the perfection of the writing, nor even the real loss I felt upon leaving the world contained in its pages. It meant something more than all that to me, something I could not, or would not, articulate. Later, I took it to the dinner table, still holding on to it, as we do sometimes with books we are not quite ready to relinquish.

"So?" my mother asked.

I told her it was basically sound.

At fourteen, I did Zora Neale Hurston a critical disservice. I feared my "extraliterary" feelings for her. I wanted to be an objective aesthete and not a sentimental fool. I disliked the idea of "identifying" with the fiction I read:

---

2. Again, *Middlemarch* is an interesting comparison. Readers often prefer Lydgate and are disappointed at Dorothea's choice of Ladislaw.

I wanted to like Hurston because she represented "good writing," not because
she represented me. In the two decades since, Zora Neale Hurston has gone
from being a well-kept, well-loved secret among black women of my mother's
generation to an entire literary industry—biographies[3] and films and Oprah
and African American literature departments all pay homage to her life[4] and
work as avatars of black woman-ness. In the process, a different kind of critical
disservice is being done to her, an overcompensation in the opposite direction.
In *Their Eyes Were Watching God*, Janie is depressed by Joe Starks's determination to idolize her: he intends to put her on a lonely pedestal before the
whole town and establish a symbol (the Mayor's Wife) in place of the woman
she is. Something similar has been done to Hurston herself. She is like Janie,
set on her porch-pedestal ("Ah done nearly languished tuh death up dere"),
far from the people and things she really cared about, representing only the
ideas and beliefs of her admirers, distorted by their gaze. In the space of one
volume of collected essays, we find a critic arguing that the negative criticism of Hurston's work represents an "intellectual lynching" by black men,
white men and white women; a critic dismissing Hurston's final work with
the sentence "*Seraph on the Suwanee* is not even about black people, which
is no crime, but *is* about white people who are bores, which is"; and another
explaining the "one great flaw" in *Their Eyes Were Watching God*: Hurston's
"curious insistence" on having her main character's tale told in the omniscient
third person (instead of allowing Janie her "voice outright"). We are in a critical world of some banality here, one in which most of our nineteenth-century
heroines would be judged oppressed creatures, cruelly deprived of the therapeutic first-person voice. It is also a world in which what is called the "Black
Female Literary Tradition" is beyond reproach:

> Black women writers have consistently rejected the falsification of their
> Black female experience, thereby avoiding the negative stereotypes such

3. The (very good) biography is *Wrapped in Rainbows: The Life of Zora Neale Hurston* by
Valerie Boyd. Also very good is *Zora Neale Hurston: A Life in Letters*, collected and edited by
Carla Kaplan.
4. *Dust Tracks on a Road* is Hurston's autobiography.

falsification has often created in the white American female and Black male literary traditions. Unlike many of their Black male and white female peers, Black women writers have usually refused to dispense with whatever was clearly Black and/or female in their sensibilities in an effort to achieve the mythical "neutral" voice of universal art.[5]

Gratifying as it would be to agree that black women writers "have consistently rejected the falsification" of their experience, the honest reader knows that this is simply not the case. In place of negative falsification, we have nurtured, in the past thirty years, a new fetishization. Black female protagonists are now unerringly strong and soulful; they are sexually voracious and unafraid; they take the unreal forms of earth mothers, African queens, divas, spirits of history; they process grandly through novels thick with a breed of greeting-card lyricism. They have little of the complexity, the flaws and uncertainties, depth and beauty of Janie Crawford and the novel she springs from. They are pressed into service as role models to patch over our psychic wounds; they are perfect;[6] they overcompensate. The truth is, black women writers, while writing many wonderful things,[7] have been no more or less successful at avoiding the falsification of human experience than any other group of writers. It is not the Black Female Literary Tradition that makes Hurston great. It is Hurston herself. Zora Neale Hurston—capable of expressing human vulnerability as well as its strength, lyrical without sentiment, romantic and yet rigorous and one of the few truly eloquent writers of sex—is as exceptional among black women writers as Tolstoy is among white male writers.[8]

It is, however, true that Hurston rejected the "neutral universal" for her novels—she wrote unapologetically in the black-inflected dialect in which she

5. All the critical voices quoted above can be found in *Zora Neale Hurston's* Their Eyes Were Watching God: *Modern Critical Interpretations*, edited by Harold Bloom.
6. Hurston, by contrast, wanted her writing to demonstrate the fact that "Negroes are no better nor no worse, and at times as boring as everybody else."
7. Not least of which is Alice Walker's original introduction to *Their Eyes Were Watching God*. By championing the book, she rescued Hurston from forty years of obscurity.
8. A footnote for the writers in the audience: *Their Eyes Were Watching God* was written in seven weeks.

was raised. It took bravery to do that: the result was hostility and disinterest. In 1937, black readers were embarrassed by the unlettered nature of the dialogue and white readers preferred the exoticism of her anthropological writings. Who wanted to read about the poor Negroes one saw on the corner every day? Hurston's biographers make clear that no matter what positive spin she put on it, her life was horribly difficult: she finished life working as a cleaner and died in obscurity. It is understandable that her reclaiming should be an emotive and personal journey for black readers and black critics. But still, one wants to make a neutral and solid case for her greatness, to say something more substantial than "She is my sister and I love her." As a reader, I want to claim fellowship with "good writing" without limits; to be able to say that Hurston is my sister and Baldwin is my brother, and so is Kafka my brother, and Nabokov, and Woolf my sister, and Eliot and Ozick. Like all readers, I want my limits to be drawn by my own sensibilities, not by my melanin count. These forms of criticism that make black women the privileged readers of a black woman writer go against Hurston's own grain. She saw things otherwise: "When I set my hat at a certain angle and saunter down Seventh Avenue. . . . the cosmic Zora emerges. . . . How *can* anybody deny themselves the pleasure of my company? It's beyond me!" This is exactly right. No one should deny themselves the pleasure of Zora—of whatever color or background or gender. She's too delightful not to be shared. We all deserve to savor her neologisms ("sankled," "monstropolous," "rawbony") or to read of the effects of a bad marriage, sketched with tragic accuracy:

> The years took all the fight out of Janie's face. For a while she thought it was gone from her soul. No matter what Jody did, she said nothing. She had learned how to talk some and leave some. She was a rut in the road. Plenty of life beneath the surface but it was kept beaten down by the wheels. Sometimes she stuck out into the future, imagining her life different from what it was. But mostly she lived between her hat and her heels, with her emotional disturbances like shade patterns in the woods—come and gone with the sun. She got nothing from Jody except what money could buy, and she was giving away what she didn't value.

The visual imagination on display in *Their Eyes Were Watching God* shares its clarity and iconicity with Christian storytelling—many scenes in the novel put one in mind of the bold-stroke illustrations in a children's Bible: young Janie staring at a photograph, not understanding that the black girl in the crowd is her; Joe Starks atop a dead mule's distended belly, giving a speech; Tea Cake bitten high on his cheekbone by that rabid dog. I watched the TV footage of Hurricane Katrina with a strong sense of déjà vu, thinking of Hurston's flood rather than Noah's: "Not the dead of sick and ailing with friends at the pillow and the feet . . . [but] the sodden and the bloated; the sudden dead, their eyes flung wide open in judgment. . . ."

Above all, Hurston is essential universal reading because she is neither self-conscious nor restricted. She was raised in the real Eatonville, Florida, an all-black town; this unique experience went some way to making Hurston the writer she was. She grew up a fully human being, unaware that she was meant to consider herself a minority, an other, an exotic or something depleted in rights, talents, desires and expectations. As an adult, away from Eatonville, she found the world was determined to do its best to remind her of her supposed inferiority, but Hurston was already made, and the metaphysical confidence she claimed for her life ("I am not tragically colored") is present, with equal, refreshing force, in her fiction. She liked to yell "Culllaaaah Struck!"[9] when she entered a fancy party—almost everybody was. But Hurston herself was not. "Blackness," as she understood it and wrote about it, is as natural and inevitable and complete to her as, say, "Frenchness" is to Flaubert. It is also as complicated, as full of blessings and curses. One can be no more removed from it than from one's arm, but it is no more the total measure of one's being than an arm is.

But still, after all that, there is something else to say—and the "neutral universal" of literary criticism pens me in and makes it difficult. To write critically in English is to aspire to neutrality, to the high style of, say, Lionel Trilling

9. See chapter 16 for a sad portrayal of a truly color-struck lady, Mrs. Turner.

or Edmund Wilson. In the high style, one's loves never seem partial or personal, or even like "loves," because white novelists are not white novelists but simply "novelists," and white characters are not white characters but simply "human," and criticism of both is not partial or personal but a matter of aesthetics. Such critics will always sound like the neutral universal, and the black women who have championed *Their Eyes Were Watching God* in the past, and the one doing so now, will seem like black women talking about a black book. When I began this piece, it felt important to distance myself from that idea. By doing so, I misrepresent a vital aspect of my response to this book, one that is entirely personal, as any response to a novel shall be. Fact is, I *am* a black woman,[10] and a slither of this book goes straight into my soul, I suspect, for that reason. And though it is, to me, a mistake to say, "Unless you are a black woman, you will never fully comprehend this novel," it is also disingenuous to claim that many black women do not respond to this book in a particularly powerful manner that would seem "extraliterary." Those aspects of *Their Eyes Were Watching God* that plumb so profoundly the ancient buildup of cultural residue that is (for convenience's sake) called "Blackness"[11] are the parts that my own "Blackness," as far as it goes, cannot help but respond to personally. At fourteen I couldn't find words (or words I liked) for the marvelous feeling of recognition that came with these characters who had my hair, my eyes, my skin, even the ancestors of the rhythm of my speech.[12] These forms of identification are so natural to white readers—(Of course Rabbit Angstrom is like me! Of course Madame Bovary is like me!)—that they believe themselves above personal identification, or at least believe that they are identifying only at the highest, existential levels (His soul is like my soul. He is human; I am human). White readers often believe they are colorblind.[13] I always thought I was a colorblind reader—until I read this novel, and that ultimate cliché of

---

10. I think this was the point my mother was trying to make.
11. As Kafka's *The Trial* plumbs that ancient buildup of cultural residue that is called "Jewishness."
12. Down on the muck, Janie and Tea Cake befriend the "Saws," workers from the Caribbean.
13. Until they read books featuring nonwhite characters. I once overheard a young white man at a book festival say to his friend, "Have you read the new Kureishi? Same old thing—loads of Indian people." To which you want to reply, "Have you read the new Franzen? Same old thing—loads of white people."

black life that is inscribed in the word *soulful* took on new weight and sense for me. But what does *soulful* even mean? The dictionary has it this way: "expressing or appearing to express deep and often sorrowful feeling." The culturally black meaning adds several more shades of color. First shade: *soulfulness* is sorrowful feeling transformed into something beautiful, creative and self-renewing, and—as it reaches a pitch—ecstatic. It is an alchemy of pain. In *Their Eyes Were Watching God*, when the townsfolk sing for the death of the mule, this is an example of *soulfulness*. Another shade: to be soulful is to follow and *fall in line* with a feeling, to go where it takes you and not to go against its grain.[14] When young Janie takes her lead from the blossoming tree and sits on her gatepost to kiss a passing boy, this is an example of *soulfulness*. A final shade: the word *soulful*, like its Jewish cousin, *schmaltz*,[15] has its roots in the digestive tract. "Soul food" is simple, flavorsome, hearty, unfussy, with spice. When Janie puts on her overalls and joyfully goes to work in the muck with Tea Cake, this is an example of *soulfulness*.[16]

This is a beautiful novel about soulfulness. That it should be so is a tribute to Hurston's skill. She makes "culture"—that slow and particular[17] and artificial accretion of habit and circumstance—seem as natural and organic and beautiful as the sunrise. She allows me to indulge in what Philip Roth once called "the romance of onself," a literary value I dislike and yet, confronted with this beguiling book, cannot resist. She makes "black woman-ness" appear a real, tangible quality, an essence I can almost believe I share, however improbably, with millions of complex individuals across centuries and continents and languages and religions. . . .

Almost—but not quite. Better to say, when I'm reading this book, I believe it, with my whole soul. It allows me to say things I wouldn't normally. Things like *"She is my sister and I love her."*

---

14. At its most common and banal: catching a beat, following a rhythm.
15. In the *Oxford English Dictionary*: "**Schmaltz n.** informal. excessive sentimentality, esp. in music or movies. ORIGIN 1930s: from Yiddish *schmaltz*, from German *Schmalz* 'dripping, lard.'"
16. Is there anything less soulful than attempting to define soulfulness?
17. In literary terms, we know that there is a tipping point at which the cultural particular—while becoming no less culturally particular—is accepted by readers as the neutral universal. The previously "Jewish fiction" of Philip Roth is now "fiction." We have moved from the particular complaints of Portnoy to the universal claims of Everyman.

Two

E. M. FORSTER,
MIDDLE MANAGER

1

In the taxonomy of English writing, E. M. Forster is not an exotic creature. We file him under Notable English Novelist, common or garden variety.
Yet there is a sense in which Forster was something of a rare bird. He was
largely free of vices commonly found in novelists of his generation—what's
unusual about Forster is what he *didn't* do. He didn't lean rightward with the
years or allow nostalgia to morph into misanthropy; he never knelt for the
pope or queen, nor did he flirt (ideologically speaking) with Hitler, Stalin or
Mao; he never believed the novel was dead or the hills alive, continued to read
contemporary fiction after the age of fifty, harbored no special hatred for the
generation below or above him, did not come to feel that England had gone
to hell in a handbasket, that its language was doomed, that lunatics were running the asylum or foreigners swamping the cities.

Still, like all notable English novelists, he was a tricky bugger. He made
a faith of personal sincerity and a career of disingenuousness. He was an

Edwardian among modernists, and yet—in matters of pacifism, class, education and race—a progressive among conservatives. Suburban and parochial, his vistas stretched far into the East. A passionate defender of "Love, the beloved republic," he nevertheless persisted in keeping his own loves secret, long after the laws that had prohibited honesty were gone. Between the bold and the tame, the brave and the cowardly, the engaged and the complacent, Forster walked the middling line. At times—when defending his liberal humanism against fundamentalists of the right and left—that middle line was, in its quiet, Forsterish way, the most radical place to be. At other times—in the laissez-faire coziness of his literary ideas—it seemed merely the most comfortable. In a letter to Goldsworthy Lowes Dickinson, Forster lays out his casual aesthetics, casually:

> All I write is, to me, sentimental. A book which doesn't leave people either happier or better than it found them, which doesn't add some permanent treasure to the world, isn't worth doing. . . . This is my "theory," and I maintain it's sentimental—at all events it isn't Flaubert's. How can he fag himself to write "Un Coeur Simple"?

To his detractors, the small, mild oeuvre of E. M. Forster is proof that when it comes to aesthetics, one really *better* be fagged: the zeal of the fanatic is what's required. "E. M. Forster never gets any further than warming the teapot," thought Katherine Mansfield, a fanatic if ever there was one. "He's a rare fine hand at that. Feel this teapot. Is it not beautifully warm? Yes, but there aint going to be no tea." There's something middling about Forster; he is halfway to where people want him to be. Even the editors of this exhaustive collection of his broadcasts find it necessary to address the middlebrow elephant in the room with almost unseemly haste (page 9):

> Forster, though recognized as a central player in his literary milieu, has been classed by most cultural historians of this period as secondary to Virginia Woolf, James Joyce, or TS Eliot . . . relegated not quite to the

lesser lights of modernism, but perhaps to the "middle lights," if we might
invent this term.[1]

Conscientious editors, they defend their subject fiercely and at length. It
feels incongruous, for never was there a notable English novelist who wore
his status more lightly. To love Forster is to reconcile oneself to the admix-
ture of banality and brilliance that was his, as he had done himself. In this
volume that blend is perhaps more perfectly represented than ever before.
Whether that's a good thing or not is difficult to say. At any rate, what we
have here is a four-hundred-page selection of the talks Forster delivered over
the wireless. The great majority of them were about books (he titled the series
Some Books); a quarter of them concern—and were broadcast to—India and
its people. Scattered among the remainder is a miscellaneous hodgepodge
of topics that tickled Forster's fancy: the Great Frost of 1929, the music of
Benjamin Britten, the free wartime concerts given in the National Gallery,
and so on. The tone is resolutely conversational, frothy and without academic
pretension ("Now you have to be cool over Yeats. He was a great poet, he lived
poetry, but there was an element of bunkum in him." "What is the use of Art?
There's a nasty one"), the sort of thing one can imagine made T. S. Eliot—
also broadcasting for the BBC during this period—sigh wearily as he passed
Forster's recording booth on the way to his own. Eliot was very serious about
literary criticism; Forster could be, too, but in these broadcasts he is not, at
least not in any sense Eliot would recognize. For one thing, he won't call what
he is doing literary criticism, or even reviewing. His are "recommendations"
only. Each episode ends with Forster diligently reading out the titles of the
books he has dealt with, along with their exact price in pounds and shillings.
In place of Eliot's severe public intellectual we have Forster the chatty librar-
ian, leaning over the counter, advising you on whether a book is worth the
bother or not—a peculiarly English aesthetic category. It's a self-imposed role
entirely lacking in intellectual vanity ("Regard me as a parasite," he tells his

---

1. The book in question is *The BBC Talks of E. M. Forster, 1929–1960*, University of Missouri
Press.

audience, "savoury or unsavoury who battens on higher forms of life"), but it's a mistake to think it a lazy or accidental one. Connection, as everyone knows, was Forster's great theme; between people, nations, heart and head, labor and art. Radio presented him with the opportunity of mass connection. It went against his grain to put any obstacle between his listeners and himself. From the start, Forster's concern—to use the parlance of modern broadcasting—was where to pitch it. Essentially it was the problem of his fiction, writ large, for he was the sort to send one manuscript to Virginia Woolf, another to his good friend the policeman Bob Buckingham, and fear the literary judgment of both. On the air, as on the page, Forster was never free from the anxiety of audience. His rupture from his modernist peers happens here, in his acute conception of audience, in his inability *not* to conceive of an audience. When Nora Barnacle asked her husband, "Why don't you write sensible books that people can understand?" her husband ignored her and wrote *Finnegans Wake*. Joyce's ideal reader was himself—that was his purity. Forster's ideal reader was a kind of projection, and not one entirely sympathetic to him. I think of this reader as, if not definitively English, then of a type that abounds in England. Lucy Honeychurch (*A Room with a View*) is one of them. So are Philip Herriton (*Where Angels Fear to Tread*) and Henry Wilcox (*Howards End*) and Maurice Hall (*Maurice*). Forster's novels are full of people who'd think twice before borrowing a Forster novel from the library. Well—they'd want to know—is it worth the bother or not? Neither intellectuals nor philistines, they are the kind to "know what they like" and have the "courage of their convictions," though their convictions are not entirely their own and their courage mostly fear. They are capable of cruelty born of laziness, but also of an unexpected spiritual greatness born of love. The right book at the right moment *might* change everything for them (Forster only gave the credence of certainty to Love). It's worth thinking of these cautious English souls, with their various potential for greatness and shabbiness, love and spite, as Forster's radio audience: it makes his approach comprehensible. Think of Maurice Hall and his groundskeeper lover, Alec Scudder, settled by their Bakelite radio waiting for the latest installment of *Some Books*. Maurice, thanks to his superior education, catches the literary references but, in his suburban slowness, misses much of the spirit. Alec, not having read Wordsworth, yet grasps the soul of that poet as he listens to Forster recount a visit to the Lake District, Wordsworth country: "Grey sheets of rain trailed in front of the mountains, waterfalls slid down them and shone in the sun, and the sky was always sending shafts of light into the valleys." Early on, Forster voiced his determination to plow the middle course: "I've had nice letters from people regretting that my talks are above them, and others equally nice regretting that they are below; so hadn't I better pursue the even tenor of my way?"

Well, hadn't he?

2

I've made up an imaginary person whom I call "you" and I'm going to tell you about it. Your age, your sex, your position, your job, your training—I know nothing about all that, but I have formed the notion that you're a person who wants to read new books but doesn't intend to buy them.

But here Forster is too humble: he knew more of his audience than the contents of their passports. Take his talk on Coleridge of August 13, 1931. A new *Collected* is out, it's a nicely printed edition, costs only three shillings sixpence, and he'd like to talk to you about it. But he senses that you are already sighing, and he knows why:

Perhaps you'll say "I don't want a complete Coleridge, I've got 'The Ancient Mariner' in some anthology or other, and that's enough. 'The Ancient Mariner' and 'Kubla Khan' and perhaps the first half of 'Christabel'— that's all in Coleridge that really matters. The rest is rubbish and not even good dry rubbish, it's moist clammy rubbish, it's depressing." So if I tell you that there are 600 pages in this new edition, you'll only reply "I'm sorry to hear it."

Still—600 pages makes one think.

The first half of Christabel—how perfect that is, and how it makes one laugh. A mix of empathy and ventriloquism fuels the comic engines of his novels; here in the broadcasts it's reemployed as sly technique, allowing Forster to approach the congenital anti-intellectualism of the English from an oblique angle, one that flatters them with complicity. Here he is, up to the same thing with D. H. Lawrence:

> Much of his work is tedious, and some of it shocks people, so that we are inclined to say: "What a pity! What a pity to go on about the subconscious and the solar plexus and maleness and femaleness and African darkness and the cosmic battle when you can write with such insight about human beings and so beautifully about flowers.

Have you had that thought? Don't worry if you have; so has E. M. Forster. Still, it's a mistake:

> You can't say, "Let's drop his theories and enjoy his art," because the two are one. Disbelieve his theories, if you like, but never brush them aside. . . . He resembles a natural process much more nearly than do most writers . . . and one might as well scold a flower for growing on a manure heap, or a manure heap for producing a flower.

It's a gentle correction, but a serious one, aimed democratically at both listener and speaker. And like this, pursuing a gentle push and pull, iron fist hidden in velvet glove, Forster presses on in his determined, middling way. He's educating you, but surreptitiously, and unlike the writings of his childhood hero, Matthew Arnold, it never feels painful. The *leggerezza* of his prose lightens every load. Speaking on the twentieth of June, 1945, Forster outlines Arnold's more muscular approach:

> One of his complaints against his countrymen was that they were eccentric and didn't desire to be anything else. They didn't want to be better

informed or urbane, or to know what is great in human achievement. They didn't want culture. And he flung at them another of his famous accusations: Philistines. The philistine is the sort of person who says "I know what I know and I like what I like, and that's the kind of chap I am." And Matthew Arnold, a Victorian David, slung his pebble bang in the middle of Goliath's forehead.

Forster was no pebble slinger. For him, not only the means but also the aims were to be different. It really didn't matter to Forster if a fellow had read Lawrence or not (he is consistently sentimental about the unlettered: peasants, sailors, gardeners, natives). But to *deny* Lawrence, because he was not to your taste, or to deny poetry itself, out of fear and incomprehension— that mattered terribly. The only philistinism that counted was the kind that deformed the heart, trapping us in an attitude of scorn and fear until scorn and fear are all we know. On the twelfth of February 1947, recommending *Billy Budd*, Forster finds an unlikely ally in Melville:

> He also shows that . . . innocence is not safe in a civilization like ours, where a man must practice a "ruled undemonstrative distrustfulness" in order to defend himself against traps. This "ruled undemonstrative distrustfulness" is not confined to business men, but exists everywhere. We all exercise it. I know I do, and I should be surprised if you, who are listening to me, didn't. All we can do (and Melville gives us this hint) is to exercise it consciously, as Captain Vere did. It is unconscious distrustfulness that corrodes the heart and destroys the heart's insight, and prevents it from saluting goodness.

Unconscious distrustfulness is what Lucy Honeychurch feels toward George Emerson, what Philip Herriton feels in Italy, what Maurice Hall feels for his own soul. Forster nudges his characters toward a consciousness of this weakness in themselves; they do battle against it and win. They learn to salute goodness. Sometimes this is achieved with delicacy and the illusion of freedom, as it is in *A Room with a View*; at other times, in *Maurice*, say, happiness arrives a good deal more dogmatically (though no less pleasurably). But it is always Forster's game by Forster's rules. In radio, though, each man's consciousness is his own. There are no Lucy Honeychurches to play with—only nameless, faceless listeners whose sensibilities can only be guessed at, only assumed. In the anxiety of this unfamiliar situation, a comic novelist, with his natural weakness for caricature, is apt to assume too much. The broadcasts suffer from empathic condescension: Forster is unconvinced that we might also, like him, be capable of a broad sympathetic sensibility. Recommending two memoirs, one by Sir Henry Newbolt (a patriotic, public-school adventurer with "a touch of the medieval knight about him"), and another by Mr. Grant Richards (a "gay and irresponsible" fin de siècle journalist who "loves Paris with a fervour"), he predicts two camps of readers, split by sensibility, unable to understand each other:

> Mr. Grant Richards is a very different story. The title he has given his memoirs proves that: he calls them *Memoirs of a Misspent Youth*. . . . Like Sir Henry Newbolt he is a friend of Rothenstein and was fond of birdnesting, but those are the only bond between them. . . . The atmosphere of the book one might call Bohemian, and if you find yourself in complete sympathy with Sir Henry Newbolt you won't care for *Memories of a Misspent Youth* and vice versa.

There is an element of the nervous party host in Forster; he fears people won't speak to each other unless he's there to facilitate the introduction. Occasionally his image of the general reader is almost too general to recognize. Who dreads philosophy so much they need easing into Plato like this?

> The word *Plato* has rather a boring sound. For some reason or other "Plato" always suggests to me a man with a large head and a noble face who never stops talking and from whom it is impossible to escape.

Who's (this) afraid of *The Magic Flute*?

It's a lovely book,[2] I implore you to read it, but rather unluckily it's based on an opera by Mozart. I say "unluckily" not because the opera is bad, it is Mozart's best, but because many readers of the book won't have heard of the opera, and so won't catch on the allusions. You'll have to be prepared for some queer names.

No one reading these words, perhaps. On the other side of the class and educational divide—a line that so preoccupied Forster—it's easy to forget what it's like not to know. Forster was always thinking of those who did not know. He worries that simply by having this one-way conversation he pushes the Alec Scudders in his audience still further into the shadows. Frequently he asks the (necessarily) rhetorical question "And what do you think?" We can be sure that Eliot, in the next booth over, never asked that. But isn't there a point where empathy becomes equivocation? Can't you hear Henry Wilcox, fuming: "Good God, man, it's not what *I* think that matters! I'm paying my license fee to hear what *you* think!"

Henry would want a few strong opinions, the better to repeat them to his wife and pass them off as his own. Forster does have strong opinions to offer. At first glance, they seem the sort of thing of which Henry would approve:

I like a novel to be a novel. I expect it to be about something or some-one. . . . I get annoyed. It is foolish to get annoyed. One can cure oneself, and should. It is foolish to insist that a novel must be a novel. One must take what comes along, and see if it's good.

But halfway through that paragraph Forster has given Henry the slip.

●

In the foreword to this volume, P. N. Furbank calls Forster "the great simplifier." It's true he wrote simply, had a gift for the simple expression of complex ideas, but he never made a religion of simplicity itself. He under-

---

2. He refers to the narrative version by Goldsworthy Lowes Dickinson.

stood and defended the expression of complexity in its own terms. He was
E. M. Forster: he didn't need everyone else to be like him. Which would
appear the simplest, most obvious principle in the world—yet how few English novelists prove capable of holding it! In English fiction, realists defend
realism and experimentalists defend experimentalism; those who write
simple sentences praise the virtues of concision, and those who are fond
of their adjectives claim the lyrical as the highest value in literature. Forster was different. Several times he reminds his listeners of the *Bhagavad
Gita* and in particular the advice Krishna gives Arjina: "But thou hast only
the right to work; but none to the fruit thereof; let not then the fruit of thy
action be thy motive; nor yet be thou enamoured in inaction." Forster took
that advice: he could sit in his own literary corner without claiming its superiority to any other. Stubbornly he defends Joyce, though he doesn't much
like him, and Woolf, though she bemuses him, and Eliot, though he fears
him. His recommendation of Paul Valéry's *An Evening with Monsieur Teste* is
representative:

> Well, the first line is illuminating. "La bêtise n'est pas mon fort." Stupid-
> ity is not my strong point. No it wasn't. Valery was never never stupid. If he
> had been stupid sometimes, he would no doubt have been more in touch
> with the rest of us, who are stupid so frequently. That was his limitation.
> Remember on the other hand what limitations are ours, and how much
> we lose by our failure to follow the action of a superior mind.

Forster was not Valéry, but he defended Valéry's right to be Valéry. He
understood the beauty of complexity and saluted it where he saw it. His own
preference for simplicity he recognized for what it was, a preference, linked to
a dream of mass connection. He placed no particular force behind it:

> And it's Mister Heard's[3] sympathy that I want to stress. He doesn't write
> because he is learned and clever and fanciful, although he is all these

---

3. The book recommended is *The Social Substance of Religion* by Gerald Heard.

things. He writes because he knows of our troubles from within and wants
to help with them. I wish he wrote more simply, because then more of us
might be helped. That, really, is my only quarrel with him.

3

Occupying "a midway position" between the aristocrat's memoir and that
of the bohemian, Forster recommends *As We Are,* the memoir of Mr. E. F.
Benson ("The book's uneven—bits of it are perfunctory, but bits are awfully
good"). He finds one paragraph particularly wise on "the problem of growing
old" and quotes it:

> Unfortunately there comes to the majority of those of middle age an ine-
> lasticity not of physical muscle and sinew alone but of mental fibre. Expe-
> rience has its dangers: it may bring wisdom, but it may also bring stiffness
> and cause hardened deposits in the mind, and its resulting inelasticity is
> crippling.

Is it inelasticity that drives English writers to religion (Greene, Waugh,
Eliot), to an anticulture stance (Wells, K. Amis, Larkin), to the rejection of
accepted modes of literary seriousness (Wodehouse, Greene)? Better, I think,
to credit it to a healthy English perversity, a bloody-minded war against cliché. It's a cliché to think liking Keats makes you cultured (Larkin and Amis
defaced their college copy of *The Eve of St. Agnes*[4]), a commonplace to think
submission to God incompatible with intellectual vitality. Then again, it's
hard to deny that in many of these writers a calcification occurs, playful poses
become rigid attitudes. Forster feared the sea change. In the year Forster finished broadcasting, in the same BBC studios, Evelyn Waugh submits to an
interviewer interested in his "notable rejection of life":

---

4. Next to the phrase "into her dream he melted" was written "You mean he fucked her, do
you?"

Interviewer: What do you feel is your worst fault?

Waugh: Irritability.

Interviewer: Irritability with your family? With strangers?

Waugh: Absolutely everything. Inanimate objects and people, animals, everything . . .

Forster worked hard to avoid this fate, first through natural inclination and then, later, by way of a willed enthusiasm, an openness to everything that itself skirts perilously close to banality. He did not believe in the "rejection of life," not for reasons of irritability, asceticism, intellectual fastidiousness or even mystical attachments. He quotes approvingly this discussion, from *The Magic Flute*, between Jesus and Buddha:

"Lord Buddha, was your gospel true?"

"True and False."

"What was true in it?"

"Selflessness and Love."

"What false?"

"Flight from Life."

In the wartime broadcasts in particular Forster gets into life, though with difficulty: you sense in more peaceful times he would have left the public speaking to those more suited to it. Passing H. G. Wells in the street in the early forties, Forster recalls Wells "calling after me in his squeaky voice 'Still in your ivory tower?' 'Still on your private roundabout?' I might have retorted, but did not think of it till now."

During the war Forster got onto his own roundabout, broadcasting mild English propaganda to India, ridiculing Nazi "philosophy" from the early thirties onward, attacking the prison and police systems, defending the Third Program, speaking up for mass education, the rights of refugees, free concerts for the poor and art for the masses. Recognizing that "humanism has its dangers; the humanist shirks responsibility, dislikes making decisions, and is sometimes a coward," he was anyway determined to hold faith with the "failed" liberal values so many of his peers now jettisoned. "Do we, in these terrible times, want to be humanists or fanatics? I have no doubt as to my own wish, I would rather be a humanist with all his faults, than a fanatic with all his virtues." Forster, an Edwardian, lived through two cataclysmic wars, watched England's transformation from elegant playground of the fortunate few to the mass factory of everybody. And still he kept faith with the future. In the greatest of his broadcasts, "What I Believe," a much longer piece absent from this volume, he sympathizes with our natural reactionary instincts but doesn't submit to them: "This is such a difficult moment to live in, one cannot help getting gloomy and also a bit rattled, and perhaps short-sighted." As our present crop of English novelists get a bit rattled, Forster's example begins to look exemplary.

On Forster's centenary, again in the same studio, another notable English novelist good-humoredly recognizes his own U-turn, motivated by gloom:

> **Interviewer:** In 1964, in an essay called "No More Parades" you said you
>   felt that British culture was the property of some sort of exclusive club
>   and you'd always bitterly resented that fact; I get the impression from
>   certain things you've written recently that you resent the fact that it's *not*
>   the property of an exclusive club any longer. . . .
> **Kingsley Amis:** (laughing) That's right, yes. . . .

But Forster was clever about even this kind of literary insincerity: "The simple view is that creation can only proceed from sincerity. But the facts don't always bear this out. The insincere, the half sincere, may on occasion contribute." Lucky for the English that this should be so. On the third of October 1932, Forster considers a critical study of Wordsworth, a writer who, like Amis, "moved from being a Bolshie . . . to being a die-hard." The study argues that Wordsworth "had a great deal to cover up," having had an affair and an illegitimate child with a French woman, Annette Vallon, all of which he kept hidden. Back in England he made a hypocritical fetish of his own puritanism and lived "to be a respectable and intolerant old man." Something calcified in

Wordsworth: he ended up hating the France he'd loved as a youth, becoming a "poet of conventional morality," more concerned with public reputation than with poetry itself. Forster too had a good deal to hide and kept it hidden; one feels in his attention to the Wordsworth story the recognition of a morality tale. It is almost as if, with the door of his private sexuality firmly closed, Forster willed himself to open every window. This curious inverse effect is most noticeable in the honesty and flexibility of his criticism. On his affection for Jane Austen: "She's English, I'm English, and my fondness for her may well be a family affair." On a naval book that celebrates the simplicity of the sailor's life: "I don't know whether I am overpraising the book. Its values happen to coincide with my own, and one does then tend to overpraise." He is gently amused to learn of J. Donald Adams's (then editor of the *New York Times Book Review*) suspicion of the recent crop of American fiction:

> The twenties and thirties of this century were unsatisfactory, Mr Adams thinks, because they contributed nothing positive; they pricked holes in the old complacency (like Sinclair Lewis) or indulged in private fantasies (like James Branch Cabell) or played about frivolously like Scott Fitzgerald.

Here's the funny thing about literary criticism: it hates its own times, only realizing their worth twenty years later. And then, twenty years after that, it wildly sentimentalizes them, out of nostalgia for a collective youth. Condemned cliques become halcyon "movements," annoying young men, august geniuses. Unlike Adams, Forster had the gift of recognizing good writing while it was still young. Enthusiastically he hails Rosamond Lehmann, William Plomer, Christopher Isherwood. And it's only 1932! He defends their modern quality against English nostalgia: "If they still believe in what Keats called the holiness of the heart's imagination, then aren't we with them, and does it make any difference to us that they don't use Keats' words?"

Which reminds us of the simplest and greatest pleasure of this book: Forster gets it right, often. He's right about Strachey's *Queen Victoria*, right about the worth of H. G. Wells and Rebecca West and Aldous Huxley; right about

Eliot's *Ash Wednesday* and Russell's *History of Western Philosophy*. Sitting on a 1944 panel titled "Is the novel dead?"[5] he is right to answer in the negative.

The editors of this volume, making heavy weather of it, claim "Forster's talks engaged and helped shape British culture." I imagine Forster would have been surprised by that statement and perplexed by their concern for his literary status. He thought the words *highbrow* and *lowbrow* "responsible for more unkind feelings and more silly thinking than any other pair of words I know." He was not the sort to get riled up on that subject. He was a popular novelist. Who could say he didn't know his craft? And not in the workaday way Somerset Maugham knew his. There's magic and beauty in Forster, and weakness, and a little laziness, and some stupidity. He's like us. Many people love him for it. We might finish with what Forster himself would say about these talks, what in fact he *did* say: "There is something cajoling and ingratiating about them which cannot be exorcised by editing, and they have been the devil to reproduce." But Forster was always a little too humble, a tad disingenuous. His talks are humane and charming, like everything he wrote, and on top of that, they're good fun to read, and if not quite right for a lecture hall, they're perfect for a lazy afternoon in an armchair. The title again, for those who missed it: *The BBC Talks of E. M. Forster.* The price is $59.95.

---

5. The other panelists: Desmond MacCarthy, Rose Macaulay, Graham Greene, Evelyn Waugh and Philip Toynbee.

Three

MIDDLEMARCH
AND EVERYBODY

HENRY & GEORGE

In 1873, the young Henry James reviewed George Eliot's *Middlemarch*. An odd review, neither rave nor pan. Eliot represented the past—James hoped to be the future. "It sets a limit," he wrote, "to the development of the old-fashioned English novel." James's objection to *Middlemarch* is familiar: there's too much of it. He found "its diffuseness makes it too copious a dose of pure fiction." He would have preferred a more "organized, moulded, balanced composition." Such a lot of characters! And so often lacking the grander human qualities. With one exception: Dorothea. She alone has an "indefinable moral elevation" and "exhales a sort of aroma of spiritual sweetness." It is of the "career of [this] obscure St. Theresa" that he should have liked to read more. Finding Dorothea the most admirable character, he imagines she "was to have been the central figure." He wonders what went wrong. Certainly the doctor Lydgate is interesting enough, but his story "yields in dignity" to Dorothea's, and as for hapless Fred Vincy—why are we presented with such a "fullness of detail" on "this common-place young gentleman, with his some-what meagre tribulations and his rather neutral egotism"?

A famous query opens chapter 29 of *Middlemarch:* "But why always Dorothea?" It's neat that James's complaint—essentially "But why always Fred?"—should be the inverse reflection of it. You might say of Henry and George what the novel says of Lydgate and Rosamund: *between him and her indeed there was that total missing of each other's mental track. . . .* James can't understand why *Middlemarch* should stray so far from Dorothea, lingering on Lydgate, Fred and the rest. Cautiously he asks: was it an unconscious instinct or a deliberate plan?

•

Questions concerning the gestation of novels aren't often answerable, but *Middlemarch* is an exception. Eliot kept a journal, and in 1869 she records work on "a novel called Middlemarch" competing with research for "a long poem on Timolean." This *Middlemarch* is the tale of a young, progressive doctor called Lydgate whose arrival in a provincial town coincides with the 1832 Reform Bill debates. Work on it goes slowly, painfully—there's more hope for the poem. By the end of the year they're both abandoned. What happens next is interesting. In November, Eliot begins a second story, *Miss Brooke,* and finds she can write a hundred pages of it in a month. To a novelist, fluidity is the ultimate good omen; suddenly difficult problems are simply solved, intractable structural knots loosen themselves, and you come upon the key without even recognizing that this is what you hold. By late 1871, the Lydgate and Dorothea stories are joined (by the creaky yet workable plot device of Mr. Brooke's dinner party), and like the two hands of a piece for the piano, a contrapuntal structure is set in motion, in which many melodic lines make equal claim on our attention. The result is that famous Eliot effect, the narrative equivalent of surround sound. Here is the English novel at its limit, employing an unprecedented diversity of "central characters," so different from the centrifugal narratives of Austen. The novel is a riot of subjectivity. To Mary Garth, Fred Vincy is the central character in *Middlemarch.* To Ladislaw, it is Dorothea. To Lydgate, it is Rosamund Vincy. To Rosamund, it is herself. And authorial attention is certainly diffuse; it seems to focus not simply on those who are most good, or most attractive or even most interesting, but on those who are "there." Unconscious instinct or deliberate plan? That Lydgate and Dorothea's stories existed separately, that Dorothea's story came second, points firmly at deliberation. Yet to say so is to give a question of fiction a factual answer, and the proper rebuff to James comes from a different place, not the place of fact, but the seat of feeling. James mistakes the sensibility of the novel:

> The reader is sometimes tempted to complain of a tendency which we are at a loss exactly to express—a tendency to make light of the serious elements of the story and to sacrifice them to the more trivial ones.

To James, Dorothea is a serious element, Fred a trivial one. It's strange to see wise Henry reading like a dogmatic young man, with a young man's certainty of what elements, in our lives, will prove the most significant. But then, *Middlemarch* is a book *about* the effects of experience that changes *with* experience. It gets better as you age, being, as Woolf knew, "One of the few English novels written for grown-up people." *Jane Eyre* is understood by the fourteen-year-old as effectively as by the forty-year-old, possibly better. Surely few fourteen-year-olds can make real sense of the marriage of Lydgate and Rosamund. When you're young, the domestic seems such a trivial thing. And as for Fred, the rereader grows steadily less certain that the problems of a Fred Vincy are necessarily more trivial than the angst of a Dorothea Brooke. With time, we're less tempted to find serious only those matters clothed in the garments of Seriousness. And this is fitting because it mirrors Eliot's own journey: as a young woman she shared Dorothea's puritan, self-conscious seriousness, those lofty principles untempered by actual living. The young Marian Evans was all for God, and then, with equal violence, all against Him; she adopted a severe mode of dress and a Quaker-style cape and dreamed of martyrdom (*Middlemarch* opens with a memorable sideswipe at the Art of Serious Dressing); like Dorothea she tried to offer herself as "lamp-holder" to a great man—it's lucky for literature that the great men she chose found her too ugly. Serially rejected, Marian grew convinced that the life of the affections would never be hers. Finally, she gave up on experience and settled for the comforts of the intellect: reading, translating, reviewing. She was no stranger to the proud opinion she later placed in Lydgate's mind: *books are stuff and life is stupid.* It's the necessary, defensive position of those whom (like Eliot) experience seems to refuse, and also those (like Lydgate) who refuse experience. But then, in her forties, things changed for Eliot. It was a mixture of ideas and experience that did it, of love and philosophy. By the time she writes *Middlemarch,* at age fifty, she can look upon her young self with satirical good humor (Dorothea is, in large part, a satirical self-portrait) and clinical self-knowledge. She is able to identify her own mistake:

> The first impulse of a young and ingenuous mind is to withhold the slightest sanction from all that contains even a mixture of supposed error. When the soul is just liberated from the wretched giant's bed of dogmas on which it has been racked and stretched ever since it began to think there is a feeling of exultation and strong hope.

The young Eliot could exult only in the perfect truths we glean from certain books in our libraries; the mature Eliot had learned to have sympathy for the stumbling errors of human beings. These days, when reading critically, the fashion is to remain aloof from the human experiences of novelists. Eliot herself was less squeamish. It was her contention that human experience is as powerful a force as theory or revealed fact. Experience transforms perspective, and transformations in perspective, to Eliot, constitute real changes in the world. "Our subtlest analysis of schools and sects," she wrote, "must miss the essential truth, unless it be lit up by the love that sees in all forms of human thought and work the life and death struggles of separate human beings." Experience, for Eliot, was a powerful way of knowing. She had no doubt that she had learned as much from loving her partner George Lewes, for example, as she had from translating Spinoza. When Dorothea truly becomes great (only really in the last third of the novel, when she comes to the aid of Lydgate and Rosamund), it is because she has at last recognized the value of emotional experience:

All the active thought with which she had before been representing to herself the trials of Lydgate's lot . . . all this vivid sympathetic experience returned to her now as a power: it asserted itself as acquired knowledge asserts itself and will not let us see as we saw in the day of our ignorance.

Once she saw through a glass, darkly, now she is the less deceived. . . . Of how many Victorian novels could that sentence serve as shorthand. One of the reasons we idolize the nineteenth-century English novel is the way its methods, aims and expression seem so beautifully integrated. Author, characters and reader are all striving in the same direction. Eliot, speaking of Dorothea's mind, describes the process this way: "The reaching forward of the whole consciousness towards the fullest truth, the least partial good." It is a fine description of what all good novelists try to do, after their own fashion. But Eliot made a religion of this process; it replaced the old-time religion in which she was raised. Her imagination was particularly compelled by those moments when, as we have it in the vernacular, "the scales fall from our eyes." Bulstrode realizing the true nature of his choices, Rosamund realizing other people exist as she does, Lydgate realizing he has mistaken his wife in every particular, Dorothea realizing the very same of her own husband ("Having embarked on your marital voyage, it is impossible not to be aware that you make no way and that the sea is not within sight—that, in fact, you are exploring an enclosed basin"), even old Mr. Brooke realizing the peasants who live on his land don't actually like him. . . . With a scalpel Eliot dissects degrees of human velleity, finding the conscious action hidden within the impulse hidden within the desire hidden within the will tucked away deep inside the decision that we have obfuscated even from ourselves. (She is very modern in this; she articulates the obsessive circles of self-consciousness and self-deception as sharply as that other master of diffusion, David Foster Wallace. Or maybe we should say that David Foster Wallace is very Victorian.) She pulls it all into the light, as Christ determined to pluck our sins even from our souls. Eliot is the secular laureate of revelation. I love that ecstatic final conversation between Dorothea and her sister:

"I cannot think how it all came about." Celia thought it would be pleasant to hear the story.

"I daresay not," said Dorothea, pinching her sister's chin. "If you knew how it came about, it would not seem wonderful to you."

"Can't you tell me?" said Celia, settling her arms cozily.

"No dear, you would have to feel with me, else you would never know."

Oh, you have to feel it to know it! "Ten years of experience," Eliot wrote to a friend, "have wrought great changes in my inward self." She believed it was a significant change of perspective that enabled the martyred, self-involved Marian Evans to become George Eliot, wisest of writers, who has time for Fred, time for everybody. Here she is, post-*Middlemarch*, replying to a young male correspondent (who had written asking for advice on a personal matter, as many did, post-*Middlemarch*), assuring him that even the simplest aspects of his problem and of her advice to him are of interest to her:

> You should share my reliance on those old, old truths which shallow, drawing-room talk contemptuously dismisses as "commonplaces", though they have more marrow in them, and are quite as seldom wrought into the mental habits as any of the subtleties that pretend to novelty.

That might be a Fred Vincy writing in, troubled by his love problem with Mary Garth. For the mature George Eliot, the trivial problems of a Fred, the commonplaces he thinks and speaks, these are human experience, too, and therefore sacred. For the young Henry James, who has not yet patience for the commonplace, it is a mystery why there must be Fred (or so *much* Fred). But Fred, to Eliot, is a member of "mixed and erring humanity"—her favorite Goethe quote. She always hoped that her work would demonstrate the "remedial influences of pure, natural human relations." Still, it took a great deal of Art to arrange *Middlemarch* so that it might resemble Nature in all its diffusion, all its naturalness. Eliot's Nature is a thing highly stylized, highly intellectual. She was a writer of ideas, maybe more so than any novelist in our canon. In order to be attentive to Fred, Eliot had to take the long way round. It was a philosopher, Spinoza, who first convinced her of the importance of experience. It was theory that brought her to practice. These days, *writer of ideas* has become a term of abuse: we think "Ideas" are the opposite of something we call "Life." It wasn't that way with Eliot. In fact, her ability to animate ideas is so acute she is able to fool the great Henry James into believing Fred Vincy a commonplace young man who has wandered into *Middlemarch* with no purpose, when really nothing could be further from the truth.

MARIAN AND FRED AND SPINOZA

But you can see why Henry hadn't much time for Fred. He's not Henry's type of thing at all—just a simple boy, with a streak of selfishness. He likes to ride and play cards and spend more money than he has. Fred is in love with a bright, plain girl called Mary Garth who is not convinced Fred is worthy of her love. On reflection, Fred agrees. Of the Three Love Problems that dominate *Middlemarch*—Dorothea and Causabon, Lydgate and Rosamund, Fred and Mary—Fred's would seem the least edifying. Yet to Eliot all were equal, and of equal interest, and worthy of an equal number of pages. All her people are striving toward the fullest truth, the least partial good. Except when Eliot thought of striving, she had more in mind than Austen's hope of happy marriages, or Dickens's dream of resolved mysteries. She was thinking of Spinoza's kind of striving, *conatus*. From Spinoza, Eliot took the idea that the good we strive for should be nothing more than "what we certainly know will be useful to us," not a fixed point, no specific moral system, not, properly speaking, a morality at all. It cannot be found in the pursuit of transcendental reward, as Dorothea believes it to be, or in one's ability to conform to a set of rules, as Lydgate attempts when he submits to a conventional marriage. Instead, wise men pursue what is best in and *best for* their own natures. They think of the good as a dynamic, unpredictable combination of forces, different, in practice, for each of us. It's *that* principle that illuminates *Middlemarch*. Like Spinoza's wise men, Eliot's people are always seeking to match what is good in themselves in joyful combinations with other good things in the world. In *Ethics*,

the book Eliot spent years trying to translate (she never finished), the wise walk
in gardens, see plays, eat pleasantly, do work that is meaningful to them and so
on, as their sensibilities allow and demand. They love and are attentive to the
laws of nature, because these alone are eternal and therefore an attribute of the
Supreme Good. All of this was the riposte Eliot needed to the arid rigors of her
family's Methodism; she responded passionately to the idea of worldly striving,
of cleaving to those qualities in others, and in the world, that complemented
one's own strengths. It was what she herself had done. And it cast two things for
which she cared deeply—natural science and human relationships—in a new,
holy light. Spinoza seemed to understand Marian's way of being in the world.
Her shocking common-law "marriage of true minds" to George Lewes (who also
translated Spinoza) was exactly the right kind of *conatus*: a power-strengthening
union characterized by joy. Her rejection of the organized church, so horrifying
to her family, was really a turning away from false, abstract moral values. Her
interest in the new natural sciences was, in Spinozian terms, a form of worship.
When Marian found Spinoza she found the closest philosophical expression of
her own experiences:

> Indeed, the human body is composed of a great many parts of different
> natures, which require continuous and varied food, so that the whole body
> may be capable of doing everything which can follow from its nature, and
> consequently, so that the mind may also be equally capable of conceiving
> many things.

In her intellectual and personal life, Eliot demanded continuous and varied
food—and she conceived of many things. One of these things was Fred Vincy,
a commonplace young man who would seem more suited to a penny-farthing
romance. But it's worth looking again at the facts, which means, in the world
of *Middlemarch*, the emotional facts. Fred is in love with a good girl, a girl
who does not love him because he is not worthy; Fred agrees with her. Maybe
the point is this: of all the people striving in *Middlemarch*, *only Fred is striving for a thing worth striving for*. Dorothea mistakes Causabon terribly, as
Lydgate mistakes Rosamund, but Fred thinks Mary is worth having, that she

is probably a good in the world, or at least, good for him ("She is the best girl I know!")—and he's right. Of all of them Fred has neither chosen a chimerical good nor radically mistaken his own nature. He's not as dim as he seems. He doesn't idealize his good as Dorothea does when she imagines Causabon a second Milton, and he doesn't settle on a good a priori, like Lydgate, who has long believed that a doting, mindless girl is just what a man of science needs. What Fred surmises of the good he stumbles upon almost by accident, and only as a consequence of being fully in life and around life, by being open to its vagaries simply because he is in possession of no theory to impose upon it. In many ways bumbling Fred is Eliot's ideal Spinozian subject. Here is Gilles Deleuze on Spinoza's wise man; he could just as well be speaking of Fred:

> That is why Spinoza calls out to us in the way he does: you do not know beforehand what good or bad you are capable of; you do not know beforehand what a body or mind can do, in a given encounter, a given arrangement, a given combination.

Fred has no idea what he is capable of. His moral luck is all encounter, arrangement, combination. Mary Garth *is* that encounter; she is Fred's reason to be good. It is through her, and for her, that he is able to change:

> Even much stronger mortals than Fred Vincy hold half their rectitude in the being they love best. "The theatre of all my actions is fallen," said an antique personage when his chief friend was dead; and they are fortunate who get a theatre where the audience demands their best. Certainly it would have made a considerable difference to Fred at that time if Mary Garth had had no decided notions as to what was admirable in character.

Simply put, if Fred didn't love Mary, he'd be half the man he is (and Fred is also the occasion to soften some of Mary's hard dogmatic edges, for it surprises her, too, that she could love someone like Fred). And the rigors of love combine with other duties and redouble themselves. Because Fred loves Mary, when he recklessly borrows money from her family and is unable to pay it back, he finds the weight of his misdeed surprisingly heavy upon him. This is not biblical morality but practical morality: Fred has done something wrong in the world, and his true punishment lies not in the next world but in this one. It's in the pain he has caused:

> Curiously enough, his pain in the affair beforehand had consisted almost entirely in the sense that he must have been dishonourable, and sink in the opinion of the Garths: he had not occupied himself with the inconvenience and possible injury that his breach might occasion them, for this exercise of the imagination on other people's needs is not common with hopeful young gentlemen. Indeed we are most of us brought up in the notion that the highest motive for not doing a wrong is something irrespective of the beings who would suffer the wrong. But at this moment he suddenly saw himself as a pitiful rascal who was robbing two women of their savings.

In *Middlemarch* love enables knowledge. Love *is* a kind of knowledge. If Fred didn't love Mary, he would have no reason to exercise his imagination on her family. It's love that makes him realize that two women without their savings are a real thing in the world and not merely incidental to his own sense of dishonor. It's love that enables him to feel another's pain as if it were his own. For Eliot, in the absence of God, all our moral tests must take place on this earth and have their rewards and punishments here. We are one another's lesson, one another's duty. This turns out to be a doctrine peculiarly suited to a certain kind of novel writing. *Middlemarch* is a dazzling dramatization of earthly human striving, of *conatus* in combination. Eliot's complex structure allows for so many examples—each reader will have his or her favorite—but there is one in particular, dropped deep into the middle of the novel like a pebble in a great pond, that seems to me the most beautiful, for its ripples fan outward and outward and reveal the unity in Eliot's diffusion. When the vicar Farebrother decides, for the sake of his good friend Fred, to give up the hope of ever marrying Mary Garth (for he loves her, too), a sage little aperçu occurs to him: "To think of the part one little woman can play in the life of a man, so that to renounce her may be a very good imitation of heroism, and to win her may be a discipline!" Farebrother's satisfaction here, like all the satisfactions *Middlemarch* offers, is not transcendental, but of the earth. Eliot has replaced metaphysics with human relationships. In doing this she took from Spinoza—whose metaphysics are, in fact, extensive—what she wanted and left what she couldn't use. To make it work, she utilized a cast of saints and princes but also fools and criminals, and every shade of human in between. She needed Fred quite as much as Dorothea.

MIDDLEMARCH AND EVERYBODY

These must be the most famous lines in *Middlemarch*:

If we had a keen vision and feeling for all ordinary human life, it would be like hearing the grass grow and the squirrel's heart beat, and we should die of that roar which lies on the other side of silence. As it is, the quickest of us walk about well wadded with stupidity.

Why do we like them so much? Because they seem so humane. We are moved that it should pain Eliot so to draw a border around her attention, that she is so alive to the mass of existence lying unnarrated on the other side of silence. She seems to care for people, indiscriminately and in their entirety, as it was once said God did. She finds it a sin to write always of Dorothea! As literary atonement, Eliot fills her novel with more objects of attention than a novel can comfortably hold. Because we must give Henry his due: *Middlemarch is* messy, decentered, unnerving. It seems to hint at those doubts of the efficacy of narrative that were to follow in the next century. Why always Dorothea, why heroes, why the centrality of a certain character in a narrative, why narrative at all? Eliot, being a Victorian, did not go all the way down that road. For Eliot, in 1870, people are still all that people really have; our knowledge of, and feelings for, one another. A hopeful creed that has bonded readers to Eliot for over a century. Doesn't she seem to solve the head/heart schism of our literature? Neither as sentimental as our popular novelists, nor as dryly cerebral as our experimentalists. Under the influence of Spinoza, via an understanding of Fred, she thought with her heart and felt with her head. It's a fictional procedure perfectly described by one of her creations, Will Ladislaw:

> To be a poet is to have a soul so quick to discern, that no shade of quality escapes it, and so quick to feel, that discernment is but a hand playing with finely ordered variety on the chords of emotion—a soul in which knowledge passes instantaneously into feeling, and feeling flashes back as a new organ of knowledge. One may have that condition by fits only.

Any writer of the classic nineteenth-century English novel had to be able to access this organic relation between what one felt one knew of human behavior and what one knew one felt. That nineteenth-century English novels continue to be written today with troubling frequency is a tribute to the strength of Eliot's example and to the nostalgia we feel for that noble form. Eliot would be proud. But should we be? For where is *our* fiction, our twenty-first-century fiction? We glimpse it here and there. Certainly not as often as you might expect, given the times we live in. As writers and readers and critics, we English remain terribly proud of our conservative tastes. Every year the polls tell us *Middlemarch* is the country's favorite novel, followed by *Pride and Prejudice*, followed by *Jane Eyre* (sometimes this order is reversed). Oh, the universality of the themes. Oh, the timelessness of the prose. But there is a misunderstanding, in England, about the words *universality* and *timelessness* as they relate to our canon. What is universal and timeless in literature is *need*—we continue to *need* novelists who seem to know and feel, and who move between these two modes of operation with wondrous fluidity. What is not universal or timeless, though, is form. Forms, styles, structures—whatever word you prefer—should change like skirt lengths. They have to; otherwise we make a rule, a religion, of one form; we say, "This form here, *this* is what reality is like," and it pleases us to say that (especially if we're English) because it means we don't have to read anymore, or think, or feel. Eventually we become like Mr. Brooke, and Literature something we "went into a great deal, at one time. . . ." George Eliot: now, *there* was a writer. Why don't they write 'em like that anymore? Except the George Eliot of today—so alive to every shade of human feeling, so serious about our dependence on one another—she won't be like the George Eliot of yesterday. Her form will be quite different. She won't be writing the classic nineteenth-century novel. She might not even be English. She might be like Mary Gaitskill, say, or Laura Hird, or A. L. Kennedy. George Eliot may look cozy and conservative from a century's distance, but she was on the border of the New—so will her descendants be. In her essay "Silly Novels By Lady Novelists," Eliot laid out her radical program for great fiction, radical because it was no program at all: "Like crystalline masses, it may take any form, and yet be beautiful."

What twenty-first-century novelists inherit from Eliot is the radical freedom to push the novel's form to its limits, wherever they may be. It's a mistake to hate *Middlemarch* because the Ichabods love it. That would be to denude oneself of one of those good things of the world that Spinoza advised we cling to. *Feeling into knowledge, knowledge into feeling* . . . When we say Eliot was the greatest of Victorian novelists, we mean this process worked more fluidly in her than anyone else.

Four

REREADING BARTHES
AND NABOKOV

The birth of the reader must be at the cost of the death of the Author.
                    —ROLAND BARTHES, "The Death of the Author"

Curiously enough, one cannot read a book: one can only reread it. A good reader, a major reader, an active and creative reader is a rereader.
                    —VLADIMIR NABOKOV, "Good Readers and Good Writers"

1

The novels we know best have an architecture. Not only a door going in and another leading out, but rooms, hallways, stairs, little gardens front and back, trapdoors, hidden passageways, et cetera. It's a fortunate rereader who knows half a dozen novels this way in their lifetime. I know one, *Pnin*, having read it half a dozen times. When you enter a beloved novel many times, you can come to feel that you possess it, that nobody else has ever lived there. You try not to notice the party of impatient tourists trooping through the kitchen (*Pnin* a minor scenic attraction en route to the canyon *Lolita*), or that shuffling academic army, moving in perfect phalanx, as they stalk a squirrel around the backyard (or a series of squirrels, depending on their methodology). Even the architect's claim on his creation seems secondary to your wonderful way of living in it.

To a rereader of this type, Roland Barthes's authorial death sentence will not seem especially polemical. Long before Barthes told them they could, rereaders had been squatting in the houses of beloved novels, each with their own ideas of the floor plan. "A text's unity lies not in its origin but in its destination." Well, yes! And, apart from anything else, we're already living here! On first reading Barthes, in college, the essay struck me as the confirmation of an old desire, to possess a novel entirely. Now when I teach the essay to writing students, the room splits evenly between those who take it in their stride as a perfectly obvious experiential truth and those who take it as an affront. For the first type, the kind of reader I have tried to describe above, Barthes's apparently radical transaction of power is an exchange they have always already assumed. They have always walked into books boldly, without knocking or bothering too much about the owner. But to those students who have the tendency to feel humbled before the act of writing, "The Death of the Author" is a perverse assault on the privileges of authorship, on the possibility of fixed meaning, even upon "Truth" itself. For a polemic a mere seven pages long, it has a great power to disturb, seeming to take from a delicate student her sense of the text as an intelligible thing, as well as her sense of herself as a significant individual capable of receiving meaning:

> Yet this destination cannot any longer be personal: the reader is without history, biography, psychology; he is simply that *someone* who holds together in a single field all the traces by which the written text is constituted.

Meanwhile, on the other side of the room, those bold readers remain unruffled and unsurprised to find themselves described as "destinations"— on the contrary, the impersonality suits them. They were never likely to say, in a college class, "I guess, for me, as a lapsed Catholic feminist from Iowa this book didn't really work." All texts are grist to their mill: personal sensibilities have never come into it. They are excited to add to the *text's* sudden indeterminacy, their *own* indeterminacy as well. To observe these two natural, unschooled reactions is fascinating: they reveal within the famous ideological debate a more intimate and important question of character, into which a teacher should not necessarily intrude. Why not allow each student to find out for himself what kind of rereader he is? No bad blood need be spilled over it (as it was when I was in college). After all, you can storm the house of a novel like Barthes, rearranging the furniture as you choose, or you can enter on your knees, like the pilgrim Nabokov thought you were, and try to figure out the cunning design of the place—the house will stand either way.

In my own reading life, I've been pulled first in one direction, then in the other. Reading has always been my passion, my pleasure, and I am constitutionally drawn to any thesis that gives power to readers, increasing their freedom of movement. But when I became a writer, writing became my discipline, my practice, and I felt the need to believe in it as an intentional, directional act, an expression of an individual consciousness. And the tension between these two modes grows particularly acute when I try to read the author Nabokov as the critic Barthes recommends. On the one hand there is Barthes's radical invocation of reader's rights ("The removal of the Author . . . is not merely an historical fact or an act of writing; it utterly transforms the modern text or—which is the same thing—the text is henceforth made and read in such a way that at all levels its Author is absent.") On the other, Nabokov's bold assertion of authorial privilege ("My characters are galley slaves"). You can hardly get going at all. This despite the fact that the great critic and the great author have a theme in common: both equally concerned with *jouissance*, with literary bliss (though they define it differently), and the creative act of reading. Barthes spoke of the pleasure of the text, Nabokov of asking his students to read "with your brain and spine . . . the tingle in the spine really tells you what the author felt and wished you to feel." Barthes, though, had no interest in what the author felt or wished you to feel, which is where my trouble starts.

It's easy to read "The Death of the Author" as a series of revolutionary demands, but it's worth remembering that it was also simply a licked forefinger held up to test a wind already blowing. For along with authorial assassination, Barthes lays out his vision for a new kind of "text," and it is one that the reader of 1968 would have recognized:

> Multi-dimensional space in which a variety of writings, none of them original, blend and clash. [It is] a tissue of quotations drawn from the innumerable centres of culture. . . . In the multiplicity of writing, everything is to be *disentangled*, nothing *deciphered*; the structure can be followed, "run" (like the thread of a stocking) at every point and at every level, but there is nothing beneath: the space of writing is to be ranged over, not pierced.

This was the thrilling space of the *nouveau roman*, of Robbe-Grillet and Sarraute and Claude Simon—the new writing was already with us. To read these new texts properly, though, it was necessary that the Author step aside, and here survey gave way to manifesto. The Author was dead, and in his place came the "scriptor," born simultaneously with the text (so that "every text is eternally written *here and now*"), and with no real existence before or after it:

> Succeeding the Author, the scriptor no longer bears within him passions, humours, feelings, impressions, but rather this immense dictionary from which he draws a writing that can know no halt: life never does more than imitate the book, and the book itself is only a tissue of signs, an imitation that is lost, infinitely deferred.

Long live the scriptor! Like a lot of rereaders of my college generation, I fell for this "new" French criticism hard (although much of it was already, by the time we got to Kristeva, Foucault, Derrida and the rest, thirty years old.) For myself, I read it enthusiastically and badly, taking a wide variety of complex philosophical ideas as a kind of personal poetic license. Barthes was my favorite, both for his relative accessibility and the unlimited power he appeared to be placing at my feet. If the text was eternally written here and now, well then this surely meant I didn't have to worry about its historical specificity, and so could turn to A *Sentimental Education* in perfect ignorance of the 1848 Revolution, or *The Cherry Orchard* without reading a blessed word about the emancipation of the serfs. His theory of the text, too, appealed to me strongly: antic, decentered, many-voiced, perverse. I sought out the "new" fiction that would justify and exemplify it. Nabokov, with his unreliable narrators, with his reversal of the traditional life/art hierarchies ("I am no more guilty of imitating 'real life' than 'real life' is responsible for plagiarizing me," he once claimed), with that referential style that even the noble-winged seraphs envied—Nabokov *should* have been exhibit number one. But there was, there is, a problem. Superficially the ideal Barthesian *text* suits Nabokov quite well. But what about the man who writes it? *Scriptor?* Stripped of his inalienable passions, humors, feelings, and impressions? It's difficult to imagine Nabokov in this club or any club.[1] It's a brave critic who dares tell Vladimir Vladimirovich that he is "diminishing like a figurine at the far end of the literary stage," no longer "the past of his own book" but only incidental to it. Hard, too, to imagine an all-powerful Reader more able than Nabokov to "disentangle" his own cat's cradles. "Genius," he wrote, "still means to me—in my Russian fastidiousness and pride of phrase—a unique dazzling gift." To Nabokov, an author was more than a bricolage artiste, more than a recombiner of older materials. His sensibility, his sensations, his memories, and his mode for expressing it all—these had to be unique. So proud of his own genius, so particular about his interpretations, Nabokov refused to lie down and die.

2

Part of the difficulty to be had linking Nabokov with the French criticism is that criticism's tendentious politics. Barthes's argument flirts heavily with

---

1. "I don't belong to any club or group. I don't fish, cook, dance, endorse books, sign books, co-sign declarations, eat oysters, get drunk, go to church, go to analysts, or take part in demonstrations."

a leftist aesthetic and this is hard to fit to a man who liked to torture his left-leaning friends with paeans to capitalism generally and the Vietnam War specifically. Where Nabokov saw the Author as the very principle of individualized Western freedom, Barthes saw precisely the same thing, but didn't like it:

> The Author is a modern figure, a product of our society in so far as, emerging from the Middle Ages with English empiricism, French rationalism and the personal faith of the Reformation, it discovered the prestige of the individual, of, as it is more nobly put, the "human person." It is thus logical that in literature it should be this positivism, the epitome and culmination of capitalist ideology, which has attached the greatest importance to the "person" of the Author.

Nabokov, having fled the Communist revolution, was not sympathetic to ideologies that made light of Western freedoms and individual privilege, up to and including the individuality of the author. But in a deeper sense, the disjunction between Nabokov and *la nouvelle critique* is philosophical. It has to do with how Nabokov thought about reality:

> Reality is a very subjective affair. I can only define it as a kind of gradual accumulation of information, and as specialization. If we take a lily, for instance, or any other kind of natural object, a lily is more real to a naturalist than it is to an ordinary person. But it is still more real to a botanist. And yet another stage of reality is reached with that botanist who is a specialist in lilies. You can get nearer and nearer, so to speak, to reality; but you never get near enough because reality is an infinite succession of steps, levels of perception, false bottoms, and hence unquenchable, unattainable. You can know more and more about one thing but you can never know everything about one thing: it's hopeless.

But this is a different kind of interpretive hopelessness. For Barthes, hermeneutics and epistemology have been subjected to a twin crisis: there is no *there* there. With the Author dead, no longer the past of his own text, nor its source of nourishment or final meaning, the scriptor merely "traces a field without origin—or which, at least, has no other origin than language itself, language which ceaselessly calls into question all origins." And this crisis in authorship, for Barthes, has consequences far beyond the little world of novels and their readers:

> In precisely this way literature (it would be better from now on to say *writing*), by refusing to assign a "secret," an ultimate meaning, to the text (and to the world as text), liberates what may be called an anti-theological activity, an activity that is truly revolutionary since to refuse to fix meaning is, in the end, to refuse God and his hypostases—reason, science, law.

Just as we must give up the urge to know the reality of the text, we must also give up the hope of knowing the world in its ultimate reality. There can be no more "deciphering," we must settle for "disentangling." Power is relinquished. Not so in Nabokov's world. In Nabokov's portrait of subjectivity you can still decipher by *degrees*. The lily can be *more or less real*, and there *exists* an ultimate reality even if we can never know it. Still, we can come close. To approach the reality of a novel, as readers, Nabokov asked that we bring biographical,[2] historical, cultural, entomological, and linguistic knowledge to the task, not to mention attentive care, empathy, synesthetic acuity, and a keen visual sense. There can be ever more accurate readings of the lily. And there can be, consequently, philistine misreadings, a fact Barthes's portrait of the prepotent reader (blissed out, picking her way through a riot of potential meanings, constructing a text playfully, without limits) refuses to acknowledge.

But Nabokov was no cold-blooded empiricist and he was not blind to the indeterminacy of writing. For him, too, there existed a blissful, unfettered, nonhierarchical experience of meaning—but it came earlier in the process.

2. His translated poetry reader of 1944, *Three Russian Poets: Selections from Pushkin, Lermontov and Tyutchev*, takes care to include three sparklingly written mini-biographies of the poets.

Not while the reader reads, but before the writer writes, in a moment that precedes composition: "Inspiration." Nabokov split this old-fashioned word into two Russian parts. The first half of inspiration, for him, is *vorstorg* (initial rapture). *Vorstorg* describes that moment in which the book as a whole is conceived:

> A combined sensation of having the whole universe entering you and of yourself wholly dissolving in the universe surrounding you. It is the prison wall of the ego suddenly crumbling away and the non-ego rushing in from the outside to save the prisoner—who is already dancing in the open.

Here the author dies, momentarily; *here* meaning is indeterminate and free flowing. *Vorstorg* "has no conscious purpose in view"; in *vorstorg* "the entire circle of time is conceived, which is another way of saying time ceases to exist." But after this comes the second stage: *vdokhnovenie* (recapture). And it's here that the actual writing gets done. In Nabokov's experience, the two had quite different natures. *Vorstorg* was "hot and brief." *Vdokhnovenie* "cool and sustained." In the first you lose yourself. In the second, you are doing the conscious work of construction. And while making the choices good writing requires, the Author exists, he circumscribes, he controls, he puts walls on either side of the playground. The reader, to read him properly, would do well to recognize the existence of these walls. The Author limits the possibility of the reader's play.

In *The Pleasure of the Text* and "S/Z," meanwhile, we find Barthes assigning this work of construction to readers themselves. Here a rather wonderful Barthesian distinction is made between the "readerly" and the "writerly" text. Readerly texts ask little or nothing of their readers; they are smooth and fixed in meaning and can be read passively (most magazine copy and bad genre writing is of this kind). By contrast, the writerly text openly displays its *written-ness*, demanding a great effort from its reader, a creative engagement. In a writerly text the reader, through reading, is actually reconstructing the act of writing, a thrilling idea with which Nabokov would sympathize, for that was the kind of active reader his own work required.[3] But then Barthes imagines a further step: that by reading across the various "codes" he believed were inscribed in the writerly text (the linguistic, symbolic, social, historical, et cetera), a reader, in an active sense, constructs the text *entirely anew* with each reading. In this way Barthes reverses the hierarchy of the writer-reader dynamic. The reader becomes "no longer the consumer but the producer of text."

Hard to know for sure what Nabokov would have made of *that*. My guess is he would have found it unhinged. He disliked literary theory in general. ("Every good reader has enjoyed a few good books in his life so why analyse the pleasures that both sides know?") It's probably for the best that he didn't live to see the kind of post-Barthes (and post-Foucault) campus criticism that flowered on both sides of the pond during the eighties and nineties. Wild analogy; aggressive reading against the grain and across codes and discourses; a fondness for cultural codes over textual particulars. You remember the sort of thing:

> *The Trans-gendered Suitor: Refractions of Darcy as Elizabeth's True Sister*
>   *in* Pride and Prejudice.
> *Daisy, the Dollar, and Foucault's Repressive Hypothesis: Portraits of*
>   *Sexualised Capital in* The Great Gatsby.
> *Please Sir Can I Have Some More: Bulimic Rejections of Self in* Oliver
>   Twist.

I've written a lot of essays like this. And found it a wonderful thing, to feel so free. The novel was mine to do with as I wished, to read upside down, back to front or in entirely anachronistic terms. That kind of freedom makes writers of readers, liberating us from the passive and authoritarian reading

---

3. Another way of thinking about the distinction might be: there is a style that believes writing should mimic the quick pace, the ease, and the fluidity of reading (or even of speech). And then there is a style that believes reading should mimic the obstruction and slow struggle of writing. Raymond Carver would be on that first axis. Nabokov is *way out* on the second. Joyce is even further.

styles we are taught in school (*Hard Times* = British education system in Victorian England). When we read instead in an active way we get to reinscribe dusty old novels into our own interests and concerns. There is a joy in getting someone to hand us *their* butterfly so we can spend twenty pages making the case for its being *our* giraffe.

But Nabokov believed in the butterfly qua butterfly. For this reason, when I first read his *Lectures on Literature* I was disappointed.[4] Was this really Nabokov? The apparent analytic simplicity, the lengthy quoting without commentary. The obsession with (what seemed to me) utterly banal details: the shape of Gregor Samsa's shell, a map of Dublin, the exact geographical location of *Mansfield Park*. And the questions he set his students! What color are Emma Bovary's eyes? What kind of house was Bleak House? How many *rooms* are in there? You have to reset your brain, away from the overheated hustle of English departments, before you can see how beautiful those lectures are. How attentive. How particular. When it comes to rereading, Nabokov felt, "one should notice and fondle details." These lectures are a marvelous, concrete example of that principle.

For Barthes, ideologically tied to a post-Marxist analysis, a bad reader was a consumer and an ideal one, a producer. For Nabokov, the reader is neither. Nabokov's ideal reader is something resembling a butterfly collector, with an interest both empirical and aesthetic. For his ideal reader, the text is a highly particular thing, and the job is to appreciate and note its particularities. If nothing else, in these lectures we find a mirror image of how Nabokov himself hoped to be read. For he felt his own work to be multiplex but not truly multivalent—the buck stopped at Nabokov, the man who had placed the details there in the first place. His texts had their unity (their truest reality) in him.

Consequently, seriously variant interpretations of his novels were only so much *poshlust*[5] to him, to be filed next to "Freudian symbolism, moth-eaten

---

4. These were originally conceived as lectures for Nabokov's Cornell undergraduates on the Masters of European Fiction. They were collected and published after his death.
5. Properly *poshlost*, from the Russian for vulgarity. Nabokov's definition: "Not only the obviously trashy but mainly the falsely important, the falsely beautiful, the falsely clever, the falsely attractive."

mythologies, social comment, humanistic messages, political allegories, over concern with class or race, and the journalistic generalities we all know." This makes him a hard author to write about. He seems to admit no ideal reader except himself. I think of him as one of the last, great twentieth-century believers in the autonomy of the Author, as Frank Lloyd Wright was one of the last believers in the Architect. They both specialized in theatrical interviews, struck self-regarding and self-mythologizing poses, all of which would mean nothing (the Author being dead, you don't have to listen to his self-descriptions) if it weren't for the fact that they wove the restrictions and privileges of authorship into the very fabric of the things they built. For it's true that each time I enter *Pnin* I feel its author controlling (via an obsessive specificity) all my reactions, just as, in Wright's Unity Temple, one enters through a small, low side door, forced to approach the magnificence of the interior by way of a series of awkward right-angled turns. There is extraordinary, almost overwhelming beauty in Nabokov—there is also an oppressive rigidity. You will live in his house his way. Nabokov's way means giving up the reader's traditional linear right-of-way through a novel (starting at the first page and ending at the last) and confronting instead a network of connected leitmotifs, quotations, clues, and puzzles that are not so much to be read as deciphered. Faced with a Nabokov novel it's impossible to rid yourself of the feeling that you've been set a problem, as a chess master sets a problem in a newspaper. I am always tormented by the sense I have missed something— and Nabokov makes me feel my failure. The Author, he claimed, "clashes with readerdom because he is his own ideal reader and those other readers are so very often mere lip-moving ghosts and amnesiacs." He claimed to be writing, instead, "mainly for artists, fellow-artists and follow artists," whose job it was to "share not the emotions of the people in the book but the emotions of its author—the joys and difficulties of creation." *Follow* artists! In practice this means subsuming your existence in his, until you become, in effect, Nabokov's double, knowing what he knows, loving as he loves and hating his way, too,[6]

6. Nabokov nerds often slavishly parrot his strong opinions. I don't think I'm the first person to have my mind poisoned, by Nabokov, against Dostoyevsky.

following each nuance, pursuing each reference, in what amounts to a reader's mimeograph of the Author's creative act. (And there exist many people who hate Nabokov for precisely this reason.) It is a reversal of the Barthes formulation: here it is the *reader* who must die so that the *Author* may live. There is a sensible school of thought that argues *all* writing makes us do this[7]—but few writers make you feel your subjection as Nabokov does. The only perfect tenant of the house that Nabokov built is Nabokov.[8]

3

When you teach Nabokov to students, along with the usual complaint that his vocabulary is unnecessarily baroque, they want to know whether all this game playing, all this punning complexity is, in the end, truly *for* the reader at all. They scrunch up their noses and direct you to a particular passage: "Now, isn't this just Nabokov basically getting himself *off*?" The question is a fair one. The elusive, allusive, pleasures of the Nabokovian text—whose pleasures are these, really? When asked about "the pleasures of writing" in his *Playboy* interview, Nabokov answered: "They correspond exactly to the pleasures of reading, the bliss, the felicity of a phrase is shared by writer and reader: by the satisfied writer and the grateful reader."

But isn't the aside vital? Doesn't satisfaction trump gratitude? With our twenty-first-century passion for equality, gratitude seems a slavish sort of attitude to take to an author. Is that truly our reward for being Nabokovians, for reading and rereading, pursuing every butterfly, every long-vanished Russian émigré poet? Nabokov thought so; he felt that what he offered his reader, and especially his *reader*, was not the antic pleasure of their own interpretations, but the serious satisfaction of *twinning the emotion of creation*:

7. "In many ways writing is the act of saying *I*, of imposing oneself upon other people, of saying *listen to me, see it my way, change your mind.* It's an aggressive, even a hostile act. You can disguise its aggressiveness all you want with veils of subordinate clauses and qualifiers and tentative subjunctives, with ellipses and evasions—with the whole manner of intimating rather than claiming, of alluding rather than stating—but there's no getting around the fact that setting words on paper is the tactic of a secret bully, an invasion, an imposition of the writer's sensibility on the reader's most private space."—Joan Didion
8. Vera, his wife and "first and best reader" being a close second.

I would say that the main favour I ask of the serious critic is sufficient per-
ceptiveness to understand that whatever term or trope I use, my purpose
is not to be facetiously flashy or grotesquely obscure but to express what I
feel and think with the utmost truthfulness and perception.

By following all his threads, you are doing more than reading, you are given
the opportunity to precisely reconstruct the bliss of *vdokhnovenie*, of Nabokov's
own writerly act. (And maybe even a trace of *vorstorg*. Nabokov thought that
the "force and originality involved in the primary spasm of inspiration is directly
proportional to the worth of the book the author will write." We might hope,
then, for a trace of the propellant to be left after the explosion.) The difference
is that Nabokov asks that we admit it is the *author's* gift in the design, rather
than *our* gift at connecting the dots, that is truly meaningful, and meaning pro-
ducing. No matter how I try to slot them together, Nabokov goes a certain way
along with Barthes and no further. Reading is creative! insists Barthes. Yes, but
writing creates, replies Nabokov, smoothly, and turns back to his note cards.

Maybe we can say that Nabokov makes his readers so very creative that
we are liable to feel that we ourselves have made something. *Pnin* rereaders can follow the Lermontov hints (to a poem called "The Triple Dream")
and the Tolstoy hints (to "The Death of Ivan Ilyich") and find in those texts
miniature versions of *Pnin*'s Russian doll structure, *mise-en-abymes* placed
by Nabokov into his novel with the care of Van Eyck.[9, 10] They are so hard to

---

9. Warning: this footnote for *Pnin* nerds only. Galya Diment's illuminating study *Pniniad*
reveals that Nabokov meant to kill Pnin, and was committed to this plan until quite far along
in the novel. It appears to be a case of a writer becoming too charmed by his own creation
to kill him. But it also means that the Tolstoy and Lermontov echoes (this sense of being
spoken about casually, or caricatured, by other people, while you yourself are experiencing an
extremely personal and ulterior reality) are deprived their final satisfaction (as Pnin's escape
from the jaws of death finds its own echo in the glass bowl that improbably survives the
washing up). We can faintly imagine what the last chapter was to have been: the narrator and
Jack Cockerell doing their sordid, lame little impressions of Pnin, while Pnin lies dying, or
perhaps has already died. (Which leads to the question: what is it about having people speak
of you as you lie dying that is particularly Russian?)
10. Of course an *actual* Van Eyck turns up at Pnin's successful little party, when Laurence
Clements, lost in thought while holding a dictionary, is compared to the master's portrait
of Canon van der Paele. At the same party, a little later on, bored Laurence is to be found
"flipping through an album of *Flemish Masterpieces*."

see, such particular details, that you feel you placed them there yourself. And the experience of rereading *Pnin* is never perfect or finished—there's always some new detail to fondle. A newcomer to Nabokov will notice only the actual butterflies fluttering around; as you get further in, you'll start to notice the entomology sunk deep into the weft and weave. Those Nabokovian words, pressed into service for quite other purposes, which, upon closer inspection, reveal their hidden wings and abdomens (bole, crepitation, Punchinello[11]). And it's only on this most recent rereading that I think to kneel in front of my desk, place a glass of water at eye level and position a comb, on end, behind it. *Zebra cocktail!*[12] Nabokov saw it—now I do. And it's beautiful. Gratitude does not seem out of place.

Whether one quite approves of it or not, it's a Nabokovian assumption that if you work to give him back what he has given to you, this should be reward enough (for you). His students learned this soon enough.[13] And of course Vera lived it. (The character most closely modeled on Vera—Zina, from *The Gift*—is praised by the narrator for having a "perfect understanding . . . for everything that he himself loved.") Here Barthes comes up against a wall of pure Nabokov. Barthes scorned that "image of literature, to be found in ordinary culture, [which] is tyrannically centred on the author, his person, his life, his hates, his passions." And then Foucault, in the essay that answered

11. All appear in *Pnin*. *Bole* is used for "the trunk of a tree" but is also the small eye on a butterfly wing; *crepitation* is a Nabokov favorite, but aside from crackling generally, it's the word for what a (bombardier) beetle does when he "ejects a pungent fluid with a sudden sharp report." *Punchinello*, in *Pnin*, is of course the ugly Italian commedia character, who is short and stout, and so, in the simile under consideration, reminiscent of a tongue. But it is also a very pretty butterfly.
12. From *Pnin*: "He placed various objects in turn—an apple, a pencil, a chess pawn, a comb—behind a glass of water and peered through it at each studiously: the red apple became a clear-cut red band bounded by a straight horizon, half a glass of Red Sea, Arabia Felix. The short pencil, if held obliquely, curved like a stylized snake, but if held vertically became monstrously fat—almost pyramidal. The black pawn, if moved to and fro, divided into a couple of black ants. The comb, stood on end, resulted in the glass's seeming to fill with beautifully striped liquid, a zebra cocktail."
13. "My method of teaching precluded genuine contact with my students. At best, they regurgitated a few bits of my brain during examinations."

Barthes's own, and deepened it, identified the Author (or "Author-function") as "the principle of thrift in the proliferation of meaning."[14] In Nabokov's case, the arrow hits its bull's-eye: this author's high-handed rules about reading, his various strictures concerning interpretation, and his defensive humiliations of his own potential readers (especially on the topic of Freudian critics and *Lolita*[15])—these all work to "impede the free circulation, the free manipulation, the composition, decomposition, and recomposition of fiction."[16] But a question I never asked as a college rereader, now bothers me as a writer: *and what of it?*

It was meant to be obvious, to the college rereaders we once were, that any restriction on the multivalent free flow of literary meaning was not to be stood for. But to speak for myself, I've changed my mind. The assumption that what a reader wants most is unfettered freedom, rather than limited, directed, play,[17] or that one should automatically feel nostalgia for a bygone age of collective, anonymous authorship[18]—none of this feels at all obvious to me anymore. The house rules of a novel, the laying down of the author's peculiar terms—all of this is what interests me. This is where my pleasure is. Yet it must also be true that part of the change in my attitude represents a vocational need to believe in Nabokov's vision of total control. Nabokov's profound hostility to Freud was no random whim—it was the theory of the unconscious itself that horrified him. He couldn't stand to admit the existence of a secondary power directing and diverting his own. Few writers can. I think of that lovely idea of Kundera's: "Great novels are always a little more intelligent than their authors." This, in part, is what Barthes had to tell us

14. Foucault, "What Is an Author?," 1969. The English translation quoted is by Joseph V. Harari, first published in 1979.
15. "Ferrety, human-interest fiends, those jolly vulgarians," as he called them. And that cagey afterword to *Lolita* performs a similar function.
16. Foucault, "What Is an Author?"
17. In Nabokov's case, it's more like S&M—an experience you'd hope Foucault could get behind.
18. A largely romantic concept. And wasn't it always the same examples? Either it was Homer; some unspecified "ethnographic societies" within which "narrative is never assumed by a person but by a mediator, shaman or relator whose 'performance'—the mastery of the narrative code—may possibly be admired but never his 'genius'" (Barthes); or else the rather weak model of Beaumont and Fletcher.

and what Nabokov wanted to dispute. Maybe every author needs to keep faith with Nabokov, and every reader with Barthes. For how can you write, believing in Barthes? Still, I'm glad I'm not the reader I was in college anymore, and I'll tell you why: it made me feel lonely. Back then I wanted to tear down the icon of the author and abolish, too, the idea of a privileged reader—the text was to be a free, wild thing, open to everyone, belonging to no one, refusing an ultimate meaning. Which was a powerful feeling, but also rather isolating, because it jettisons the very idea of communication, of any possible genuine link between the person who writes and the person who reads. Nowadays I know the true reason I read is to feel less alone, to make a connection with a consciousness other than my own. To this end I find myself placing a cautious faith in the difficult partnership between reader and writer, that discrete struggle to reveal an individual's experience of the world through the unstable medium of language. Not a refusal of meaning, then, but a quest for it. Whether it is "ultimate" or "secret" meaning, seems to me besides the point and rather a sleight of hand on the part of Barthes; by using such terms he forces a monumental, essentialist, and theological discourse on a relationship that is in fact far more hesitant and delicate than he allows. Nabokov is not God, and I am not his creation. He is an Author and I am his reader, and we are stumbling toward meaning simultaneously, together. Zebra cocktail!

Five

F. KAFKA, EVERYMAN

1

How to describe Kafka, the man? Like this, perhaps:

It is as if he had spent his entire life wondering what he looked like, without ever discovering there are such things as mirrors.
A naked man among a multitude who are dressed.
A mind living in sin with the soul of Abraham.
Franz was a saint.[1]

Or then again, using details of his life, as found in Louis Begley's refreshingly factual *The Tremendous World I Have Inside My Head: Franz Kafka: A Biographical Essay*: over six feet tall, handsome, elegantly dressed; an unexceptional student, a strong swimmer, an aerobics enthusiast, a vegetarian; a frequent visitor to movie houses, cabarets, all-night cafés, literary soirees and brothels; the

---

1. Respectively, Walter Benjamin, Milena Jesenská, Erich Heller and Felice Bauer.

published author of seven books during his brief lifetime; engaged three times (twice to the same woman); valued by his employers, promoted at work.

But this last Kafka is as difficult to keep in mind as the Pynchon who grocery shops and attends baseball games, the Salinger who grew old and raised a family in Cornish, New Hampshire. Readers are incurable fabulists. Kafka's case, though, extends beyond literary mystique. He is more than a man of mystery—he's metaphysical. Readers who are particularly attached to this supra-Kafka find the introduction of a quotidian Kafka hard to swallow. And vice versa. I spoke once at a Jewish literary society on the subject of time in Kafka, an exploration of the idea—as the critic Michael Hofmann has it—that "it is almost always too late in Kafka." Afterward a spry woman in her nineties, with a thick old-world accent, hurried across the room and tugged my sleeve: "But you're quite wrong! I knew Mr. Kafka in Prague—and he was *never* late."

Recent years have seen some Kafka revisionism, although what's up for grabs is not the quality of the work,[2] but rather its precise nature. What kind of a writer *is* Kafka? Above all, it's a revision of Mr. Kafka's biographical aura. From a witty essay of this kind, by the young novelist and critic Adam Thirlwell:

> It is now necessary to state some accepted truths about Franz Kafka, and the Kafkaesque. . . . Kafka's work lies outside literature: it is not fully part of the history of European fiction. He has no predecessors—his work appears as if from nowhere—and he has no true successors. . . . These fictions express the alienation of modern man; they are a prophecy of a) the totalitarian police state, and b) the Nazi Holocaust. His work expresses a Jewish mysticism, a non-denominational mysticism, an anguish of man without God. His work is very serious. He never smiles in photographs. . . . It is crucial to know the facts of Kafka's emotional life when reading his fiction. In some sense, all his stories are autobiographical. He is a genius, outside ordinary limits of literature, and a saint, outside ordinary limits of human behaviour. All of these truths, all of them, are wrong.

2. This has not been seriously assailed since Edmund Wilson's "A Dissenting Opinion on Kafka."

Thirlwell blames the banality of the Kafkaesque on Max Brod, Kafka's friend, first biographer and literary executor, in which latter capacity he defied Kafka's will (Kafka wanted his work burned), a fact that continues to stain Brod, however faintly, with bad faith. For his part, Brod always maintained that Kafka knew there would be no bonfire: if his friend was serious, he would have chosen another executor. Far harder to defend is Brod's subsequent decision to publish the correspondence,[3] the diaries and the acutely personal *Letter to My Father* (though posthumous literary morality is a slippery thing: when what is found in a drawer is very bad, the shame of it outlives both reader and publisher; when it's as good as *Letter to My Father*, the world winks at it).

If few readers of Kafka can be truly sorry for the existence of the unpublished work, many regret the manner in which Brod chose to present it. The problem is not solely Brod's flat-footed interpretations; it's his interventions in the texts themselves. For when it came to editing the novels, Brod's sympathy for the theological would seem to have guided his hand. Kafka's system of ordering chapters was often unclear, occasionally nonexistent; it was Brod who collated *The Trial* in the form with which we are familiar. If it feels like a journey toward an absent God—so the argument goes—that's because Brod placed the God-shaped hole at the end. The penultimate chapter, containing the pseudohaggadic parable "Before the Law," might have gone anywhere, and placing it anywhere else skews the trajectory of ascension; no longer a journey toward the supreme incomprehensibility, but a journey without destination, into which a mystery is thrust and then succeeded by the quotidian once more. Of course, there's also the possibility that Kafka would have placed this chapter near the end, exactly as Brod did, but lovers of Kafka are not inclined to credit him with Brod's variety of common sense. The whole *point* of Kafka is his uncommonness. Whatever Brod explains we feel sure Kafka would leave unexplained; whichever conventional interpretation he foists on the works the

---

3. Begley tells us that Brod did not directly publish Kafka's letters to Milena and Felice, but neither did he press them to "surrender his letters for destruction, or to destroy the letters themselves." As a result, Brod lost control of them. As the German army entered Prague, Milena entrusted them to Willy Haas, who published them in 1952; Felice, who emigrated to America, sold her letters herself, in 1955, to Schocken Books.

works themselves repel. We think of Shakespeare this way, too: a writer sullied by our attempts to define him. In this sense the idea of a literary genius is a gift we give ourselves, a space so wide we can play in it forever. Thirlwell again:

> It is important, when reading Kafka, not to read him too Brodly.
> Take this passage from Brod's 1947 biography: "It is a new kind of smile that distinguishes Kafka's work, a smile close to the ultimate things— a metaphysical smile so to speak—indeed sometimes when he used to read out one of his tales for us friends of his, it rose above a smile and we laughed aloud. But we were soon quiet again. It is no laughter befitting human beings. Only angels may laugh this way. . . ." Angels! It is often underestimated, how much talent is required to be a great reader. And Brod was not a great reader, let alone a great writer.

True. Maybe we can say instead that Brod was a great talent spotter.[4] Of his own literary capacities, Brod had few illusions. His friendship with Kafka was monstrously one-sided from the start, a thing carved from pure awe. They met after a lecture on Schopenhauer, given by Brod, after which Kafka approached the lecturer and accompanied him home. "Something seems to have attracted him to me," writes Brod. "He was more open than usual, filling the endless walk home by disagreeing strongly with my all too rough formulations." The familiar pilgrim's pose, two steps behind the prophet, catching wisdom as it falls.[5] These days we tire of Brod's rough formulations: for too long they set the tone. We don't want to read Kafka Brodly anymore, as the postwar Americans did so keenly. It's tempting to think, had we ourselves been those first readers, we would have recognized at once—without such heavy prompting—the literary greatness of an ex-ape talking to the academy or tiny Josephine "piping" for her mouse people. I wonder.

---

4. Brod championed many artists, including Leoš Janáček, Franz Werfel and Karl Kraus.
5. The truly hagiographic text is Gustav Janouch's *Conversations with Kafka*. The young Gustav befriended Kafka in Berlin in the final year of the writer's life. In this essay, where I quote from the book, it is with the understanding that this is "reported speech" and most probably prettified for publication.

There exists a second Brod account of Kafka reading aloud:

We friends of his laughed quite immoderately when he first let us hear the
first chapter of *The Trial*. And he himself laughed so much that there were
moments when he couldn't read any further. Astonishing enough, when
you think of the fearful earnestness of this chapter.

Here the crime of Kafka's first biographer is rather benign: a slight overdose of
literary respect. Brod couldn't quite believe Kafka was being funny when he was
being funny. For how could Kafka, in his fearful earnestness, be funny? But it's
strange: Kafka revisionism is also, after a fashion, in love with Kafkaesque purity.
We can't credit the Brodish idea that Kafka writes of "the alienation of modern
man"—too obvious. And how could Kafka be obvious? How could Kafka be anything that we are? Even our demystifications of Kafka are full of mystery.

2

But if we're not to read Kafka too Brodly, how are we to read him? We might
do worse than read him Begley. Gently skeptical of the biographical legend, Begley yet believes in the "metaphysical smile" of the work, the possibility that it
expresses our modern alienation—here prophet Kafka and quotidian Kafka are
not in conflict. He deals first, and most successfully, with the quotidian. The
Kafka who, like other diarists, indulged a relentless dramaturgy of the self; the
compulsive letter writer who once asked a correspondent, "Don't you get pleasure out of exaggerating painful things as much as possible?" For Kafka, the pros-
pect of a journey from Berlin to Prague is "a foolhardiness whose parallel you can
only find by leafing back through the pages of history, say to Napoleon's march
to Russia." A brief visit to his fiancée "couldn't have been worse. The next thing
will be impalement." The diaries are the same, only more so: few people, even in
that solipsistic form, can have written "I" as frequently as he. People and events
appear rarely; the beginning of the First World War is a matter to be weighed
equally with the fact he went swimming that day. The Kafka who wrote the fictions was a man of many stories; the private Kafka sang the song of himself:

I completely dwell in every idea, but also fill every idea. . . . I not only feel
myself at my boundary, but at the boundary of the human in general.

I am the end or the beginning.

Life is merely terrible; I feel it as few others do. Often—and in my
inmost self perhaps all the time—I doubt that I am a human being.

One could quote pages of similar sentiments: Kafka scholars usually do.
Thankfully, Begley has more of a comic sense than most Kafka scholars, tend-
ing to plump instead for Kafka in quite other moods; at times whiny, occasionally wheedling, often slyly disingenuous, and every now and then frankly
mendacious. The result is something we don't expect. It's a little funny:

It turns out we really do keep writing the same thing. Sometimes I
ask whether you're sick and then you write about it, sometimes I want
to die and then you do, sometimes I want stamps and then you want
stamps. . . .

This, writes Begley, is "Kafka's characterization (in a moment of despond-
ency) of the letters that he and Milena exchanged [and it] is not far off the
mark for many of them, and applies with even greater force to many of the
letters to Felice." Certainly the love letters are repetitive; there is something
mechanical in them, not deeply felt, at least, not toward their intended
recipients—the sense is of a man writing to himself. Impossible to believe
Kafka was in love with poor Felice Bauer, she of the "bony, empty face,
that wore its emptiness openly. . . . Almost broken nose. Blonde, somewhat
straight, unattractive hair, strong chin"; Felice with her bourgeois mores, her
offer to sit by him as he worked ("In that case," he wrote back, "I could not
write at all"), her poor taste in "heavy furniture" ("A perfect tombstone,"
writes Kafka, describing a sideboard of her choosing, "or a memorial to the
life of a Prague official"). For Kafka she is symbol: the whetstone upon which
he sharpens his sense of himself. The occasion of their engagement is the cue
to explain to her (and to her father) why he should never marry. The pros-
pect of living with her inspires pages of encomia on solitude. Begley, a fiction

writer himself, has an eye for the way fiction writers obsessively preserve their personal space, even while seeming to give it away. You might say he has Kafka's number: "It's all there in a nutshell: the charm offensive Kafka commenced with the conquest of Felice as its goal; reflexive flight from that goal as soon as it is within reach; insistence on dealing with her and their future only on his terms; and self-denigration as a potent defense against intimacy that requires more than words." Poor Felice! She never stood a chance. In his introductory letter Kafka claims: "I am an erratic letter writer. . . . On the other hand, I never expect a letter to be answered by return. . . . I am never disappointed when it doesn't come." In fact, counters Begley, "The opposite was true: Kafka wrote letters compulsively and copiously, and turned into a hysterical despot if they were not answered forthwith, bombarding Felice with cables and remonstrances." Kafka frantically pursued Felice, and then he tried to escape her, Begley writes, "with the single-minded purpose and passion of a fox biting off his own leg to free himself from a trap"—a line with more than a little Kafka spirit in it. "Women are traps," Kafka said once, "which lie in wait for men everywhere, in order to drag them down into the Finite."[6] It's a perfectly ordinary expression of misogyny, dispiriting in a mind that more often took the less-traveled path. À propros: having had it suggested to him by a young friend that Picasso was "a willful distortionist" who painted "rose-coloured women with gigantic feet," Kafka replied:

> I do not think so. . . . He only registers the deformities which have not yet penetrated our consciousness. Art is a mirror, which goes "fast," like a watch—sometimes.[7]

Kafka's mind was like that; it went wondrous fast—still, when it came to women, it went no faster than the times allowed. Those who find the personal failures of writers personally offensive will turn from Kafka here, as readers turn from Philip Larkin for similar reasons (the family resemblance between the two

6. *Conversations with Kafka*, Gustav Janouch.
7. Ibid.

writers was noted by Larkin himself[8]). In this matter, Kafka has a less judgmental biographer than Larkin found in Andrew Motion; Begley, though perfectly clear on Kafka's "problems with girls" does not much agonize over them. Literary nerds may enjoy the curious fact that for both those literary miserabilists (close neighbors on any decent bookshelf) modern heating appliances appear to have served as synecdoche for what one might call the Feminine Mundane:

He married a woman to stop her getting away
Now she's there all day
And the money he gets for wasting his life on work
She takes as her perk
To pay for the kiddies' clobber and the drier
And the electric fire[9]

I yield not a particle of my demand for a fantastic life arranged solely in the interest of my work; she, indifferent to every mute request, wants the average: a comfortable home, an interest on my part in the factory, good food, bed at eleven, central heating. . . .[10]

Yet as it was with Larkin, Kafka's ideas about women and his experiences of them turn out to be different things. Women were his preferred correspondents and inspiration (in 1912, the Felice correspondence[11] competes with the writing of Amerika; in 1913, it wins), his most stimulating intellectual sparring partners (Milena Jesenská, with whom he discussed "the Jewish question"), his closest friends (his favorite sister, Ottla) and finally the means of his escape

8. Although, naturally, Larkin felt his own case to be by far the more extreme, as he makes clear in his poem "The Literary World": My dear Kafka / When you've had five years of it, not five months, / Five years of an irresistible force meeting an / Immoveable object right in your belly, / Then you'll know about depression.
9. "Self's the Man" by Philip Larkin.
10. From Kafka's diary. "She" is Felice.
11. Traditionally, critics credit Felice Bauer with being at least partial inspiration for "The Judgement"—the first story of his that satisfied Kafka. The evidence is circumstantial but convincing: it was dedicated to Felice, its composition dates to the beginning of their correspondence, and its heroine, to whom the hero is engaged, shares her initials: "Frieda Brandenfeld, a girl from a well-to-do family."

(Dora Diamant, with whom, in the final year of his life, he moved to Berlin). No, women did not drag Kafka into the finite. As Begley would have it: *the opposite was true.* Usefully, Begley is a rather frequent and politic employer of modifiers and corrections. *In reality, the truth was, the opposite was true.* Kafka told his diary the only way he could live was as a sexually ascetic bachelor. *The truth was* he was no stranger to brothels. Begley is particularly astute on the bizarre organization of Kafka's writing day. At the Assicurazioni Generali, Kafka despaired of his twelve-hour shifts that left no time for writing; two years later, promoted to the position of chief clerk at the Insurance Institute, he was now on the one-shift system, 8:30 A.M. until 2:30 P.M. And then what? Lunch until 3:30, then a sleep until 7:30, then exercises, then a family dinner. After which he started work around 11:00 P.M. (as Begley points out, the letter and diary writing took up at least an hour a day, and more usually two), and then "depending on my strength, inclination, and luck, until one, two or three o' clock, once even till six in the morning." Then, finding it an "unimaginable effort to go to sleep," he fitfully rested before leaving to go to the office once more. This routine left him permanently on the verge of collapse. Yet "when Felice wrote to him . . . arguing that a more rational organization of his day might be possible, he bristled: 'The present way is the only possible one; if I can't bear it, so much the worse; but I will bear it somehow.'" It was Brod's opinion that Kafka's parents should gift him a lump sum "so that he could leave the office, go off to some cheap little place on the Riviera to create those works that God, using Franz's brain, wishes the world to have." Begley, leaving God out of it, politely disagrees, finding Brod's wish

> probably misguided. Kafka's failure to make even an attempt to break out of the twin prisons of the Institute and his room at the family apartment may have been nothing less than the choice of the way of life that paradoxically best suited him. It is rare that writers of fiction sit behind their desks, actually writing, for more than a few hours a day. Had Kafka been able to use his time efficiently, the work schedule at the Institute would have left him with enough free time for writing. As he recognized, the truth was that he wasted time.

The truth was that he wasted time! The writer's equivalent of the dater's revelation: *He's just not that into you.* "Having the Institute and the conditions at his parents' apartment to blame for the long fallow periods when he couldn't write gave Kafka cover: it enabled him to preserve his self-esteem." And here Begley introduces yet another Kafka we rarely think of, a writer in competition with other writers in a small Prague literary scene, measuring himself against the achievements of his peers. For in 1908, Kafka had published only eight short prose pieces in *Hyperion*, while Brod had been publishing since he was twenty; his close friend Oskar Baum was the successful author of one book of short stories and one novel, and Franz Werfel—seven years Kafka's junior—had a critically acclaimed collection of poems. In 1911, Kafka writes in his diary: "I hate Werfel, not because I envy him, but I envy him too. He is healthy, young and rich, everything that I am not." And later in that same year: "Envy of the apparent success of Baum whom I like so much. With this, the feeling of having in the middle of my body a ball of wool that quickly winds itself up, its innumerable threads pulling from the surface of my body to itself." Of course, that wool ball—a throwaway line in a diary!—reminds us how little call he had to envy anyone.

3

The impossibility of not writing, the impossibility of writing German, the impossibility of writing differently. One might add a fourth impossibility, the impossibility of writing. . . . Thus what has resulted was a literature impossible in all respects, a gypsy literature which had stolen the German child out of its cradle and in great haste put it through some kind of training, for someone had to dance on the tightrope. (But it wasn't a German child, it was nothing; people merely said that somebody was dancing.)

A perfect slice of Kafka. On May 3, 1913, Kafka's diary conceives of a butcher's knife "quickly and with mechanical regularity chop[ping] into me from the side," slicing thin, parma ham style, *pezzi di Kafka*. . . . The quote above is like that: it has the marbled mark of Kafka running through it. It traces a typical Kafka journey, from the concrete, to the metaphorical, to the allegorical, to the notional, which last—as so often with Kafka— seems to grow obscure the more precisely it is expressed. From this same quote Begley efficiently unpacks Kafka's "frightful inner predicament," born of his strange historical moment. A middle-class Prague Jew (*"The most Western Jewish of them all"*) both enamored of and horrified by an Eastern shtetl life he never knew; a Jew in a period of virulent anti-Semitism ("I've been spending every afternoon outside in the streets, wallowing in anti-Semitic hate") who remained ambivalent toward the Zionist project; a German speaker surrounded by Czech nationalists. The impossible "gypsy literature" an aspect of an impossible gypsy self, an assimilated Judaism that was fatally neither one thing or the other.

In Kafka's world there were really two "Jewish questions." The first was external, asked by Gentiles, and is familiar: "What is to be done with the Jews?" For which the answer was either persecution or "toleration," that vile word.[12] (Writing to Brod from an Italian *pensione*, Kafka describes being barely tolerated at lunch by an Austrian colonel who has just found out he is Jewish: "Out of politeness he brought our little chat to a sort of end before he hurried out with long strides. . . . Why must I be a thorn in their flesh?"). The second Jewish question, the one that Kafka asked himself, was existential: *What have I in common with Jews?* Begley does not shy from citing this and many of the other quotations "used by scholars to buttress the argument that Kafka was himself a Jewish anti-Semite, a self-hating Jew":

I admire Zionism and am nauseated by it.

At times I'd like to stuff them all, simply as Jews (me included) into, say, the drawer of the laundry chest. Next I'd wait, open the drawer a little to see if they've suffocated, and if not, shut the drawer again and keep doing this to the end.

---

12. Now more commonly used for recent immigrants to Western democracies.

Isn't it natural to leave a place where one is so hated? The heroism of staying is nonetheless merely the heroism of cockroaches which cannot be exterminated, even from the bathroom.

To this evidence, Freudians add exhibit number one: fantasies of self-slaughter ("*Between throat and chin would seem to be the most rewarding place to stab*"), shadowing Kafka's lineage (grandson of the butcher of Wossek) and those tales of Jewish ritual murder that are as old as anti-Semitism itself.[13] For Begley, though, the accusation of auto-anti-Semitism is "unfair and, in the end, beside the point." He sees rather the conflicted drama of assimilation: "The fear was of a crack in the veneer . . . through which might enter the miasma of the shtetl or the medieval ghetto." In this version, affection and repulsion are sides of the same coin:

> It would have been surprising if he, who was so repelled by his own father's vulgarity at table and in speech, had not been similarly repelled by the oddities of dress, habits, gestures and speech of the very Jews of whom he made a fetish, because of the community spirit, cohesiveness, and genuine emotional warmth he was convinced they possessed.

It's an awkward argument that struggles to recast repulsion as "the cumulative effect on Kafka of the ubiquitous anti-Semitism" all around him, which in turn caused a kind of "profound fatigue," compelling him to "transcend his Jewish experience and his Jewish identity" so that he might write " about the human condition"—a conclusion that misses the point entirely, for Kafka found the brotherhood of man quite as incomprehensible as the brotherhood of Jews. For Kafka, the impossible thing was collectivity itself:

> What have I in common with Jews? I have hardly anything in common with myself, and should stand very quietly in a corner, content than I can breathe.

---

13. Begley: "Three 'ritual murder trials,' throwbacks to the Middle Ages, and unimaginable for Jews believing that they lived in an era of moral as well as material progress, took place within his lifetime."

Kafka's horror is not Jewishness per se, because it is not a horror *only* of Jewishness: it is a horror of all shared experience, all shared being, all *genus*. In a time and place in which national, linguistic and racial groups were defined with ever more absurd precision, how could the very idea of commonness not turn equally absurd? In his *Memoirs of an Anti-Semite,* fellow Austro-Hungarian Gregor von Rezzori presented the disquieting idea that the philo-Semite and the anti-Semite have something essential in common (the narrator is both): a belief in a *collective Jewish nature, a Semiteness.* Kafka, by contrast, had stopped believing. The choice of belonging to a people, of partaking of a shared nature, was no longer available to him. He often wished it was not so (hence his sentimental affection for shtetl life), but it *was* so. On this point, Begley quotes Hannah Arendt approvingly, though he does not pursue her brilliant conclusion:

> . . . These men [assimilated German Jews] did not wish to "return" either to the ranks of the Jewish people or to Judaism, and could not desire to do so . . . not because they were too "assimilated" and too alienated from their Jewish heritage, but because all traditions and cultures as well as all "belonging" had become equally questionable to them.[14]

Jewishness itself had become the question. It is a mark of how disconcerting this genuinely Kafkaesque concept is that it should provoke conflict in Begley himself.

"My people," wrote Kafka, "provided that I have one." What does it mean, to have a people? On no subject are we more sentimental and less able to articulate what we mean. In what, for example, does the continuity of "Blackness" exist? Or "Irishness"? Or "Arabness"? Blood, culture, history, genes? Judaism, with its matrilineal line, has been historically fortunate to have at its root a beautiful answer, elegant in its circularity: Jewishness is the gift of a Jewish mother. But what is a Jewish mother? Kafka found her so unstable a thing, a mistranslation might undo her:

14. From her introduction to Walter Benjamin's *Illuminations: Essays and Reflections.* As Begley points out, Benjamin and Kafka were "near enough contemporaries for Arendt's comments to be considered directly relevant" to Kafka's case.

Yesterday it occurred to me that I did not always love my mother as she deserved and as I could, only because the German language prevented it. The Jewish mother is no "Mutter," to call her "Mutter" makes her a little comical. . . . "Mutter" is peculiarly German for the Jew, it unconsciously contains, together with the Christian splendor, Christian coldness also, the Jewish woman who is called "Mutter" therefore becomes not only comical but strange. . . . I believe it is only the memories of the ghetto that still preserve the Jewish family, for the word "Vater" too is far from meaning the Jewish father.

Kafka's Jewishness was a kind of dream, whose authentic moment was located always in the nostalgic past. His survey of the insectile situation of young Jews in Inner Bohemia can hardly be improved upon: "With their posterior legs they were still glued to their father's Jewishness, and with their waving anterior legs they found no new ground."

Alienation from oneself, the conflicted assimilation of migrants, losing one place without gaining another . . . This feels like Kafka in the genuine clothes of an existential prophet, Kafka in his twenty-first-century aspect (if we are to assume, as with Shakespeare, that every new century will bring a Kafka close to our own concerns). For there is a sense in which Kafka's Jewish question ("What have I in common with Jews?") has become everybody's question, Jewish alienation the template for all our doubts.[15] What is Muslimness? What is femaleness? What is Polishness? What is Englishness? These days we all find our anterior legs flailing before us. We're all insects, all *Ungeziefer*,[16] now.

---

15. Sylvia Plath hinted at this: "I think I may well be a Jew."
16. As Gregor Samsa awoke one morning from uneasy dreams he found himself transformed in his bed into a gigantic *Ungeziefer*. Variously translated as *insect, cockroach*—much to the horror of Nabokov, who insisted the thing had wings—*bug, dung-beetle*, the literal translation is *vermin*. Only the David Wyllie, Joachim Neugroschel and Stanley Corngold translations retain this literal meaning.

Six

TWO DIRECTIONS FOR THE NOVEL

Those who knew
what was going on here
must give way to
those who know little.
And less than little.
And finally as little as nothing.

—Wislawa Szymborska, "The End and the Beginning"

1

From two recent novels, a story emerges about the future for the Anglophone Novel. Both are the result of long journeys. *Netherland*, by Joseph O'Neill, took seven years to write; *Remainder*, by Tom McCarthy, took seven years to find a mainstream publisher. The two novels are antipodal—indeed, one is the strong refusal of the other. The violence of the rejection *Remainder* represents to a novel like *Netherland* is, in part, a function of our ailing literary culture. All novels attempt to cut neural routes through the brain, to convince us down *this* road the true future of the Novel lies. In healthy times, we cut multiple roads, allowing for the possibility of a Jean Genet as surely as a Graham Greene. These aren't particularly healthy times. A breed of lyrical realism has had the freedom of the highway for some time now, with most other exits blocked. For *Netherland*, our receptive pathways are so solidly established that to read this novel is to feel a powerful, somewhat dispiriting sense of recognition. It is perfectly done—in a sense, that's the problem. It's so precisely the image of what we have been taught to value in fiction that it throws that image into a kind of existential crisis, as the photograph gifts a nervous breakdown to the painted portrait.

Netherland is nominally the tale of Hans van den Broek, a Dutch stock analyst, transplanted from London to downtown New York with his wife and young son. When the towers fall, the family relocates to the Chelsea Hotel; soon after, a trial separation occurs. Wife and son depart once more for London, leaving Hans stranded in a world turned immaterial, phantasmagoric: "Life itself had become disembodied. My family, the spine of my days, had crumbled. I was lost in invertebrate time." Every other weekend he visits his family, hoping "that flying high into the atmosphere, over boundless massifs of vapor or small clouds dispersed like the droppings of Pegasus on an unseen platform of air, might also lift me above my personal haze"—the first of many baroque descriptions of clouds, light and water. On the alternative weekends, he plays cricket in Staten Island, the sole white man in a cricket club that includes Chuck Ramkissoon, a Trinidadian wiseacre, whose outsize dreams of building a cricket stadium in the city represent a Gatsbyesque commitment to the American Dream/human possibility/narrative with which Hans himself is struggling to keep faith. The stage is set, then, for a "meditation" on identities both personal and national, immigrant relations, terror, anxiety, the attack of futility on the human consciousness and the defense against same: meaning. In other words, it's the post-9/11 novel we hoped for. (Were there calls, in 1915, for the Lusitania novel? In 1985, was the Bhopal novel keenly anticipated?) It's as if, by an act of collective prayer, we have willed it into existence. But *Netherland* is only superficially about 9/11 or immigrants or cricket as a symbol of good citizenship. It certainly *is* about anxiety, but its worries are formal and revolve obsessively around the question of authenticity. *Netherland* sits at an anxiety crossroads where a community in recent crisis— the Anglo-American liberal middle class—meets a literary form in long-term crisis, the nineteenth-century lyrical realism of Balzac and Flaubert. Critiques of this form by now amount to a long tradition in and of themselves. Beginning with what Robbe-Grillet called "the destitution of the old myths of 'depth,'" they blossomed into a phenomenology skeptical of realism's metaphysical tendencies; they peaked in that radical deconstructive doubt that questions the capacity of language itself to describe the world in any accuracy. They all of them note the (often unexamined) credos upon which realism is built: the transcendent importance of form, the incantatory power of language to reveal truth, the essential fullness and continuity of the self. Yet despite these theoretical assaults, the American metafiction that stood in opposition to realism has been relegated to a safe corner of literary history, to be studied in postmodernity modules, and dismissed, by our most prominent public critics, as a fascinating failure, intellectual brinkmanship that lacked heart. Barth, Barthelme, Pynchon, Gaddis, David Foster Wallace—all misguided ideologists, the novelist equivalent of the socialists in Francis Fukuyama's *The End of History and the Last Man*. In this version of our literary history the last man standing is the Balzac-Flaubert model, on the evidence of its extraordinary persistence. But the critiques persist, too. Is it really the closest model we have to our condition? Or simply the bedtime story that comforts us most?

Netherland, unlike much lyrical realism, has some consciousness of these arguments, and so it is an anxious novel, unusually so. It is absolutely a post-catastrophe novel, but the catastrophe isn't terror, it's realism. In its opening pages, we get the first hint of this. Hans, packing up his London office in preparation to move to New York, finds himself buttonholed by a senior vice president "who reminisced for several minutes about his loft on Wooster Street and his outings to the 'original' Dean & DeLuca." Hans finds this nostalgia irritating: "Principally he was pitiable—like one of those Petersburgians of yesteryear whose duties have washed him up on the wrong side of the Urals." But then:

It turns out he was right, in a way. Now that I, too, have left that city, I find it hard to rid myself of the feeling that life carries a taint of aftermath. This last-mentioned word, somebody once told me, refers literally to a second mowing of grass in the same season. You might say, if you're the type prone to general observations, that New York City insists on memory's repetitive mower—on the sort of purposeful postmortem that has the effect, so one is told and forlornly hopes, of cutting the grassy past to manageable proportions. For it keeps growing back, of course. None of this means that I wish I were back there now; and naturally I'd like to believe that my own retrospection is in some way more important than the old S.V.P.'s, which, when I was exposed to it, seemed to amount to not much more than a cheap longing. But there's no such thing as a cheap longing, I'm tempted to conclude these days, not even if you're sobbing over a cracked fingernail. Who knows what happened to that fellow over there? Who knows what lay behind his story about shopping for balsamic vinegar? He made it sound like an elixir, the poor bastard.

This paragraph is structured like a recognized cliché (i.e., We had come, as they say, to the end of the road). It places before us what it fears might be a tired effect: in this case, the nostalgia-fused narrative of one man's retrospection (which is to form the basis of this novel). It recognizes that effect's inauthenticity, its lack of novelty, even its possible dullness—and it employs the effect anyway. By stating its fears Netherland intends to neutralize them. It's a novel that wants you to know that it knows you know it knows. Hans invites us to sneer lightly at those who are "prone to general observations," but only as a prelude to just such an observation, presented in language frankly genteel and faintly archaic ("so one is told and forlornly hopes"). Is it cheap longing? It can't be because—and this is the founding, consoling myth of lyrical realism—the self is a bottomless pool. What you can't find in the heavens (anymore), you'll find in the soul. Yet there remains, in Netherland, a great anxiety about the depth or otherwise of the soul in question (and thus Netherland's entire narrative project). Balsamic vinegar and Dean & DeLuca in the first two pages are no accident. All the class markers are openly displayed, and it's a preemptive strike: is the reader suggesting that white middle-class futures traders are less authentic, less interesting, less capable of interiority than anyone else?

Enter Chuck Ramkissoon. Chuck has no such anxieties. He is unselfconscious. He moves through the novel simply *being*, and with abandon, saying those things that the novel—given its late place in the history of the novel—daren't, for fear of seeming naive. It's Chuck who openly states the central metaphor of the novel, that cricket is "a lesson in civility. We all know this; I do not need to say more about it." It's left to Chuck to make explicit the analogy between good behavior on pitch and immigrant citizenship: "And if we step out of line, believe me, this indulgence disappears. What this means . . . is we have an extra responsibility to play the game right." Through Chuck idealisms and enthusiasms can be expressed without anxiety:

> "I love the national bird," Chuck clarified. "The noble bald eagle represents the spirit of freedom, living as it does in the boundless void of the sky."
> I turned to see whether he was joking. He wasn't. From time to time, Chuck actually spoke like this.

And again:

> "It's an impossible idea, right? But I'm convinced it will work. Totally convinced. You know what my motto is?"
> "I didn't think people had mottoes anymore," I said.
> "Think fantastic," Chuck said. "My motto is, Think Fantastic."

Chuck functions here as a kind of authenticity fetish, allowing Hans (and the reader) the nostalgic pleasure of returning to a narrative time when symbols and mottoes were full of meaning and novels weren't neurotic, but could aim themselves simply and purely at transcendent feeling. This culminates in a reverie on the cricket pitch. Chuck instructs Hans to put his old-world fears aside and hit the ball high ("How else are you going to get runs? This is America"), and Hans does this, and the movement is fluid, unexpected,

formally perfect, and Hans permits himself an epiphany, expressed, like all
epiphanies, in one long, breathless, run-on sentence:

> All of which may explain why I began to dream in all seriousness of a sta-
> dium and black and brown and even a few white faces crowded in bleach-
> ers, and Chuck and me laughing over drinks in the members' enclosure
> and waving to people we know, and stiff flags on the pavilion roof, and
> fresh white sight-screens, and the captains in blazers looking up at a quar-
> ter spinning in the air, and a stadium-wide flutter of expectancy as the two
> umpires walk onto the turf square and its omelet-colored batting track,
> whereupon, with clouds scrambling in from the west, there is a roar as the
> cricket stars trot down the pavilion steps onto this impossible grass field in
> America, and everything is suddenly clear, and I am at last naturalized.

There are those clouds again. Under them, Hans is rendered authentic,
real, *natural*. It's the dream that Plato started, and Hans is still having it.

But *Netherland* is anxious. It knows the world has changed and we do not
stand in the same relation to it as we did when Balzac was writing. In *Père
Goriot*, Balzac makes the wallpaper of the Pension Vauquer speak of the lives
of the guests inside. Hans does not have quite this metaphysical confidence:
he can't be Chuck's flawless interpreter. And so *Netherland* plants inside itself
its own partial critique, in the form of Hans's wife Rachel, whose "truest self
resisted triteness, even of the inventive romantic variety, as a kind of false-
hood." It is she who informs Hans of what the reader has begun to suspect:

> "Basically, you didn't take him seriously."
> She has accused me of exoticizing Chuck Ramkissoon, of giving him a
> pass, of failing to grant him a respectful measure of distrust, of perpetrat-
> ing a white man's infantilizing elevation of a black man.

Hans denies the charge, but this conversation signals the end of Chuck's
privileged position (gifted to him by identity politics, the only authenticity to
survive the twentieth century). The authenticity of ethnicity is shown to be a

fake—Chuck's seeming naturalness is simply an excess of ego, which overflows soon enough into thuggery and fraud. For a while Chuck made Hans feel authentic, but then, later, the submerged anger arrives, as it always does: what makes Chuck more authentic than Hans anyway? It makes sense that Hans's greatest moment of antipathy toward Chuck (he is angry because Chuck has drawn him into his shady, violent business dealings) should come after three pages of monologue, in which Chuck tells a tale of island life, full of authentic Spanish names and local customs and animals and plants, which reads like a Trinidadian novel:

> Very little was said during the rest of that journey to New York City. Chuck never apologized or explained. It's probable that he felt his presence in the car amounted to an apology and his story to an explanation— or, at the very least, that he'd privileged me with an opportunity to reflect on the stuff of his soul. I wasn't interested in drawing a line from his childhood to the sense of authorization that permitted him, as an American, to do what I had seen him do. He was expecting *me* to make the moral adjustment—and here was an adjustment I really couldn't make.

Once the possibility of Chuck's cultural authenticity is out of play, a possible substitute is introduced: world events. Are *they* the real thing? During a snowstorm, Hans and Rachel have the argument everyone has ("She said, 'Bush wants to attack Iraq as part of a right-wing plan to destroy international law and order as we know it and replace it with the global rule of American force'"), which ends for Hans as it ends for many people, though you get the sense Hans believes his confession to be in some way transgressive:

> Did Iraq have weapons of mass destruction that posed a real threat? I had no idea; and to be truthful, and to touch on my real difficulty, I had little interest. I didn't care.

But this conclusion is never in doubt: even as Rachel rages on, Hans's mind wanders repeatedly to the storm, its specks of snow like "small and dark flies," and also like "a cold toga draped [over] the city." The nineteenth-century flaneur's ennui has been transplanted to the twenty-first-century bourgeois's political apathy—and made beautiful. Other people's political engagement is revealed to be simply another form of inauthenticity. ("World events had finally contrived a meaningful test of their capacity for conscientious political thought. Many of my acquaintances, I realized, had passed the last decade or two in a state of intellectual and psychic yearning for such a moment.") The only sophisticated thing to do, the only *literary* thing to do, is to stop listening to Rachel and think of a night sky:

> A memory of Rachel and me flying to Hong Kong for our honeymoon, and how in the dimmed cabin I looked out of my window and saw lights, in small glimmering webs, on the placeless darkness miles below. I pointed them out to Rachel. I wanted to say something about these creaturely cosmic glows, which made me feel, I wanted to say, as if we had been removed by translation into another world.

This sky serves the same purpose as another one near the end of the novel in which "a single cavaliering cloud trailed a tattered blue cloak of rain" and to which a "tantalizing metaphysical significance" attaches, offering Hans "a sanctuary: for where else, outside of reverie's holy space, was I to find it?" Where else indeed? These are tough times for Anglo-American liberals. All we've got left to believe in is ourselves.

In *Netherland*, only one's own subjectivity is really authentic, and only the personal offers this possibility of transcendence, this "translation into another world." Which is why personal things are so relentlessly aestheticised: this is how their importance is signified, and their depth. The world is covered in language. Lip service is paid to the sanctity of mystery:

> One result [of growing up in Holland] in a temperament such as my own, was a sense that mystery is treasurable, even necessary: for mystery, in such a crowded, see-through little country, is, among other things, space.

But in practice *Netherland* colonizes all space by way of voracious image. This results in many beauties ("a static turnstile like a monster's unearthed skeleton") and some oddities (a cricket ball arrives "like a gigantic meteoritic cranberry"), though in both cases, there is an anxiety of excess. Everything must be made literary. Nothing escapes. On TV "dark Baghdad glitter[s] with American bombs." Even the mini traumas of a middle-class life are given the high lyrical treatment, in what feels, at its best, like a grim satire on the profound fatuity of twenty-first-century bourgeois existence. The surprise discovery of his wife's lactose intolerance becomes "an unknown hinterland to our marriage"; a slightly unpleasant experience of American bureaucracy at the DMV brings Hans (metaphorically) close to the war on terror:

And so I was in a state of fuming helplessness when I stepped out into the inverted obscurity of the afternoon. . . . I was seized for the first time by a nauseating sense of America, my gleaming adopted country, under the secret actuation of unjust, indifferent powers. The rinsed taxis, hissing over fresh slush, shone like grapefruits; but if you looked down into the space between the road and the undercarriage, where icy matter stuck to the pipes and water streamed down the mud flaps, you saw a foul mechanical dark.

To which one wants to say, isn't it hard to see the dark when it's so lyrically presented? And also: grapefruits?

In an essay written half a century ago, Robbe-Grillet imagined a future for the novel in which objects would no longer "be merely the vague reflection of the hero's vague soul, the image of his torments, the shadow of his desires." He dreaded the "total and unique adjective, which attempt[s] to unite all the inner qualities, the entire hidden soul of things." But this adjectival mania is still our dominant mode, and *Netherland* is its most masterful recent example. And why shouldn't it be? The received wisdom of literary history is that *Finnegans Wake* did not fundamentally disturb realism's course as Duchamp's urinal disturbed realism in the visual arts: the novel is made out of language, the smallest units of which still convey meaning, and so they will always carry the trace of the Real. But if literary realism survived the assault of Joyce, it retained the wound. *Netherland* bears this anxiety trace; it foregrounds its narrative nostalgia, asking us to note it, and look kindly upon it:

> I was startled afresh by the existence of this waterside vista, which on a
> blurred morning such as this had the effect, once we passed under the
> George Washington Bridge, of canceling out centuries. . . .

The centuries are duly canceled. What follows is a page of landscape portraiture, seen from a train's window ("Clouds steaming on the clifftops foxed all sense of perspective, so that it seemed to me that I saw distant and fabulously high mountains"). Insert it into any nineteenth-century novel (again, a test first suggested by Robbe-Grillet) and you wouldn't see the joins. The passage ends with a glimpse of a "near-naked white man" walking through the trees by the track; he is never explained and never mentioned again, and this is another rule of lyrical realism: that the random detail confers the authenticity of the Real. As perfect as it all seems, in a strange way it makes you wish for urinals.

Halfway through the novel, Hans imagines being a professional cricketer, lyrically and at length. He dreams of the ball hanging "before me like a Christmas bauble," of a bat preternaturally responsive by means of "a special dedication of memory," and after he's done, he asks for our indulgence:

> How many of us are completely free of such scenarios? Who hasn't known,
> a little shamefully, the joys they bring?

It's a credit to *Netherland* that it is so anxious. Most lyrical realism blithely continues on its merry road, with not a metaphysical care in the world, and few of its practitioners write as finely as Joseph O'Neill. I have written in this tradition myself and cautiously hope for its survival, but if it's to survive, lyrical realists will have to push a little harder on their subject. *Netherland* recognizes the tenuous nature of a self, that "fine white thread running, through years and years," and Hans flirts with the possibility that language may not precisely describe the world ("I was assaulted by the notion, arriving in the form of a terrifying stroke of consciousness, that substance—everything of

so-called concreteness—was indistinct from its unnameable opposite") but in
the end *Netherland* wants always to comfort us, to assure us of our beautiful
plenitude. At a certain point in his *Pervert's Guide to Cinema*, the philosopher
Slavoj Žižek passes quickly and dismissively over exactly this personal fullness
we hold so dear in the literary arts ("You know . . . the wealth of human personality and so on and so forth . . ."), directing our attention instead to those
cinematic masters of the antisublime (Hitchcock, Tarkovsky, David Lynch)
who look into the eyes of the Other and see no self at all, only an unknowable
absence, an abyss. *Netherland* flirts with that idea, too. Not knowing what to
do with photographs of his young son, Hans gives them to Chuck's girlfriend,
Eliza, who organizes photo albums for a living:

> "People want a story," she said. "They like a story."
>
> I was thinking of the miserable apprehension we have of even those
> existences that matter most to us. To witness a life, even in love—even
> with a camera—was to witness a monstrous crime without noticing the
> particulars required for justice.
>
> "A story," I said suddenly. "Yes. That's what I need."
>
> I wasn't kidding.

An interesting thought is trying to reach us here, but the ghost of the literary burns it away, leaving only its remainder: a nicely constructed sentence,
rich in sound and syntax, signifying (almost) nothing. *Netherland* doesn't
really want to know about misapprehension. It wants to offer us the authentic
story of a self. But is this really what having a self feels like? Do selves always
seek their good, in the end? Are they never perverse? Do they always want
meaning? Do they not sometimes want its opposite? And is this how memory
works? Do our childhoods often return to us in the form of coherent, lyrical
reveries? Is this how time feels? Do the things of the world really come to us
like this, embroidered in the verbal fancy of times past? Is this really realism?

In the end what is impressive about *Netherland* is how precisely it knows
the fears and weaknesses of its readers. What is disappointing is how much it
indulges them. Out of a familiar love, like a lapsed High Anglican, *Netherland*

hangs on to the rituals and garments of transcendence, though it well knows they are empty. In its final, saccharine image (Hans and his family, reunited on the mandala of the London Eye), *Netherland* demonstrates its sly ability to have its metaphysical cake and eat it, too:

> A self-evident and prefabricated symbolism attaches itself to this slow climb to the zenith, and we are not so foolishly ironic, or confident, as to miss the opportunity to glimpse significantly into the eyes of the other and share the thought that occurs to all at this summit, which is, of course, that they have made it thus far, to a point where they can see horizons previously unseen, and the old earth reveals itself newly.

And this epiphany naturally reminds Hans of another, which occurred years earlier as the Staten Island Ferry approached New York, and the sky colored like a "Caran d'Ache box" of pencils, purples fading into blues:

Concentrat[ing] most glamorously of all, it goes without saying, in the lilac acres of two amazingly high towers going up above all others, on one of which, as the boat drew us nearer, the sun began to make a brilliant yellow mess. To speculate about the meaning of such a moment would be a stained, suspect business; but there is, I think, no need to speculate. Factual assertions can be made. I can state that I wasn't the only person on that ferry who'd seen a pink watery sunset in his time, and I can state that I wasn't the only one of us to make out and accept an extraordinary promise in what we saw—the tall approaching cape, a people risen in light.

There was the chance to let the towers be what they were: towers. But they were covered in literary language when they fell, and they continue to be here.

2

If *Netherland* is a novel only partially aware of the ideas that underpin it, *Remainder* is fully conscious of its own. But how to write about it?

Immediately an obstacle presents itself. When we write about lyrical realism our great tool is the quote, so richly patterned. But *Remainder* is not filled with pretty quotes; it works by accumulation and repetition, closing in on its subject in ever-decreasing revolutions, like a trauma victim circling the blank horror of the traumatic event. It plays a long, meticulous game, opening with a deadpan paragraph of comic simplicity:

> About the accident itself I can say very little. Almost nothing. It involved something falling from the sky. Technology, parts, bits. That's it, really: all I can divulge. Not much, I know.
>
> It's not that I'm being shy. It's just that—well, for one, I don't even remember the event. It's a blank: a white slate, a black hole. I have vague images, half-impressions: of being, or having been—or, more precisely, being *about* to be—hit; blue light; railings; lights of other colours; being held above some kind of tray or bed.

This is our protagonist, though that's a word from another kind of novel. Better to use *enactor*. This is our Enactor. He has no name, he lives in Brixton and recently he has been hit on the head by some kind of enormous *thing*. For a long time he was in a coma, his mind "still asleep but getting restless and inventing spaces for me to inhabit . . . cricket grounds with white crease and boundary lines painted on the grass." After a time, he recovers, though he has to learn to move and walk again. But there is a remainder: it appears that the "parties, institutions, organizations—let's call them the *bodies*— responsible for what happened" are offering him a settlement on the condition of his silence (though he can't remember what happened). His lawyer phones to tell him the amount. It is eight and a half million pounds. The Enactor turns suddenly to the window, accidentally pulling the phone out of the wall:

> The connection had been cut. I stood there for some time, I don't know how long, holding the dead receiver in my hand and looking down at what the wall had spilt. It looked kind of disgusting, like something that's come out of something.

For the first fifty pages or so, this is *Remainder*'s game, a kind of antiliterature hoax, a windup (which is, however, impeccably written). Meticulously it works through the things we expect of a novel, gleefully taking them apart, brick by brick. Hearing of the settlement, he "felt neutral. . . . I looked around me at the sky: it was neutral too—a neutral spring day, sunny but not bright, neither cold nor warm." It's a huge sum of money, but he doesn't like clothes or shoes or cars or yachts. A series of narrative epiphany MacGuffins follow. He goes to the pub with a halfhearted love interest and his best friend. The girl thinks he should use the money to build an African village; the friend thinks he should use it to snort coke off the bodily surfaces of strippers. Altruism and hedonism prove equally empty. We hear of his physiotherapy—the part of his brain that controls motor function is damaged and needs to be rerouted: "To cut and lay the new circuits [in the brain], what they do is make you visualize things. Simple things like lifting a carrot to your mouth." You have to visualize every component of this action, over and over, and yet, he finds, when they finally put a real carrot in your hand, "gnarled, dirty and irregular in ways your imaginary carrot never was," it short-circuits the visualization. He has to start from the top, integrating these new factors. All this is recounted in a straightforward first person that reminds us that most avant-garde challenges to realism concentrate on voice, on where this "I" is coming from, this mysterious third person. Spirals of interiority are the result (think of David Foster Wallace's classic short story "The Depressed Person": a first person consciousness rendered in obsessive third person, speaking to itself). *Remainder*, by contrast, empties out interiority entirely: the narrator finds all his own gestures to be completely inauthentic, and everyone else's too. Only while watching *Mean Streets* at the Brixton Ritzy does he have a sense of human fluidity, of manufactured truth—the way De Niro opens a fridge door, the way he lights a cigarette. So natural! But the Enactor finds he can't be natural like De Niro, he isn't fluid. He's only good at completing cycles and series, reenacting actions. For example, he gets a certain tingling pleasure (this is literal; he gets it in his body) from having his reward card stamped in a certain "themed Seattle coffee bar," on the corner of Frith Street and Old Compton. Ten stamps, ten cappuccinos, a new card, start the series again. He sits at the window people watching. He sees inauthenticity everywhere:

Media types . . . their bodies and faces buzzed with glee, exhilaration—a jubilant awareness that for once, just now, at this particular right-angled intersection, they didn't have to sit in a cinema or living room in front of a TV and watch other beautiful people laughing and hanging out: they could be the beautiful young people themselves. See? Just like me: completely second-hand.

The clubbers, the scene gays, the old boys heading to their drinking clubs— all formatted. Then suddenly he notices a group of homeless people, the way they take messages up and down the street to each other, with a sense of purpose, really seeming to *own* the street, interacting with it genuinely. He makes contact with one of them. He takes him to a local restaurant, buys him a meal. He wants to ask the boy something, but he can't get it out. Then the wine spills:

The waiter came back over. He was . . . She was young, with large dark glasses, an Italian woman. Large breasts. Small.

"What do you want to know?" my homeless person asked.

"I want to know . . ." I started, but the waiter leant across me as he took the tablecloth away. She took the table away too. There wasn't any table. The truth is, I've been making all this up—the stuff about the homeless person. He existed all right, sitting camouflaged against the shop fronts and the dustbins—but I didn't go across to him.

Because, in fact, the homeless are just like everyone else:

They had a point to prove: that they were one with the street; that they and only they spoke its true language; that they really *owned* the space around them. Crap: total crap . . . And then their swaggering, their arrogance: a cover. Usurpers. Frauds.

Large breasts. Small. The narrative has a nervous breakdown. It's the final MacGuffin, the end of the beginning, as if the novel were saying: *Satisfied? Can I write this novel my way now? Remainder*'s way turns out to be an extreme form of dialectical materialism—it's a book about a man who builds in order to feel. A few days after the fake homeless epiphany, at a party, while in the host's bathroom, the Enactor sees a crack in the plaster in the wall. It reminds him of another crack, in the wall of "his" apartment in a very specific six-story building he has yet no memory of ever living in or seeing. In this building many people lived doing many things—cooking liver, playing the piano, fixing a bike. And there were cats on the roof! It all comes back to him, though it was never there in the first place. And now *Remainder really* begins, in the mission to rebuild this building, to place reenactors in it reenacting those actions he wants them to enact (cooking liver, playing the piano, fixing a bike), doing them over and over till it feels real, while he, in his apartment, fluidly closes and reopens a fridge door, just like De Niro. Eight and a half a million quid should cover this, especially as he has entrusted his money to a man much like Hans van den Broek—a stock trader—who makes money for the Reenactor (for that's what he is now) almost as quickly as he can spend it. To facilitate his reenactment, the Reenactor hires Nazrul Ram Vyas, an Indian "from a high-caste family" who works as a facilitator for a company dedicated to personal inauthenticity: Time Control UK. It takes people's lives and manages them for them. Nazrul is no more a character (in realism's sense of the word) than I am a chair, but he is the most exquisite facilitator, and it is through him that every detail of the reenactment is processed. He thinks of everything. In place of the pleasure of the rich adjective we have an imagined world in which logistical details and logical consequences are pursued with care and precision: if you were to rebuild an entire house and fill it with people reenacting actions you have chosen for them, this is exactly how it would play out. Every detail is attended to except the one we've come to think of as the only one that matters in a novel: how it *feels.* The Reenactor in *Remainder* only ever has one feeling—the tingling—which occurs whenever his reenactments are going particularly well. The feeling is addictive; the enactments escalate, in a fascinating direction. A black man is shot by two other black men near the Reenactor's house. The Reenactor at once asks Naz to "lay the ground for the re-enactment of the black man's death. I think I'd have gone mad otherwise, so strong was my compulsion to re-enact it." In this reenactment, the Reenactor himself assumes the role of the "dead black man" (who is everywhere referred to like this). His tingling goes off the charts. It's so good, he begins to fall into trances. It's impossible not to note here that the nonwhite subject is still the bad conscience of the contemporary novel, obviously so in the realist tradition, but also more subtly here in the avant-garde. Why is the greatest facilitator of inauthenticity Asian? Why is the closest thing to epiphany a dead black man? Because *Remainder*, too, wants to destroy the myth of cultural authenticity—though for purer reasons than *Netherland*. If your project is to rid the self of its sacredness, to flatten selfhood out, it's philosophical hypocrisy to let any selves escape, whatever color they may be. The nameless "dead black man" is a deliberate provocation on McCarthy's part, and in its lack of coy sentiment there is a genuine transgressive thrill. Still, it does seem rather hard to have to give up on subjectivity when you've only recently gotten free of objectification. I suppose history only goes in one direction. But to *Remainder's* provocation it's tempting to answer with another: that beneath the conscious ideas of this novel, a subconscious trace remains, revealing a faint racial antipathy that is psychological and social rather than theoretical. (If *Netherland* can be read against its own grain, which is to say, theoretically, why not read *Remainder* psychologically?) For though these novels seem far apart, their authors are curiously similar. Similar age; similar class; one went to Oxford, the other, Cambridge; both are by now a part of the publishing mainstream, share a fondness for cricket and are subject to a typically British class/race anxiety that has left its residue. A flashback-inclined Freudian might conjure up the image of two brilliant young men, straight out of college, both eager to write the Novel of the Future, who discover, to their great dismay, that the authenticity baton (which is, of course, entirely phony) has been passed on. Passed to women, to those of color, to people of different sexualities, to people from far off, war-torn places. . . . The frustrated sense of having come to the authenticity party exactly a century late!

3

Aspects of this constructive frustration were aired publicly at the Drawing Center in New York, on September 25, 2007, when two men, Tom McCarthy and the philosopher Simon Critchley, sat at a table in semidarkness and took turns reading "The Joint Statement of Inauthenticity," latest manifesto of the International Necronautical Society (INS). The men identified themselves only as the society's general secretary and chief philosopher. Their voices were flat, nasal, utterly British; they placed sudden emphasis on certain words. It was like listening to a Smiths song.

"We begin," announced the general secretary, "with the experience of failed transcendence, a failure that is at the core of the general secretary's novels[1] and the chief philosopher's tomes. *Being* is not full transcendence, the plenitude of the one or cosmic abundance, but rather an *ellipsis*, an absence, an incomprehensibly vast lack, scattered with—" and here the general secretary tripped over his tongue, corrected himself and continued, "—with debris and detritus. *Philosophy*, as the thinking of *Being*, has to begin from the experience of *disappointment* that is at once *Religious* (God is dead, the One is gone); *Epistemic* (we know very little, almost nothing; all knowledge claims have to begin from the experience of limitation); and *Political* (blood is being spilt in the streets as if it were champagne)." On the scratchy live recording,[2] the audience coughs nervously and is silent: there is not much else to be done when someone's reading a manifesto at you. The INS members continue: through the brief (by now traditional) faux demolition of the Greek idealists, specifically Plato and Aristotle, who believed form and essence to be more real than anything else, and therefore perfect. "But if form is perfect," asks the general secretary, "if it is perfection itself, then how does one explain the obvious imperfection of the world, for the world is not perfect? This is where matter, our undoing, enters into the picture. For the Greeks, the principle of imperfection was matter. Matter was the source of the corruption of form."

Necronauts, as you might guess from the name, feel differently. They are "modern lovers of debris," and what is most real for them is not form or God but "the brute materiality of the external world . . . In short, against idealism in philosophy, and idealists or transcendent conceptions of art—of art as pure

---

1. McCarthy is also the author of the novel *Men in Space*.
2. This can be heard at http://www.listen.to/necronauts.

perfect form—we set a doctrine of materialism. . . ." So, while Dorian Gray projects his perfect image into the world, Necronauts keep faith with the "rotting flesh assemblage hanging up in his attic"; as Ernest Shackleton forces his dominance fantasy onto the indifferent polar expanse, Necronauts concern themselves with the "blackened, frost-bitten toes he and his crew were forced to chop from their own feet, cook on their stove and eat." And so on. Like Chuck Ramkissoon, they have a motto: "We are all Necronauts, always, already," which is recycled Derrida (as "blood like champagne" is recycled Dostoyevsky). That is to say, we are all death-marked creatures, defined by matter—though most of us most of the time pretend not to be.

In *Remainder*, the INS general secretary puts his theoretical ideas to lively yet unobtrusive use. For the Reenactor himself does not realize he is a Necronaut; he is simply a bloke, and with Naz facilitating at his side he hopes, like the rest of us, to dominate matter, the better to disembody it. To demonstrate the folly of this, in the middle of the novel *Remainder* allows itself a stripped-down allegory on religion, staged in an auto shop where the Reenactor has gone to fix a flat tire. While there, he remembers his windshield wiper fluid reservoir is empty and asks for a fill-up. Two liters of blue liquid are poured into the reservoir, but when he presses the "spurter button" nothing spurts. The two liters haven't leaked, but neither do they appear to be in the reservoir:

> They'd vaporized, evaporated. And do you know what? It felt wonderful. Don't ask me why: it just did. It was as though I'd just witnessed a miracle: matter—these two litres of liquid—becoming un-matter—not surplus matter, mess or clutter, but pure, bodiless blueness. Transubstantiated.

A few minutes later, the engine catches, matter has its inevitable revenge ("It gushed all over me: my shirt, my legs, my groin") and transubstantiation shows itself for what it is: the beautiful pretense of the disappeared remainder. In the later reenactment of this scene (which Naz restages in an empty hangar at Heathrow, running it on a loop for weeks) the liquid really disappears, sprayed upward into an invisible, fine mist by the Reenactor's hired technicians.

McCarthy and his Necronauts are interested in tracing the history of the disappeared remainder through art and literature, marking the fundamental division between those who want to extinguish matter and elevate it to form ("They try and ingest all of reality into a system of thought, to eat it up, to penetrate and possess it. . . . This is what Hegel and the Marquis de Sade have in common") and those who want to let matter *matter*:

> To let the orange *orange* and the flower *flower*. . . . We take the side of *things* and try to evoke their nocturnal, mineral quality. This is for us the essence of poetry, as it is expressed in Francis Ponge, Wallace Stevens, Rilke's *Duino Elegies*, and some of the personae of Pessoa . . . of trying, and *failing*, to speak about the thing itself and not just ideas about the thing. Of saying "Jug. Bridge. Cigarette. Oyster. Fruitbat. Windowsill. *Sponge*."

That "failing" there is very important. It's what makes a book like *Remainder*—which is, after all, not simply a list of proper nouns—possible. Of course, it's not unusual for avant-garde fiction writers to aspire to the concrete quality of poetry. Listening to the general secretary annunciate his list, emphasizing its clarity and unloveliness, I thought of Wislawa Szymborska, in particular the opening of "The End and The Beginning":

After every war
someone has to clean up.
Things won't
straighten themselves up, after all.

Someone has to push the rubble
to the sides of the road,
so the corpse-laden wagons
can pass.

Someone has to get mired
in scum and ashes,
sofa springs,

splintered glass,
and bloody rags.

Someone must drag in a girder
to prop up a wall.
Someone must glaze a window,
rehang a door.

Even those who are allergic to literary theory will recognize the literary sensibility, echoed in this poem, of which the INS forms an extreme, yet comprehensible, part. The connection: a perverse acknowledgment of limitations. One does not seek the secret, authentic heart of things. One believes—as Naipaul had it—that the world is what it is and, moreover, that all our relations with it are necessarily inauthentic. As a consequence, such an attitude is often mistaken for linguistic or philosophical nihilism, but its true strength comes from a rigorous attention to the damaged and the partial, the absent and the unspeakable. *Remainder* reserves its finest quality of attention for the well-worn street surface where the black man dies, its "muddy, pock-marked ridges," the chewing gum and bottle tops, the "tarmac, stone, dirt, water, mud," all of which form, in the mind of narrator, an almost overwhelming narration (*"There's too much here, too much process, just too much"*) that is yet a narration defined by absence, by partial knowledge, for we can only know it by the marks it has left. *Remainder* recognizes, with Szymborska's poem, that we know, in the end, "less than little/And finally as little as nothing," and so tries always to acknowledge the void that is not ours, the messy remainder we can't understand or control— the ultimate marker of which is Death itself. We need not ever read a word of Heidegger to step in these murky waters. They flow through the "mainstream" of our canon. Through the negations of Beckett. The paradoxical concrete abstractions of Kafka. The scatological thingy-ness of Joyce at his most antic. The most famous line of Auden ("Poetry makes nothing happen").[3]

---

3. In another INS report, this line is described as "an active construct in which 'nothing' designates an event, perhaps even a momentous one."

For those who *are* theory-minded, the INS manifesto in its entirety (only vaguely sketched out here) is to be recommended: it's intellectually agile, pompous, faintly absurd, invigorating and not at all new. As celebrators of their own inauthenticity, the INS members freely admit their repetitious, recycling nature, stealing openly from Blanchot, Bataille, Heidegger, Derrida and, of course, Robbe-Grillet. Much of what is to be found in the manifesto is more leisurely expressed in the chief philosopher's own "tomes" (in particular *Very Little . . . Almost Nothing: Death, Philosophy, Literature*). As for the general secretary, within the provocations of the INS he is a theoretical fundamentalist, especially where the material practicalities of publishing are concerned. In 2003, he expelled two INS members for signing with corporate publishers, charging that they had "become complicit with a publishing industry whereby the 'writer' becomes merely the executor of a brief dictated by corporate market research, reasserting the certainties of middle-brow aesthetics." It will be interesting to see what happens to these ideas now that McCarthy's own material circumstances are somewhat changed: in 2007, *Remainder* went to Vintage Books in America and picked up a Film Four production deal. Still, that part of the INS brief that confronts the realities of contemporary publishing is not easily dismissed. When it comes to literary careers, it's true: the pitch is queered. The literary economy sets up its stall on the road that leads to *Netherland*, along which one might wave to Jane Austen, George Eliot, F. Scott Fitzgerald, Richard Yates, Saul Bellow. Rarely has it been less aware (or less interested) in seeing what's new on the route to *Remainder*, that skewed side road where we greet Georges Perec, Clarice Lispector, Maurice Blanchot, William Burroughs, J. G. Ballard. Friction, fear and outright hatred spring up often between these two traditions—yet they have revealing points of connection. At their crossroads we find extraordinary writers claimed by both sides: Melville, Conrad, Kafka, Beckett, Joyce, Nabokov. For though manifestos feed on rupture, artworks themselves bear the trace of their own continuity. So it is with *Remainder*. The Reenactor's obsessive, amoral reenactments have ancestors: Ahab and his whale, Humbert and his girl, Marlow's trip downriver. The theater of the absurd that *Remainder* lays out is articulated with the same careful pedantry of Gregor Samsa himself. In its brutal excision of psychology it is easy to feel that *Remainder* comes to literature as an assassin, to kill the novel stone dead. I think it means rather to shake the novel out if its present complacency. It clears away a little of the deadwood, offering a glimpse of an alternate road down which the novel might, with difficulty, travel forward. We could call this constructive deconstruction, a quality that, for me, marks *Remainder* as one of the great English novels of the past ten years.

Maybe the most heartening aspect of *Remainder* is that its theoretical foundations prove no obstacle to the expression of a self-ridiculing humor. In fact, the closer it adheres to its own principles, the funnier it is. Having spent half the book in an inauthentic building with reenactors reenacting, the Reenactor decides he needs a change:

> One day I got an urge to go and check up on the outside world myself. Nothing much to report.

A minimalist narrative refusal that made me laugh out loud. *Remainder* resists its readers, but it does so with a smile. And then, toward its end, a mysterious "short councilor" appears, like one of David Lynch's dwarfs, and finally asks the questions—and receives the answers—that the novel has denied us till now. Why are you doing this? How does it make you feel? In a moment of frankness, we discover the Reenactor's greatest tingle arrived with his smallest reenactment: standing in a train station, holding his palms outward, begging for money of which he had no need. It gave him the sense "of being on the other side of something. A veil, a screen, the law—I don't know. . . ." One of the greatest authenticity dreams of the avant-garde is this possibility of becoming criminal, of throwing one's lot in with Genet and John Fante, with the freaks and the lost and the rejected. (The notable exception is J. G. Ballard, author of possibly the greatest British avant-garde novel, *The Atrocity Exhibition*, who raised three children single-handedly in the domestic tranquility of a semidetached house in Shepperton.) For the British avant-garde, autobiographical extremity has become a mark of literary authenticity, the drug use of

Alexander Trocchi and Anna Kavan being at least as important to their readers as their prose. (The INS demands "all cults of authenticity be abandoned." It does not say what is to be done about the authenticity cult of the avant-garde.) In this sense, the Reenactor has a true avant-garde spirit; he wants to become the thing beyond the pale, the inconvenient remainder impossible to contain within the social economy of meaning. But no: it is still not quite enough. The only truly authentic *indivisible* remainder, the only way of truly placing yourself outside meaning, is through death, the contemplation of which brings *Remainder*, in its finale, to one of its few expressionist moments. It also enacts a strange literary doubling, meeting *Netherland* head on:

> Forensic procedure is an art form, nothing less. No I'll go further: it's higher, more refined, than any art form. Why? Because it's real. Take just one aspect of it—say the diagrams . . . They're records of atrocities. Each line, each figure, every angle—the ink itself vibrates with an almost intolerable violence, darkly screaming from the silence of the white paper: something has happened here, someone has died.
>
> "It's just like cricket," I told Naz one day.
>
> "In what sense?" he asked.
>
> "Each time the ball's been past," I said, "and the white lines are still zinging where it hit, and the seam's left a mark, and . . ."
>
> "I don't follow," he said.
>
> "It . . . well, it just is," I told him. "Each ball is like a crime, a murder. And then they do it again, and again and again, and the commentator has to commentate, or he'll die too."

In *Netherland* cricket symbolizes the triumph of the symbol over brute fact (cricket as the deferred promise of the American Dream). In *Remainder* cricket is pure facticity, which keeps coming at you, carrying death, leaving its mark. Everything must leave a mark. Everything has a material reality. Everything happens in space. As you read it, *Remainder* makes you preternaturally aware of space, as Robbe-Grillet did in *Jealousy*, *Remainder*'s obvious progenitor. Like the sportsmen whose processes it describes and admires, *Remainder* "fills time up with space" by breaking physical movements, for example, into their component parts, slowing them down; or by examining the layers and textures of a wet, cambered road in Brixton as a series of physical events rather than emotional symbols. It forces us to recognize space as a nonneutral thing—unlike realism, which often ignores the specificities of space. Realism's obsession is convincing us that time has passed. It fills space with time.

Something has happened here, someone has died. A trauma, a repetition, a death, a commentary. Remainder wants to create zinging, charged spaces, stark, pared down, in the manner of those ancient plays it clearly admires—The Oresteia, Oedipus at Colonus, Antigone. The ancients, too, troubled themselves with trauma, repetition, death and commentary (by chorus), with the status of bodies before the law, with what is to be done with the remainder. But the ancients always end in tragedy, with the indifferent facticity of the world triumphantly crushing the noble, suffering self. Remainder ends instead in comic declension, deliberately refusing the self-mythologizing grandeur of the tragic. Fact and self persist, in comic misapprehension, circling each other in space (literally, in a hijacked plane). And it's precisely within Remainder's newly revealed spaces that the opportunity for multiple allegories arises. On literary modes (How artificial is realism?), on existence (Are we capable of genuine being?), on political discourse (What's left of the politics of identity?) and on the law (Where do we draw our borders? What, and whom, do we exclude, and why?). As surface alone, though, so fully imagined, and so imaginative, Remainder is more than sufficient.

BEING

Seven

THAT CRAFTY FEELING

What follows is a version of a lecture given to the students of Columbia University's Writing Program in New York on Monday, March 24, 2008. The brief: "to speak about some aspect of your craft."

1. MACRO PLANNERS AND MICRO MANAGERS

First, a caveat: what I have to say about craft extends no further than my own experience, which is what it is—twelve years and three novels. Although this lecture will be divided into ten short sections meant to mark the various stages in the writing of a novel, what they most accurately describe, in truth, is the writing of *my* novels. That being said, I want to offer you a pair of ugly terms for two breeds of novelist: *the Macro Planner* and the *Micro Manager*.

You will recognize a Macro Planner from his Post-its, from those Moleskines he insists on buying. A Macro Planner makes notes, organizes material, configures a plot and creates a structure—all before he writes the title page. This structural security gives him a great deal of freedom of movement. It's not uncommon for Macro Planners to start writing their novels in the middle.

As they progress, forward or backward, their difficulties multiply with their choices. I know Macro Planners who obsessively exchange possible endings for one another, who take characters out and put them back in, reverse the order of chapters and perform frequent—for me, unthinkable—radical surgery on their novels: moving the setting of a book from London to Berlin, for example, or changing the title. I can't stand to hear them speak about all this, not because I disapprove, but because other people's methods are always so incomprehensible and horrifying. I am a Micro Manager. I start at the first sentence of a novel and I finish at the last. It would never occur to me to choose among three different endings because I haven't the slightest idea of the ending until I get to it, a fact that will surprise no one who has read my novels. Macro Planners have their houses largely built from day one, and so their obsession is internal—they're forever moving the furniture. They'll put a chair in the bedroom, the lounge, the kitchen and then back in the bedroom again. Micro Managers build a house floor by floor, discretely and in its entirety. Each floor needs to be sturdy and fully decorated with all the furniture in place before the next is built on top of it. There's wallpaper in the hall even if the stairs lead nowhere at all.

Because Micro Managers have no grand plan, their novels exist only in their present moment, in a sensibility, in the novel's tonal frequency line by line. When I begin a novel I feel there is nothing of that novel outside of the sentences I am setting down. I have to be very careful: the whole nature of the thing changes by the choice of a few words. This induces a special breed of pathology for which I have another ugly name: OPD or *obsessive perspective disorder*. It occurs mainly in the first twenty pages. It's a kind of existential drama, a long answer to the short question *What kind of a novel am I writing?* It manifests itself in a compulsive fixation on perspective and voice. In one day the first twenty pages can go from first-person present tense, to third-person past tense, to third-person present tense, to first-person past tense, and so on. Several times a day I change it. Because I am an English novelist enslaved to an ancient tradition, with each novel I have ended up exactly where I began: third person, past tense. But months are spent switching back and forth. Opening other people's novels, you recognize fellow Micro Managers: that opening pileup of too-careful, obsessively worried-over sentences, a block of stilted ver-biage that only loosens and relaxes after the twenty-page mark is passed. In the case of *On Beauty*, my OPD spun completely out of control: I reworked those first twenty pages for almost two years. To look back at all past work induces nausea, but the first twenty pages in particular bring on heart palpitations. It's like taking a tour of a cell in which you were once incarcerated.

Yet while OPD is happening, somehow the work of the rest of the novel gets done. That's the strange thing. It's as if you're winding the key of a toy car tighter and tighter. . . . When you finally let it go, it travels at a crazy speed. When I finally settled on a tone, the rest of the book was finished in five months. Worrying over the first twenty pages is a way of working on the whole novel, a way of finding its structure, its plot, its characters—all of which, for a Micro Manager, are contained in the sensibility of a sentence. Once the tone is there, all else follows. You hear interior decorators say the same about a shade of paint.

2. OTHER PEOPLE'S WORDS, PART ONE

It's such a confidence trick, writing a novel. The main person you have to trick into confidence is yourself. This is hard to do alone. I gather sentences round, quotations, the literary equivalent of a cheerleading squad. Except that analogy's screwy—cheerleaders *cheer*. I put up placards that make me feel bad. For five years I had a line from *Gravity's Rainbow* stuck to my door:

> We have to find meters whose scales are unknown in the world, draw our own schematics, getting feedback, making connections, reducing the error, trying to learn the real function . . . zeroing in on what incalculable plot?

At that time, I guess I thought that it was the duty of the novel to rigorously pursue hidden information: personal, political, historical. I say *I guess* because I don't recognize that writer anymore, and already find her idea of the novel oppressive, alien, useless. I don't think this feeling is unusual, especially when you start out. Not long ago I sat next to a young Portuguese novelist at dinner and told him I intended to read his first novel. He grabbed my wrist, genuinely distressed, and said: "Oh, please don't! Back then, all I read was Faulkner. I had *no sense of humor*. My God, I was a different person!"

That's how it goes. Other people's words are so important. And then without warning they stop being important, along with all those words of yours that *their* words prompted you to write. Much of the excitement of a new novel lies in the repudiation of the one written before. Other people's words are the bridge you use to cross from where you were to wherever you're going.

Recently I came across a new quote. It's my screen saver now, my little scrap of confidence as I try to write a novel. It is a thought of Derrida's and very simple:

If a right to a secret is not maintained then we are in a totalitarian space.

Which is to say: enough of human dissection, of entering the brains of characters, cracking them open, rooting every secret out! For now, this is the new attitude. Years from now, when this book is done and another begins, another change will come.

"*My God, I was a different person!*"—I think many writers think this, from book to book. A new novel, begun in hope and enthusiasm, grows shameful and strange to its author soon enough. After each book is done, you look forward to hating it (and you never have to wait long); there is a weird, inverse confidence to be had from feeling destroyed, because being destroyed, having to start again, means you have space in front of you, somewhere to go. Think of that revelation Shakespeare put in the mouth of King John: "*Now my soul has elbow room!*" Fictionally speaking, the nightmare is losing the desire to move.

3. OTHER PEOPLE'S WORDS, PART TWO

Some writers won't read a word of any novel while they're writing their own. Not one word. They don't even want to see the cover of a novel. As they write, the world of fiction dies: no one has ever written, no one is writing, no one will ever write again. Try to recommend a good novel to a writer of this type while he's writing and he'll give you a look like you just stabbed him in the heart with a kitchen knife. It's a matter of temperament. Some writers are the kind of solo violinists who need complete silence to tune their instruments. Others want to hear every member of the orchestra—they'll take a cue from a clarinet, from an oboe, even. I am one of those. My writing desk is covered in open novels. I read lines to swim in a certain sensibility, to strike a particular note, to encourage rigor when I'm too sentimental, to bring verbal ease when I'm syntactically uptight. I think of reading like a balanced diet; if your sentences are baggy, too baroque, cut back on fatty Foster Wallace, say, and pick up Kafka, as roughage. If your aesthetic has become so refined it is stopping you from placing a single black mark on white paper, stop worrying so much about what Nabokov would say; pick up Dostoyevsky, patron saint of substance over style.

Yet you meet students who feel that reading while you write is unhealthy. Their sense is that it corrupts voice by influence and, moreover, that reading great literature creates a sense of oppression. For how can you pipe out your little mouse song when Kafka's Josephine the Mouse Singer pipes so much more loudly and beautifully than you ever could? To this way of thinking, the sovereignty of one's individuality is the vital thing, and it must be protected at any price, even if it means cutting oneself off from that literary echo chamber E. M. Forster described, in which writers speak so helpfully to one another, across time and space. Well, each to their own, I suppose.

For me, that echo chamber was essential. I was fourteen when I heard John Keats in there and in my mind I formed a bond with him, a bond based on class—though how archaic that must sound, here in America. Keats was not working-class, exactly, nor black—but in rough outline his situation seemed closer to mine than the other writers you came across. He felt none of the entitlement of, say, Virginia Woolf, or Byron, or Pope, or Evelyn Waugh or even P. G. Wodehouse and Agatha Christie. Keats offers his readers the possibility of entering writing from a side door, the one marked "Apprentices Welcome Here." For Keats went about his work like an apprentice; he took a kind of MFA of the mind, albeit alone, and for free, in his little house in Hampstead. A suburban, lower-middle-class boy, a few steps removed from the literary scene, he made his own scene out of the books of his library. He never feared influence—he devoured influences. He wanted to learn from them, even at the risk of their voices swamping his own. And the feeling of apprenticeship never left him: you see it in his early experiments in poetic form; in the letters he wrote to friends expressing his fledgling literary ideas; it's there, famously, in his reading of Chapman's Homer, and the fear that he might cease to be before his pen had gleaned his teeming brain. The term *role model* is so odious, but the truth is it's a very strong writer indeed who gets by without a model kept somewhere in mind. I think of Keats. Keats slogging away, devouring books, plagiarizing, impersonating, adapting, struggling, growing, writing many poems that made him blush and then a few that made him proud, learning everything he could from whomever he could find, dead or alive, who might have something useful to teach him.

4. MIDDLE-OF-THE-NOVEL MAGICAL THINKING

In the middle of a novel, a kind of magical thinking takes over. To clarify, the middle of the novel may not happen in the actual geographical center of the novel. By *middle of the novel* I mean whatever page you are on when you stop being part of your household and your family and your partner and children and food shopping and dog feeding and reading the post—I mean when there is nothing in the world except your book, and even as your wife tells you she's sleeping with your brother her face is a gigantic semicolon, her arms are parentheses and you are wondering whether *rummage* is a better verb than *rifle*. The middle of a novel is a state of mind. Strange things happen in it. Time collapses. You sit down to write at 9 A.M., you blink, the evening news is on and four thousand words are written, more words than you wrote in three long months, a year ago. Something has changed. And it's not restricted to the house. If you go outside, everything—I mean, *everything*—flows freely into your novel. Someone on the bus says something—it's straight out of your novel. You open the paper—*every single story in the paper is directly relevant to your novel*. If you are fortunate enough to have someone waiting to publish your novel, this is the point at which you phone them in a panic and try to get your publication date brought forward because you cannot believe *how in tune the world is with your unfinished novel right now,* and if it isn't published next Tuesday maybe the moment will pass and you will have to kill yourself.

Magical thinking makes you crazy—and renders everything possible. Incredibly knotty problems of structure now resolve themselves with inspired ease. See that one paragraph? It only needs to be moved, and the whole chapter falls into place! Why didn't you see that before? You randomly pick a poetry book off the shelf and the first line you read ends up being your epigraph—it seems to have been written for no other reason.

5. DISMANTLING THE SCAFFOLDING

When building a novel you will use a lot of scaffolding. Some of this is necessary to hold the thing up, but most isn't. The majority of it is only there to make you feel secure, and in fact the building will stand without it. Each time I've written a long piece of fiction I've felt the need for an enormous amount of scaffolding. With me, scaffolding comes in many forms. The only way to write this novel is to divide it into three sections of ten chapters each. Or five sections of seven chapters. Or the answer is to read the Old Testament and model each chapter on the books of the prophets. Or the divisions of the Bhagavad Gita. Or the Psalms. Or *Ulysses.* Or the songs of Public Enemy. Or the films of Grace Kelly. Or the Four Horsemen of the apocalypse. Or the liner notes to *The White Album.* Or the twenty-seven speeches Donald Rumsfeld gave to the press corps during his tenure.

Scaffolding holds up confidence when you have none, reduces the despair, creates a goal—however artificial—an end point. Use it to divide what seems like an endless, unmarked journey, though by doing this, like Zeno, you infinitely extend the distance you need to go.

Later, when the book is printed and old and dog-eared, it occurs to me that I really didn't need any of that scaffolding. The book would have been far better off without it. But when I was putting it up, it felt vital, and once it was there, I'd worked so hard to get it there I was loath to take it down. If you are writing a novel at the moment and putting up scaffolding, well, I hope it helps you, but don't forget to dismantle it later. Or if you're determined to leave it

out there for all to see, at least hang a nice facade over it, as the Romans do
when they fix up their palazzi.

6. FIRST TWENTY PAGES, REDUX

Late in the novel, in the last quarter, when I am rolling downhill, I turn
back to read those first twenty pages. They are packed tighter than tuna in a
can. Calmly, I take off the top, let a little air in. What's amusing about the first
twenty pages—they are funny now, three years later, now I'm no longer locked
up in them—is how little confidence you have in your readers when you begin.
You spoon-feed them *everything*. You can't let a character walk across the room
without giving her backstory as she goes. You don't trust the reader to have a
little patience, a little intelligence. This reader, who, for all you know, has read
Thomas Bernhard, *Finnegans Wake*, Gertrude Stein, Georges Perec—yet *you're*
worried that if you don't mention in the first three pages that Sarah Malone
is a social worker with a dead father, this talented reader might not be able to
follow you exactly. It's awful, the swing of the literary fraudulence pendulum:
from moment to moment you can't decide whether you're the fraudulent idiot
or your reader is the fraudulent idiot. For writers who work with character a
good deal, going back to the first twenty pages is also a lesson in how much
more delicate a thing character is than you *think* it is when you're writing it.
The idea of forming people out of grammatical clauses seems so fantastical at
the start that you hide your terror in a smokescreen of elaborate sentence making, as if character can be drawn forcibly out of the curlicues of certain adjectives piled ruthlessly on top of one another. In fact, character occurs with the
lightest of brushstrokes. Naturally, it can be destroyed lightly, too. I think of a
creature called Odradek, who at first glance appears to be a "flat star-shaped
spool for thread" but who is not quite this, Odradek who won't stop rolling
down the stairs, trailing string behind him, who has a laugh that sounds as if it
has no lungs behind it, a laugh like rustling leaves. You can find the inimitable
Odradek in a one-page story of Kafka's called "The Cares of a Family Man."
Curious Odradek is more memorable to me than characters I spent three years
on, and five hundred pages.

7. THE LAST DAY

There is one great advantage to being a Micro Manager rather than a Macro Planner: the last day of your novel truly is the last day. If you edit as you go along, there are no first, second, third drafts. There is only one draft, and when it's done, it's done. Who can find anything bad to say about the last day of a novel? It's a feeling of happiness that knocks me clean out of adjectives. I think sometimes that the best reason for writing novels is to experience those four and a half hours after you write the final word. The last time it happened to me, I uncorked a good Sancerre I'd been keeping and drank it standing up with the bottle in my hand, and then I lay down in my backyard on the paving stones and stayed there for a long time, crying. It was sunny, late autumn, and there were apples everywhere, overripe and stinky.

8. STEP AWAY FROM THE VEHICLE

You can ignore everything else in this lecture except number eight. It is the only absolutely twenty-four-karat-gold-plated piece of advice I have to give you. I've never taken it myself, though one day I hope to. The advice is as follows.

When you finish your novel, if money is not a desperate priority, if you do not need to sell it at once or be published that very second—*put it in a drawer*. For as long as you can manage. A year or more is ideal—but even three months will do. *Step away from the vehicle*. The secret to editing your work is simple: you need to become its reader instead of its writer. I can't tell you how many times I've sat backstage with a line of novelists at some festival, all of us with red pens in hand, frantically editing our published novels into fit form so that we might go onstage and read from them. It's an unfortunate thing, but it turns out that the perfect state of mind to edit your own novel is two years after it's published, ten minutes before you go onstage at a literary festival. At that moment every redundant phrase, each show-off, pointless metaphor, all the pieces of deadwood, stupidity, vanity and tedium are distressingly obvious to you. Two years earlier, when the proofs came, you looked at the same page and couldn't see a comma out of place. And by the way, that's true of the professional editors, too; after they've read a manuscript multiple times, they stop being able to see it. You need a certain head on your shoulders to edit a novel, and it's not the head of a writer in the thick of it, nor the head of a professional editor who's read it in twelve different versions. It's the head of a smart stranger who picks it off a bookshelf and begins to read. You need to get the head of that smart stranger somehow. You need to forget you ever wrote that book.

9. THE UNBEARABLE CRUELTY OF PROOFS

Proofs are so cruel! Breeding lilacs out of the dead land, mixing memory and desire, stirring dull roots with spring rain. Proofs are the wasteland where the dream of your novel dies and cold reality asserts itself. When I look at loose-leaf proofs, fresh out the envelope, bound with a thick elastic band, marked up by a conscientious copy editor, I feel quite sure I would have to become a different person entirely to do the work that needs to be done here. To correct what needs correcting, fix what needs to be fixed. The only proper response to an envelope full of marked-up pages is *"Give it back to me! Let me start again!"* But no one says this because by this point exhaustion has set it. It's not the book you hoped for, maybe something might yet be done—but the will is gone. There's simply no more will to be had. That's why proofs are so cruel, so sad: the existence of the proof itself is proof that it is already too late. I've only ever seen one happy proof, in Kings College Library: the manuscript of T. S. Eliot's *The Wasteland*. Eliot, upon reaching his own point of exhaustion, had the extreme good fortune to meet Ezra Pound, a very smart stranger, and with his red pen Ezra went to work. And what work! His pen goes everywhere, trimming, cutting, slicing, a frenzy of editing, the why and wherefore not especially obvious, at times, indeed, almost ridiculous; almost, at times, indiscriminate. . . . Whole pages struck out with a single line.

Underneath Pound's markings, *The Wasteland* is a sad proof like any other—too long, full of lines not worth keeping, badly structured. Lucky Eliot, to have Ezra Pound. Lucky Fitzgerald, to have Maxwell Perkins. Lucky Carver, we now know, to have Gordon Lish. *Hypocrite lecteur!*—*mon semblable*—*mon frère!* Where have all the smart strangers gone?

10. YEARS LATER: NAUSEA, SURPRISE AND FEELING OKAY

I find it very hard to read my books after they're published. I've never read *White Teeth*. Five years ago I tried; I got about ten sentences in before I was overwhelmed with nausea. More recently, when people tell me they have just read that book, I do try to feel pleased, but it's a distant, disconnected sensation, like when someone tells you they met your second cousin in a bar in Goa. I suspect *White Teeth* and I may never be reconciled—I think that's simply what happens when you begin writing a book at the age of twenty-one. Then, a year ago, I was in an airport somewhere and I saw a copy of *The Autograph Man*, and on a whim, I bought it. On the plane I had to drink two of those mini bottles of wine before I had the stomach to begin. I didn't manage the whole thing, but I read about two-thirds, and at that incredible speed with which you can read a book if you happen to have written it. And it was actually not such a bad experience—I laughed a few times, groaned more than I laughed and gave up when the wine wore off—but for the first time, I felt something other than nausea. I felt surprise. The book was genuinely strange to me; there were whole pages I didn't recognize, didn't remember writing. And because it was so strange I didn't feel any particular animosity toward it. So that was that: between that book and me there now exists a sort of blank truce, neither pleasant nor unpleasant.

Finally, while writing this lecture, I picked up *On Beauty*. I read maybe a third of it, not consecutively, but chapters here and there. As usual, the nausea; as usual, the feeling of fraudulence; and the too-late desire to wield the red pen all over the place—but something else, too, something new. Here and there—in very isolated pockets—I had the sense that this line, that paragraph, these were exactly what I meant to write, and the fact was, I'd written them, and I felt okay about it, felt good, even. It's a feeling I recommend to all of you. That feeling feels okay.

Eight

ONE WEEK IN LIBERIA

MONDAY

There are no direct flights from England to Liberia. Either you go to Brussels or you book with Astraeus, a specialist airline named after a Roman goddess of justice. It runs a service to Freetown, in neighboring Sierra Leone. The clientele are mostly Africans dressed as if for church. Formal hats, zirconias and Louis Vuitton holdalls are popular. A toddler waddles down the aisle in a three-piece suit and bow tie. Only non-Africans are dressed for "Africa," in khakis, sandals, wrinkled T-shirts. Their bags are ostentatiously simple: frayed rucksacks, battered cases. The luggage of a nomad people.

A cross section of travelers sit in a row. A glamorous African girl in a silky blouse, an English nun, an American aid worker and a Lebanese man, who describes himself as a "fixer": "I fix things in Freetown—electrical systems, buildings." He calls the well-dressed Africans soon-comes. "They come, they soon go. Their families assume they're rich—they try to live up to this idea." The plane prepares to land. The fixer looks out the window and murmurs, "White man's graveyard," in the same spirit that people feel compelled to say "the Big Apple" as their plane approaches JFK. This, like much else on the plane, accommodates the Africa of imagination.

In Sierra Leone everyone deplanes, taking the Africa of imagination with them, a story that has at least a familiar form. Who remains in the story of Liberia? Barely a dozen people, ushered to the front to stare at one another across the wide aisles of business class. The nun is traveling on: Sister Anne of the Corpus Christi Carmelites. Brown socks in brown sandals, brown wimple; a long, kindly face, mapped with wrinkles. She has worked in Liberia since the eighties, running a mission school in Greenville. "We left when the war became impossible—we're back now, teaching students. It's not easy. Our students have seen such terrible things. Beyond imagination, really." She looks troubled when asked to describe the Liberian character. "They are either very, very good people—or the opposite. It is very hard to be good in these conditions."

Flying low over Monrovia there are no lights visible, only flood rain and sheet lightning illuminating the branches of palm trees, the jungle in a bad movie. The airport is no bigger than a village school. The one-ring baggage carousel is open to the elements; through the aperture the lightning flashes. There are more baggage handlers than passengers. They mill without occupation, bored, soaking wet. It seems incredible that heat like this persists through rain. The only thing to see is the obligatory third-world Coke billboard, ironic in exact proportion to the distance from its proper American context. This one says COKE—MAKE IT REAL. Just after the Coke sign there is a contrary sign, an indication that irony is not a currency in Liberia. It is worn by a girl who leans against the exit in a T-shirt that says THE TRUTH MUST BE TOLD.

The truth about Liberia is disputed. It consists of simultaneously asserted, mutually exclusive "facts." The CIA World Factbook states that "in 1980, a military coup led by Samuel Doe ushered in a decade of authoritarian rule," but not—as is widely believed in Liberia—that the CIA itself funded both the coup and the regime. Doe's successor, Charles Taylor, instigator of the

1989–97 Liberian civil war, in which an estimated three hundred thousand people died, is presently in the Hague awaiting trial for crimes against humanity, yet there are supportive hand-painted billboards across Monrovia (CHARLES TAYLOR IS INNOCENT!) and hagiographic collections of his speeches for sale in the airport. In Europe and America, the Liberian civil war is described as a "tribal conflict." In Liberian classrooms children from half a dozen different tribes sit together and do not seem to know what you mean when you ask if this causes a difficulty.

•

There is no real road network in Liberia. During the late-summer rainy season much of the country is inaccessible. Tonight the torrential rain is unseasonable (it is March), but the road is the best in the country, properly surfaced: one long, straight line from the airport to the Mamba Point Hotel in Monrovia. Lysbeth Holdaway, Oxfam's press officer, sits in the back of an all-weather 4x4 outlining Liberia's present situation. She has long chestnut hair, is in youthful middle age and dresses in loose linen; she looks like the actress Penelope Wilton. She "loves gardening and *most* of Radio 4" and worked for many years at the BBC. Four or five times a year she visits some of the more benighted countries of the world. Even by the standards with which she is familiar, Liberia is exceptional. "Three quarters of the population live below the poverty line—that's one U.S. dollar a day—half are on less than fifty cents a day. What infrastructure there was has been destroyed—roads, ports, municipal electricity, water, sanitation, schools, hospitals—all desperately lacking or nonexistent; eighty-six-percent unemployment, no street lights. . . ." Through the car window dead street lamps can be seen, stripped of their components during the war. Lightning continues to reveal the scene: small huts made of mud bricks; sheets of corrugated iron and refuse; more bored young men, sitting in groups, dully watching the cars go by. The cars are of two types: huge Toyota Land Cruiser pickups like this one, usually with "UN" stamped on their hoods, or taxis, dilapidated yellow Nissans, the back windows of which reveal six people squeezed into the backseats, four in the front. Our driver, John Flomo, is asked whether the essentials—a water and sanitation system, electricity, schools—existed prior to the war. "Some, yes. In towns. Less in the country." Even the electricity that lights the airport is not municipal. It comes from a hydro plant belonging to Firestone, the American rubber company famous for its tires. Firestone purchased one million acres of this country in 1926, a ninety-nine-year lease at the bargain rate of six cents an acre. It uses its hydro plant to power its operation. The airport electricity is a "gift" to the nation, although Firestone's business could not function without an airport. "All this is Firestone," says Flomo, pointing at the darkness.

TUESDAY

The Mamba Point Hotel is an unusual Liberian building. It is air-conditioned, with toilets and clean drinking water. In the parking lot a dozen UN trucks are parked. In the breakfast room the guests are uniform: button-down collars, light khakis, MacBooks. "Here's the crazy thing," one man tells another over croissants. "Malaria isn't even a hard problem to solve." At a corner table, an older woman reels off blunt statistics to a newcomer, who notes them down: "Population, three point five million. Over a hundred thousand with HIV; male life expectancy, thirty-eight; female, forty-two. Sixty-five Liberian dollars to one U.S. Officially literacy is fifty-seven percent, but that figure is really prewar—there's this whole missing generation. . . ." In the corner bar, a dozen male Liberian waiters rest against the counter, devotedly following *Baywatch*.

All trips by foreigners, however brief, are done in the NGO Land Cruisers. The two-minute journey to Oxfam headquarters passes an open rubbish dump through which people scavenge alongside skinny pigs. The NGO buildings are lined up on "UN Drive." Each has a thick boundary wall, stamped with its own logo, patrolled by Liberian security. The American embassy goes further, annexing an entire street. Oxfam shares its compound with UNICEF. These offices resemble an English sixth-form college, a white concrete block with swinging doors and stone stairwells. On each door there is a sticker: NO FIREARMS. Here Phil Samways, the country program manager, heads a small development team. He is fifty-four, sandy-haired, lanky, wearing the short-sleeved white shirt accountants favor in the summer months. Unusually, his is not a development background: for twenty years he worked at Anglian Water. He has an unsentimental, practical manner, speaking precisely and quickly: "We are moving out of the humanitarian disaster stage now—water and sanitation and so on. Now we're interested in long-term development. We choose schemes that concentrate on education and livelihoods, and the rehabilitation of ex-combatants, of which there are thousands, many of them children. We hope you'll talk to some of them. You'll see a few of our school projects while you're here, and our rural projects in Bong County, and also West Point, which is really our flagship project. West Point is a slum—half the population of Monrovia live in slums. And as you've seen, we have extreme weather—for eight months it rains like this and the country turns into a quagmire. Cholera is a massive problem. But you have to choose the area you're going to concentrate on, and we've chosen education. We found when we asked people what they needed most, people often said education first, over toilets, basic sanitation. Which should tell you something."

The atmosphere in the hallways is jovial and enthusiastic, like a school newspaper. The staff are mostly young Liberians, educated in the early eighties, before the school system collapsed, or schooled elsewhere in Africa. They are positive about the future, with much optimism focused upon Ellen Johnson-Sirleaf, the Harvard-educated economist and first female head of state in Africa. Johnson-Sirleaf won the presidency in 2005, narrowly defeating the Liberian footballer George Weah. At present she is abroad promoting foreign investment in her country. Liberia's expectations are on hold until her return. "We hope and pray," people say when her name comes up. For the moment, her real impact is conceptual rather than actual: Liberia is having its female moment. Everywhere the talk is of a new generation of girls who will "take Liberia into the future." The popular phrase among the NGO-ers is "gender strategy." The first visit of the day is to one of the "girls' clubs" Oxfam funds.

Abraham Paye Conneh, a thirty-seven-year-old Liberian who looks fifteen years younger, will accompany the visitors. He speaks a flamboyant, expressive English, peppered with the acronym-heavy language of NGOs. Prior to becoming Oxfam's education project officer, he held down three jobs simultaneously: lecturer at the University of Zion, teacher at the Liberia Baptist Theological Seminary and director of education at the West African Training Institute, a feat that netted him ten American dollars a day. He is the team's "character." He writes poetry. He is evangelical about Oxfam's work: "It's time for the women! We're understanding gender now in Liberia. We never educated our Liberian women before; we did not see their glorious potential! But we want the women of Liberia to rise up now! Oh, yes! Like Ellen rose up! We're saying, anything a man can do, a woman can do in the same superior fashion!"

Phil Samways, who enjoys Abraham's impromptu speeches but does not tend to encourage them, returns to practicalities. "Now, security is still an issue. There's a midnight curfew for everybody here—we ask that you comply with it. We get the odd riot—small, spontaneous riots. But you'll be fine with Abraham—you might even get a poem if you're lucky."

To Lysbeth and Abraham we now add the photographer, Aubrey Wade, a thirty-one-year-old Anglo-Dutchman. He is thin, dark blond. He wears a floppy sun hat beneath which a pert nose white with sunblock peeks. He rests his lens on the car window. Hand-painted billboards line the road. HAVE YOU BEEN RAPED? Also STOP RAPE IN LIBERIA. Lysbeth asks Abraham what other "particular problems women in Liberia face." The list is long: female circumcision, marriage from the age of eleven, polygamy, spousal ownership. Girls have "traditionally been discouraged from school." In some tribes, husbands covertly push their wives into sexual affairs so they may charge the offending man an "infidelity tax," paid in the form of unwaged labor. A culture of sexual favors predates the war. Further billboards warn girls not to offer their bodies in return for school grades, a common practice. The moral of Liberia might be "Where there is weakness, exploit it." This moral is not especially Liberian in character. In May 2006 a BBC investigation uncovered "systematic sexual abuse" in Liberia: UN peacekeepers offering food to teenage refugees in return for sex. In November of the same year a local anonymous NGO worker in Liberia told the corporation: "Peacekeepers are still taking advantage of the situation to sexually exploit young girls. The acts are still rampant despite pronouncements that they have been curbed."

•

In a school in Unification Town, fourteen girls from the girls' club are picked to sit with us in the new school "library." It is a small room, very hot. Lysbeth's cheeks bloom red, her hair sticks to her forehead. Our shirts are see-through with sweat. The small, random collection of textbooks on the shelves are a decade out of date. Next door is the typewriting pool, pride of the club. Here they learn to type on ten old-fashioned typewriters. It is not a "school" as that word is commonly understood. It is a building with a thousand children in it, waiting for a school to manifest itself. The preplanned questions—*Do you enjoy studying? What's your favorite subject?*—are rendered absurd. They answer quietly and sadly in a "Liberian English" that is difficult to understand. The teacher translates unclear answers. She is equally hard to understand. *What would you like to be when you grow up?* "Pilot" is a popular answer. Also "a sailor in the navy." By sea or by air, flight is on their minds. The remainder say "nurse" or "doctor" or "in government." The two escape routes visible in Liberia: aid and government. *What do your fathers do?* They are dead, or else they are rubber tappers. A girl sighs heavily. These are not the right questions. The exasperated teacher prompts: "Ask them how often they are able to come to school." Despair invades the room. A girl lays her head on the desk. No one speaks. "Ask me." It is the girl who sighed. She is fourteen; her name is Evelyn B. Momoh; she has a heart-shaped face, doll features. She practically vibrates with intelligence and impatience. "We have to work with our mothers in the market. We need to live and there's no money. It's very hard to stay in school. There's no money, do you understand? There's no money at all." We write this down. *Is the typing pool useful?* Evelyn squints. "Yes, yes, of course—it's a good thing; we are very thankful." There is the sense that she is trying hard not to scream. This is in contrast to the other girls, who only seem exhausted. *And the books?* Evelyn answers again. "I've read all of them

now. I'm very good at math. I've read all the math books. We need more."
Are there books in your house? Evelyn blinks slowly, gives up. We file out to
the typing room. Aubrey takes pictures of Evelyn as she pretends to type. She
submits to this as a politician might to a humiliating, necessary photo op. We
file outside into the dry, maddening heat. Aubrey walks the perimeter looking for something to photograph. The school sits isolated on a dusty clearing bordered by monotonous rubber plantations. Evelyn and her girls arrange
themselves under a tree to sing a close harmony song, typical, in its melody,
of West Africa. "Fellow Liberians, the war is over! Tell your girls, fetch them
to get them to school! Your war is over—they need education!" The voices
are magnificent. The girls sing without facial affect; dead-eyed, unsmiling.
Around us the bored schoolboys skulk. Nobody speaks to them or takes their
picture. The teacher does not worry that boredom and disaffection may turn
to resentment and violence: "Oh, no, they are very happy for the girls." As the
visitors prepare to leave, Evelyn stops us at the steps. It is a strange look she
has, so willful, so much in want, and yet so completely without expectation.
The word *desperate* is often misused. This is what it means. "You will write
the things we need. You have a pencil?" The list is as follows: books, math
books, history books, science books, exercise books, copybooks, pens, pencils,
more desks, a computer, electricity, a generator for electricity, teachers.

Driving back toward Monrovia:

"Abraham—isn't there a government education budget?"

"Oh, yes! Sure. Ms. Sirleaf has promised immediate action on essential
services. But she has only a $120 million budget for the whole year. The UN
budget alone in Liberia for one year is $875 million. And we have a $3.7 billion
debt!"

"But how much did what we just saw cost?"

"Ten thousand. We built an extra section of the school, provided all the
materials, et cetera. If it had not been done by us or another NGO, it would
not be done at all."

"Do you pay teachers?"

"We are not *meant* to—we don't want a two-tier system. But we can *train* them, for example. Many of the teachers in Liberia have only been educated up to the age of twelve or thirteen themselves! We have the blind leading the blind!"

"But then you're acting like a government—you're doing *their* job. Is that what NGOs do?"

"[sigh] Look, there's no human resources, and there's no money. We all must fill in the gap: the UN, Oxfam, UNICEF, CCF, the NRC, the IRC, Médecins Sans Frontières, STC, PWJ—"

"?"

"Peace Wind Japan. Another NGO. I can make you a long list. But different aid has different obligations attached. With us, there are no obligations. The money goes directly."

"So people can send money to you earmarked for a particular project?"

"Oh, yes! [extended laughter] Please put that in your article."

WEDNESDAY

The street scene in Monrovia is postapocalyptic: people occupy the shell of a previous existence. The InterContinental Hotel is a slum, home to hundreds. The old executive mansion is broken open like a child's playhouse; young men sit on the skeletal spiral staircase, taking advantage of the shade. Abraham points out Liberia's state seal on the wall: a ship at anchor with the inscription "The Love of Liberty Brought Us Here." In 1822 freed American slaves (known as Americo-Liberians, or, colloquially, Congos) founded the colony at the instigation of the American Colonization Society, a coalition of slave owners and politicians whose motives are not hard to tease out. Even Liberia's roots are sunk in bad faith. Of the first wave of emigrants, half died of yellow fever. By the end of the 1820s, a small colony of three thousand souls survived. In Liberia they built a facsimile life: plantation-style homes, white-spired churches. Hostile local Malinke tribes resented their arrival and expansion; sporadic armed battle was common. When the ACS went bankrupt in the 1840s, it demanded the "country of Liberia" declare its independence. It was the first of many category errors: Liberia was not yet a country. Its agricultural exports were soon dwarfed by the price of imports. A pattern of European loans (and defaulting on same) began in the 1870s. The money was used to partially modernize the Black America-Liberian hinterlands while ignoring the impoverished indigenous interior. The relationship between the two communities is a lesson in the factitiousness of "race." To the America-Liberians, these were "natives"—an illicit slave trade in Malinke people continued until the 1850s. As late as 1931, the League of Nations uncovered the use of forced indigenous labor. Abraham, in the front seat, bends his head round to Lysbeth in the back: "You know what we say to that seal? *The Love of Liberty MET us here.*" This is a popular Liberian joke. He laughs immoderately. "So that's how it was. They came here, and they always kept the power away from us! They had their True Whig Party, and for 133 years we were a peaceful one-party state. But there was no justice. The indigenous are ninety-five percent of this country, but we had nothing. Oh, those Congos—they had every little bit of power. Everyone in the government was Congo. They did each other favors, gave each other money. We were not even allowed the vote until very late—the sixties!"

Lys asks a reasonable question: "But how would one *know* someone was a Congo?"

"Oh, you would *know*. They had a way of speaking, a way of dressing. They always called each other "Mister." Always the big man. And they lived *very well*. This," he says, waving at the devastation of Monrovia, "was all very nice."

The largest concrete structures—the old Ministry of Health, the old Ministry of Defense, the True Whig Party headquarters—are remnants of the peaceful, unjust regimes of President Tubman (1944–71) and President Tolbert (1971–80), for whom Liberians feel a perverse nostalgia. The university, the hospital, the schools, these were financed by a True Whig policy of massive international loans and deregulated foreign business concessions, typically given to agriculturally "extractive" companies, which ship resources directly out of the country without committing their companies to any value-added processing. For much of the twentieth century, Liberia had a nickname: Firestone Republic. The deals that condemned Liberians to poverty wages and inhumane living conditions were made in these old government buildings. The people who benefited most from these deals worked in these buildings. Now these buildings have rags hanging from their windows, bullet holes in their facades and thousands of squatters inside, without toilets, without running water. Naturally, new buildings are built, new deals are made. On January 28, 2005, while an interim "caretaker" government presided briefly over a ruined country (the elections were due later that year), Firestone rushed through a new concession: fifty cents an acre for the next thirty-seven years. A processing plant—for which Liberians have been asking since the 1970s—was not part of this deal. Ministers of finance and agriculture, who had no mandate from the people and would be out of office in a few months, negotiated the deal. It was signed in the Cabinet Room at the Executive Mansion in the presence of John Blaney, U.S. ambassador at the time. During the same period, Mittal Steel acquired the country's iron ore, giving the company virtual control of the vast Nimba concession area. The campaigning group Global Witness described the Mittal deal as a "case study in which multinational corporations seek to maximise profit by using an international regulatory void to gain concessions and contracts which strongly favour the corporation over the host nation."

It is a frustration for activists that Liberians have tended not to trace their trouble back to extractive foreign companies or their government lobbies. Liberians don't think that way. Most Liberians know how much a rubber tapper gets paid: thirty-five American dollars a month. Everyone knows how much a government minister is paid: two thousand American dollars a month—a Liberian fortune. No one can tell you Firestone's annual profit (in 2005, from its Liberia production alone: $81,242,190). In a country without a middle or working class, without *a functioning civic life*, government is all. It is all there is of money, of housing, of health care and schooling, of normal life. It is the focus of all aspirations, all fury. One of the more reliable signs of weak democracy is the synonymity of the word *government* with government buildings. Storming Downing Street and killing the prime minister would not transfer executive power. In Liberia, as in Haiti, the opposite is true. The violence of the past quarter century has in part represented a battle over Congo real estate, in particular the second, infamous Executive Mansion. It is hard to find any Liberian entirely free of the mystique of this building. In the book *Liberia: The Heart of Darkness*, a gruesome account of the 1989–97 war, the author's descriptions of 1990's catastrophic battle for Monrovia are half war report, half property magazine:

> From the university campus, [Charles Taylor's] NPFL pounded the heavily fortified Executive Mansion: the huge magnificent structure built in 1964 by the Israelis at the cost of $20 million. With its back to the brilliant white beach of the Atlantic, the Executive Mansion is located at the point where West Arica comes closest to Brazil.

In 1990, that was President Samuel K. Doe inside, refusing to leave. Ten years earlier, in 1980, when the twenty-eight-year-old Doe, a semiliterate Krahn tribesman and master sergeant in the Liberian army, staged his coup d'état, his focus was also the executive mansion. He fought his way in, disemboweling President Tolbert in his bed.

We visit Red Light market. Aubrey: "Why is it called Red Light?"
Abraham: "Because a set of traffic lights used to be here."
It is a circular piece of land, surrounded by small shops and swarming with street traders. The shops have names like The Arun Brothers and Ziad's, all Lebanese owned, as is the Mamba Point Hotel. Almost all small business in Liberia is Lebanese owned. Abraham shrugs: "They simply had money at a time when we had no money." The bleak punch line is Liberia's citizenship laws: anyone not "of African descent" cannot be a citizen. Lebanese money goes straight back to Lebanon.
Women crouch around the market's perimeter, selling little polyethylene bags of soap powder. Some are from WOCDAL (Women and Children

Development Association of Liberia), funded by Oxfam. WOCDAL lends them one hundred Liberian dollars (less than two American dollars) for a day. This gives the women a slight economic advantage in Red Light, analogous to the one the Lebanese had over the Liberians in the 1950s: money when others have none. No one else in Red Light can afford to buy a full box of soap powder. This the women then sell in pieces, keeping the profit and returning the one hundred dollars to WOCDAL. It is a curious fact that a box of soap powder, sold in many small parts, generates more money in the third world than in the first. A woman with five children tells us this enables her to send two of her three children to school. The other three work alongside her in the market. *How do you decide whom to send?* "I send the fourteen- and fifteen-year-olds to school, because they will be finished sooner. The five-, six-, and seven-year-olds work with me."

THURSDAY

From the 4x4, West Point does not look like a "flagship project." A narrow corridor of filth, lined on either side with small dwellings made of trash, mud, scrap metal. Children with distended bellies, rotting food, men breaking rocks. It stretches for miles. The vehicle sticks in an alley too narrow to pass. The visitors must walk. Close up, the scene is different. It is not one corridor. There are many networks of alley. It is a city. Food is cooking. Small stalls, chicken skewers for sale. Children trail Aubrey, wanting their photograph taken. They pose boldly: big fists on knobby, twiggy arms. No one begs. We stop by a workshop stockpiled with wooden desks and chairs, solid, not unbeautiful. They are presently being varnished a caramel brown. A very tall young white man is here to show us around, Oxfam's program manager at West Point. "*This*," he says, placing both hands hard on the nearest desk for emphasis, "is great workmanship, no?" Lysbeth peers at the wood: "Um, you do know that's not quite dry?"

•

Patrick Alix is thirty years old. He is distinctly aristocratic looking, half French, and so unrelievedly serious the urge is to say stupid things in his presence. Before working in West Point, Patrick worked in Zambia doing emergency work, qualified as a chartered accountant, worked for the World Wildlife Fund in Indonesia ("I used to be an ecology militant"), performed a management evaluation of the French nuclear fusion reactor program, produced a Reggae album in Haiti and played violin in the Liverpool Philharmonic Orchestra. The above is not an exhaustive list. He has seen the situation in Liberia progress from the direst emergency to the beginnings of "development." "Basically, we've followed the returnees from the camps—many settled in this community. Sixty-five thousand people live here, thirty thousand of them children. Now, there are nineteen schools in the slum, yes? So—" *Wait. There are schools in a slum?* Patrick frowns, stops walking. He pinches his temples. "Sure," he says. "But we're going to the only government one. The rest are private, sharing space with churches, or mosques, with volunteer teachers. There's also a teacher's council here, a commissioner, the township council—you understand the slum is a township? It's organized into blocks and zones. The area representatives call meetings. Otherwise nothing would get done."

He sets off quickly through the chaotic little alleys, sure of his way. When we arrive, Patrick says: "You should have seen it before. This is the 'after' picture!" Aubrey takes a photograph of the long, low concrete building, its four large, bare rooms. Patrick says: "So Liberia has this unique freed-slave history. . . . What this means is the government structures were simply borrowed, lots of titles—minister for this, minister for that—but that was cosmetic. . . . Now, things have changed; they've pledged ten percent of their budget to education, which is enormous percentage-wise, but still only twelve million dollars *for the whole country.* There's too much to be done right now. NGOs fill the gap. What you saw back there was part of our livelihood project: fathers are taught how to make school furniture, which we, the school, buy from them at a fair price. They also sell this furniture to all the schools in West Point. And mothers make the uniforms—if that doesn't sound too traditionally gendered. . . . "

Standing in front of the school are John Brownell, who manages the livelihood project, and Ella Coleman, who until recently was West Point's commissioner. Mr. Brownell is a celebrity in West Point: he played football for Liberia. This took him to the United States and Brazil. "Rio de Janeiro!" he says, and smiles fondly, as if speaking of heaven. He is crisp-shirted despite the heat, broad as a rugby player. Ms. Coleman is a kind of celebrity, too, well known throughout West Point. Hers is a hands-on approach to pastoral care. She will enter homes to check on suspected abuse. She keeps children at her own house if she fears for their safety. She is impassioned: "We have seven-year-old girls being raped by big men! I talk to parents—I educate people. People are so poor and desperate. They don't know. For example, if a mother is keeping her child home to earn fifty Liberian dollars at the market, I say to her: "That will keep you for a day! What about the future?" Another example: one of our very young boys here, he was always touching one of our girls—so I made him a friend. He was suspended—but sitting out there will not help. I went to his house. The whole family sleeps in one room. I said to his parents: you have exposed these children to these things too early. Anything that happens to this little girl, I will hold you responsible!"

And are some of your students ex-combatants? "Oh, my girl," says Ms. Coleman sadly, "there are ex-combatants everywhere. People live next to boys who killed their own families. We, as a people, we have so much healing to do."

Patrick explains logistics. The principal of the school is on thirty American dollars a month. To rent a shack in the slum for a month is four American dollars a week. Liberian teachers are easily bribed. You pay a little, you pass your exam. At the university level, the problem is endemic. Teaching qualifications are usually dubious. "It's dull to repeat, but this all stems from extreme poverty. If you're a teacher living in a shack on a pile of rubbish, you'd probably do the same." Mr. Brownell begins to speak hopefully of the Fast Track Initiative, to which Liberia has applied for money. He puffs out his wide chest proudly. One of the aims is to reduce class size from 344:1 to 130:1. Patrick nods quickly: "Yes, big man . . . but that will take three years—while strategies are being made, these children need something now. Look at them. They're waiting."

"This is the sad truth," says Brownell.

In the shade, four girls are instructed to speak with us. The conversation is brief. They all want to be doctors. They kick the dust, refuse to make eye contact. We have only inanities to offer them anyway. *It's good that you all want to be doctors. The doctors will teach new doctors. There'll be so many doctors in Liberia soon!*

Lysbeth sighs, murmuring: "Except there's something like twenty-three Liberian doctors. And fourteen nurses. In the whole country."

The visitors wilt slightly; sit on a wall. The schoolgirls look on with pity— an unbearable reversal. They run off to help their mothers in the market. Meanwhile, Ms. Coleman is still talking; she is explaining that at some point the government will clear this slum, this school, everything and everyone in it. She does not think the situation impossible. She does not yet suffer from "charity fatigue." She is saying, "I trust it will be for the best. We made this community from the dirt, but we can't stay here."

FRIDAY

Bong country is beautiful. Lush green forest, a sweet breeze. There are pygmy hippopotamuses here and monkeys; a sense of Liberia's possibilities. Rich in natural resources, cool in the hills, hot on the beach. Nyan P. Zikeh is the Oxfam program manager for this region. He is compactly built, handsome, boyish. He was educated during the last days of Tolbert's regime ("He was killed in my final year of high school"). Nyan helps rebuild the small village communities of Bong, a strategic area fought over by all the warring factions. People live in tiny traditional thatched huts arranged around a central ground. It is quiet and clean. The communities are close-knit and gather around the visitors to join the conversation. In one village a woman explains the food situation. She is "1-0-0," her children are (usually) "1-0-1"; there are many others who are "0-0-1." It is a binary system that describes meals per day. Still, things are improving: there are schools here now; there are latrines. Nyan's projects encourage the creation of rice paddies; the men work in them, and women take the rice to market. It is more than the subsistence farming that existed before the war. His dream is to connect all these villages in a trading ring that utilizes Bong's strategic centrality and sells produce on to Monrovia. Nyan: "You have to understand, in this area, everything was destroyed. The largest displaced camps were here. We helped people go back to where their villages formerly were; we helped them rebuild. All that you see here was done with DFID money—the Department for International Development. They are British. They funded us with £271,000 sterling—they gave us this twice. And I am happy to say we met a hundred percent of our targets. Creating infrastructure and training individuals. The money went a very long way. It helped to train Liberian staff. It helped provide assistance at the county level for the Ministry of Health. It was quite an enormous help."

"This is the good aid story," says Lysbeth. "People find that very boring."

As we leave the village, the gardener in Lysbeth looks around for signs of soil cultivation. Heavy, wet palms cascade over one another, but there are no fields. Nyan prides himself on his frankness: "We can't blame anyone else. The truth is we don't have the knowledge and skill about farming. It has always been slash, burn and plant. The only industrial farming our people have known here is the rubber plantations. That is the only major industry our people know. Everything else was not developed."

•

There are such things as third-world products. In the market where the women sell their rice, a boy's T-shirt reads DAVID BECKHAM, but the picture beneath is of Thierry Henry. The plastic buckets the women carry have bad ink jobs—the colors run like tie-dye. The products no one else wants come to Liberia. "And our meat is the same," explains Nyan, "chicken feet, pig feet. That's what people are sold. More tendon than flesh. No nutritional value."

Half a mile down the road, Mrs. Shaw, an eighty-year-old Liberian teacher, sits in front of her small home. She has taught three generations of Liberian children on a wage she describes as "less then the rubber tappers: twenty-five U.S. dollars a month." She says the children she teaches have changed over the years. Now they are "hot headed." *They are angry about their situation?* She frowns: "No, angry at each other." As we leave, Lysbeth spots three graves in the yard. "My sons—they were poisoned." Lysbeth assumes this is metaphorical, but Abraham shakes his head. He doesn't know what the poison is, exactly: maybe some kind of leaf extract. In the vehicle he explains: "Her sons, they were working in government, quite good jobs. It happens that when you're doing well, sometimes you are poisoned. They put something in your drink. I always watch my glass when I am out."

●

The visitors sit on the porch eating dinner at CooCoo's Nest, the best hotel in rural Liberia. Named after President Tubman's mistress, it is owned by his daughter; she lives in America now. In her absence it is run by Kamal E. Ghanam, a louche, chain-smoking Lebanese in a safari pantsuit, who asks you kindly not to switch on the light in your room until after 7 P.M. Kamal also manages the rubber plantation behind. He brings out the sangria as Abraham and Nyan bond. These two are members of a very small group in Liberia: the makeshift Liberian middle class, created in large part by the presence of the NGOs. "It's difficult," explains Abraham. "Even if I paint my house, people begin talking. *He is Congo now.* As soon as you have anything at all, you are isolated from the people." They show off their battle scars, knife wounds from street robberies. Aubrey, who has been photographing the plantations, arrives. He has news: he met a rubber worker in the field.

"His name is David. He doesn't know his age—but we worked out with various references to events during war that he's about thirty-five years old. He has three living children and three who died. He was born on the plantation and has worked there since he was ten or twelve, he thinks. He wants to be able to keep his own children in school, but at the current rate of pay he won't be able to afford to. He works seven days a week. He says workers on the plantation live in camps that were built in 1952. There are no schools or medical facilities nearby—anyway, he couldn't afford them. He taps about fifty pounds of raw latex per day. He said it's a long day, from sunrise until late. . . ."

Aubrey is breathless and excited: we have the feeling that we are intrepid journalists, uncovering an unknown iniquity. In fact, the conditions on Liberian rubber plantations are well documented. In a CNN report of 2005, Firestone president Dan Adomitis explained that each worker "only" taps 650–750 trees a day and that each tree takes two to three minutes. Taking the lower of these two estimates equals twenty-one hours a day of rubber tapping. In the past, parents have brought their children with them in order to help them meet the quota; when this was reported, Firestone banned the practice. Now people bring their children before dawn.

Kamal smokes, listens, sighs. He says, "Listen, this is how it is," as if talking of some unstoppable natural weather phenomenon. He pauses. Then, more strongly: "Now, be careful about this tapper. He is not from Firestone, I think. He is from a different place." Nyan smiles. "Kamal, we both know that plantation—it sells to a middleman who sells to Firestone. Everybody sells to Firestone." Kamal shrugs. Nyan turns back to the visitors: "Firestone is a taboo subject here. Everyone knows the conditions are terrible—their accommodation has no water, no electricity—but it is better paid than most work here. You would have to have a very strong lobby in the U.S. government to stop them. The whole reason Firestone came to Liberia in the first place was as a means of creating a permanent supply of rubber for the American military. The British had increased the taxes on Malaysian rubber—the Americans didn't want to pay that. They needed a permanent solution. So they planted the rubber—it's not native to Liberia. Really, they created a whole industry. It sounds strange, but these are some of the best jobs in Liberia."

Kamal goes inside to collect dessert. Abraham leans over the table.

"Do you know what people say? In 2003, when the war was at its worst, *the only places in Liberia that were safe* were the U.S. embassy and Firestone. Everywhere else there was looting and killing. The American Marines were offshore—we kept hoping they would come ashore. What were they waiting for? But we waited and then they sailed away. They did *nothing*. And that is when people got disappointed."

•

Everyone at the table is asked why they think the war happened. Nyan says: "Let me tell you first my candid feeling: every Liberian in one way or another took part in the war. Either spiritually, financially, psychologically or physically.

And to answer your question: in a sense there was no reason. Brothers killed brothers, friends killed friends, only to come back the next day and regret they ever did it in the first place. For me the only real reason was greed. And poverty. All that the warlords wanted was property. When they stormed Monrovia, they did not even pretend to fight one another. They killed people in their homes and then painted their own names on the walls. When Ms. Sirleaf took over Guttridge's rubber plantation—2.8 million a month—it was still occupied by rebel forces, and they refused to leave for a year and a half. They wanted to be in the rubber business. But they destroyed the trees—didn't tap them properly. It will take another ten years to replant."

SATURDAY

Lunch in La Pointe, the "good restaurant" in Monrovia. The view is of sheer cliff dropping to marshland, and beyond this, blue green waters. During the war the beach was scattered with human skulls. Now it is simply empty. In Jamaica, tourists marry on beaches like these. They stand barefoot in wedding outfits in white sand owned by German hotel chains and hold up champagne flutes, recreating an image from a brochure. This outcome for Liberia—a normalized, if exploitative, "tourist economy"—seems almost too good to hope for. At present, La Pointe is patronized solely by NGO workers, government officials and foreign businessmen. A Liberian passes by in a reasonably nice suit. Abraham: "He's a Supreme Court judge." Another man in a tie: "Oh, he's Nigerian. He owns an airline." Everywhere in Liberia it is the same: there are only the very poor and the very powerful. In the missing middle, for now: the "international community." The monitoring agency GEMAP is in place. No government check over five hundred dollars can be signed without GEMAP's knowledge. *It is very hard to be good in these conditions.* President Johnson-Sirleaf has promised to review the 2005 Mittal Steel and Firestone concessions. *We hope and pray.*

Behind our table an Englishman, a Lebanese and a Liberian are having a lunch meeting:

Englishman: You see, I'm worried about management morale. The troops soon feel it if management is low. At the moment it's like a bloody sauna in there. Maybe we could just give them a few things . . . a nice bed, bedsheets, something so they won't be bitten to death at night. They're so happy if you do that—you wouldn't believe it!
Liberian: My friend, *someone's* going to get malaria. It's inevitable.
Lebanese: This is true.
Liberian: I ask you please not to worry about malaria—we get it all the time in Liberia. I promise you we are used to it!

•

The history of Liberia consists of elegant variations on this conversation.

The Toyota rolls up in front of Paynesville School. Motto: *Helping our selve* [sic] *through Development*. Aubrey causes a riot in the playground: everyone wants their picture taken. Some are in uniform, others in NGO T-shirts. Fifty or so wear a shirt that says CHINA AND LIBERIA: FRIENDSHIP FOREVER. We are here only for one boy. We were given his name by Don Bosco Homes, a Catholic organization that specializes in the rehabilitation of child ex-combatants.

He is very small for fifteen, with a close-shaved, perfectly round head and long, pretty eyelashes. He has the transcendental air of a child lama. Three big men bring him to us in a corner of the yard and go to fetch a chair. He stays the wrist of one of the men with a finger and shakes his head. "It's too hot here to talk. We'll go inside."

In a small office at the back of the school, four nervous adults supervise the interview. Lysbeth, who has teenage children herself, looks as if she might cry even before Richard speaks. It's been a long week. Richard is determined to make it easy for us. He smiles gently at the Dictaphone: "It's okay. Are you sure that it's on?"

•

"My name is Richard S. Jack. I was twelve in 2003. I was living with my mother when the second civil war began. I was playing on a football field when men came and grabbed me. It was done by force—I had no desire to join that war. They called themselves the Marine Force. They took both teams of boys away. They threw us in a truck. I thought I wasn't going to see my parents anymore. They took me to Lofah Bridge. What happened there? We were taught to do certain things. We were taught to use AK-47s. I was with them for a year and a half. We were many different kinds of Liberians and Sierra Leoneans, many boys. The first one or two weeks I was so scared. After that it became a part of me. I went out of my proper and natural way. War makes people go out of their proper and natural way. It is a thing that destroys even your thoughts. People still don't know what the war was about. I know. It was a terrible misunderstanding. But it is not a part of me anymore. I don't want violence in me anymore. Whenever I sit and think about the past, I get this attitude: *I am going to raise myself up.* So I tell people about my past. They should know who I was. Sometimes it is hard. But it wasn't difficult to explain to my mother. She understood how everything was. She knew I was not a bad person in my heart. Now I want to be most wise. My dream is to become somebody good in this nation. I have a feeling that Liberia could be a great nation. But I also want to see the world. I love the study of geography. I want to become a pilot. You want me to fly you somewhere? Sure. Come and find me in ten years. I promise we will fly places."

Nine

SPEAKING IN TONGUES

The following is based on a lecture given at the New York Public Library in December 2008.

1

Hello. This voice I speak with these days, this English voice with its rounded vowels and consonants in more or less the right place—this is not the voice of my childhood. I picked it up in college, along with the unabridged *Clarissa* and a taste for port. Maybe this fact is only what it seems to be—a case of bald social climbing—but at the time, I genuinely thought this was the voice of lettered people, and that if I didn't have the voice of lettered people I would never truly be lettered. A braver person, perhaps, would have stood firm, teaching her peers a useful lesson by example: not all lettered people need be of the same class, nor speak identically. I went the other way. Partly out of cowardice and a constitutional eagerness to please, but also because I didn't quite see it as a straight swap, of this voice for that. My own childhood had been the story of this and that combined, of the synthesis of disparate things. It never occurred to me that I was leaving Willesden for Cambridge. I thought I was adding Cambridge to Willesden, this new way of talking to that old way. Adding a new kind of knowledge to a different kind I already had. And for a while, that's how it was: at home, during the holidays, I spoke with my old voice, and in the old voice seemed to feel and speak things that I couldn't express in college, and vice versa. I felt a sort of wonder at the flexibility of the thing. Like being alive twice.

But flexibility is something that requires work if it is to be maintained. Recently my double voice has deserted me for a single one, reflecting the smaller world into which my work has led me. Willesden was a big, colorful, working-class sea; Cambridge was a smaller, posher pond, and almost univocal; the literary world is a puddle. This voice I picked up along the way is no longer an exotic garment I put on like a college gown whenever I choose—now it is my only voice, whether I want it or not. I regret it; I should have kept both voices alive in my mouth. They were both a part of me. But how the culture warns against it! As George Bernard Shaw delicately put it in his preface to the play *Pygmalion*, "many thousands of [British] men and women . . . have sloughed off their native dialects and acquired a new tongue." Few, though, will admit to it. Voice adaptation is still the original British sin. Monitoring and exposing such citizens is a national pastime, as popular as sex scandals and libel cases. If you lean toward the Atlantic with your high-rising terminals, you're a sellout; if you pronounce borrowed European words in their original style—even if you try something as innocent as *parmigiano* for *parmesan*—you're a fraud. If you go (metaphorically speaking) down the British class scale, you've gone from Cockney to "mockney" and can expect a public tarring and feathering; to go the other way is to perform an unforgivable act of class betrayal. Voices are meant to be unchanging and singular. There's no quicker way to insult an expat Scotsman in London than to tell him he's lost his accent. We feel that our voices are who we are, and that to have more than one, or to use different versions of a voice for different occasions, represents, at best, a Janus-faced duplicity, and at worst, the loss of our very souls. Whoever changes their voice takes on, in Britain, a queerly tragic dimension. They have betrayed that puzzling dictum "To thine own self be true," so often quoted approvingly as if it represented the wisdom of Shakespeare rather than the hot air of Polonius. "What's to become of me? What's to become of me?" wails Eliza Doolittle, realizing her middling dilemma. With a voice too posh for the flower girls and yet too redolent of the gutter for the ladies in Mrs. Higgins's drawing room.

But Eliza—patron saint of the tragically double-voiced—is worthy of closer inspection. The first thing to note is that both Eliza and *Pygmalion* are entirely didactic, as Shaw meant them to be. "I delight," he wrote, "in throwing [*Pygmalion*] at the heads of the wiseacres who repeat the parrot cry that art should never be didactic. It goes to prove my contention that art should never be anything else." He was determined to tell the unambiguous tale of a girl who changes her voice and loses her self. And so she arrives like this:

> Don't you be so saucy. You ain't heard what I come for yet. Did you tell him I come in a taxi? . . . Oh, we are proud! He ain't above giving lessons, not him: I heard him say so. Well, I ain't come here to ask for any compliment; and if my money's not good enough I can go elsewhere. . . . Now you know, don't you? I'm come to have lessons, I am. And to pay for em too: make no mistake. . . . I want to be a lady in a flower shop stead of selling at the corner of Tottenham Court Road. But they wont take me unless I can talk more genteel.

And she leaves like this:

> I can't. I could have done it once; but now I can't go back to it. Last night, when I was wandering about, a girl spoke to me; and I tried to get back into the old way with her; but it was no use. You told me, you know, that when a child is brought to a foreign country, it picks up the language in a few weeks, and forgets its own. Well, I am a child in your country. I have forgotten my own language, and can speak nothing but yours.

By the end of his experiment, Professor Higgins has made his Eliza an awkward, in-between thing, neither flower girl nor lady, with one voice lost and another gained, at the steep price of everything she was and everything she knows. Almost as afterthought, he sends Eliza's father, Alfred Doolittle, to his doom, too, securing a three-thousand-a-year living for the man on the condition that Doolittle lecture for the Wannafeller Moral Reform World League up to six times a year. This burden brings the philosophical dustman into the close, unwanted embrace of what he disdainfully calls "middle class morality." By the time the curtain goes down, both Doolittles find themselves stuck in the middle, which is, to Shaw, a comi-tragic place to be, with the emphasis on the tragic. What are they fit for? What will become of them?

How persistent this horror of the middling spot is, this dread of the interim place! It extends through the specter of the tragic mulatto, to the plight of the transsexual, to our present anxiety—disguised as genteel concern—for the contemporary immigrant, tragically split, we are sure, between worlds, ideas, cultures, voices—whatever will become of them? Something's got to give— one voice must be sacrificed for the other. What is double must be made singular. But this, the apparent didactic moral of Eliza's story, is undercut by the fact of the play itself, which is an orchestra of many voices, simultaneously and perfectly rendered, with no shade of color or tone sacrificed. Higgins's Harley Street high-handedness is the equal of Mrs. Pearce's lower-middle-class gentility, Pickering's kindhearted aristocratic imprecision every bit as convincing as Alfred Doolittle's Nietzschean Cockney-by-way-of-Wales. Shaw had a wonderful ear, able to reproduce almost as many quirks of the English language as Shakespeare. Shaw was in possession of a gift he wouldn't, or couldn't, give Eliza: he spoke in tongues.

It gives me a strange sensation to turn from Shaw's melancholy Pygmalion story to another, infinitely more hopeful version, written by the new president of the United States of America. Of course, his ear isn't half bad either. In *Dreams from My Father*, the new president displays an enviable facility for dialogue, and puts it to good use, animating a cast every bit as various as the one James Baldwin—an obvious influence—conjured for his own many-voiced novel *Another Country*. Obama can do young Jewish male, black old lady from the South Side, white woman from Kansas, Kenyan elders, white Harvard nerds, black Columbia nerds, activist women, churchmen, security guards, bank tellers, and even a British man called Mr. Wilkerson, who on a starry night on safari says credibly British things like: "I believe that's the Milky Way." This new president doesn't just speak for his people. He can speak them. It is a disorienting talent in a president; we're so unused to it. I have to pinch myself to remember who wrote the following well-observed scene, seemingly plucked from a comic novel:

"Man, I'm not going to any more of these bullshit Punahou parties."

"Yeah, that's what you said the last time. . . . "

"I mean it this time. . . . These girls are A-1, USDA-certified racists. All of 'em. White girls. Asian girls—shoot, these Asians worse than the whites. Think we got a disease or something."

"Maybe they're looking at that big butt of yours. Man, I thought you were in training."

"Get your hands out of my fries. You ain't my bitch, nigger. . . . buy your own damn fries. Now what was I talking about?"

"Just 'cause a girl don't go out with you doesn't make her a racist."

This is the voice of Obama at seventeen, as remembered by Obama. He's still recognizably Obama; he already seeks to unpack and complicate apparently obvious things ("Just 'cause a girl don't go out with you doesn't make her a racist"); he's already gently cynical about the impassioned dogma of other people ("Yeah, that's what you said the last time"). And he has a sense of humor ("Maybe they're looking at that big butt of yours"). Only the voice is different: he has made almost as large a leap as Eliza Doolittle. The conclusions Obama draws from his own Pygmalion experience, however, are subtler than Shaw's. The tale he tells is not the old tragedy of gaining a new, false voice at the expense of a true one. The tale he tells is all about addition. His is the story of a genuinely many-voiced man. If it has a moral, it is that each man must be true to his selves, plural.

For Obama, having more than one voice in your ear is not a burden, or not solely a burden—it is also a gift. And the gift is of an interesting kind, not well served by that dull publishing-house title, *Dreams from My Father: A Story of Race and Inheritance,* with its suggestion of a simple linear inheritance, of paternal dreams and aspirations passed down to a son, and fulfilled. *Dreams from My Father* would have been a fine title for John McCain's book *Faith of My Fathers,* which concerns exactly this kind of linear masculine inheritance, in his case from soldier to soldier. For Obama's book, though, it's wrong, lopsided. He corrects its misperception early on, in the first chapter, while discussing the failure of his parents' relationship, characterized by their only son as the end of a dream. "Even as that spell was broken," he writes, "and the worlds that they thought they'd left behind reclaimed each of them, I occupied the place where their dreams had been."

To occupy a dream, to exist in a dreamed space (conjured by both father and mother), is surely a quite different thing from simply inheriting a dream. It's more interesting. What did Pauline Kael call Cary Grant? "The Man from Dream City." When Bristolian Archibald Leach became suave Cary Grant, the transformation happened in his voice, which he subjected to a strange, indefinable manipulation, resulting in that heavenly sui generis accent, neither west country nor posh, American nor English. It came from nowhere; *he* came from nowhere. Grant seemed the product of a collective dream, dreamed up by moviegoers in hard times, as it sometimes feels voters have dreamed up Obama in hard times. Both men have a strange reflective quality, typical of the self-created man—we see in them whatever we want to see. "Everyone wants to be Cary Grant," said Cary Grant. "Even I want to be Cary Grant." It's not hard to imagine Obama having that same thought, backstage at Grant Park, hearing his own name chanted by the hopeful multitude. Everyone wants to be Barack Obama. Even I want to be Barack Obama.

2

But I haven't described Dream City. I'll try to. It is a place of many voices, where the unified singular self is an illusion. Naturally, Obama was born there. So was I. When your personal multiplicity is printed on your face, in an almost too obviously thematic manner, in your DNA, in your hair and in the neither-this-nor-that beige of your skin—well, anyone can see you come from

Dream City. In Dream City everything is doubled, everything is various. You have no choice but to cross borders and speak in tongues. That's how you get from your mother to your father, from talking to one set of folks who think you're not black enough to another who figure you insufficiently white. It's the kind of town where the wise man says "I" cautiously, because *I* feels like too straight and singular a phoneme to represent the true multiplicity of his experience. Instead, citizens of Dream City prefer to use the collective pronoun *we*.

Throughout his campaign Obama was careful always to say *we*. He was noticeably wary of *I*. By speaking so, he wasn't simply avoiding a singularity he didn't feel; he was also drawing us in with him. He had the audacity to suggest that, even if you can't see it stamped on their faces, most people come from Dream City, too. Most of us have complicated backstories, messy histories, multiple narratives. It was a high-wire strategy, for Obama, this invocation of our collective human messiness. His enemies latched on to its imprecision, emphasizing the exotic, un-American nature of Dream City, this ill-defined place where you could be from Hawaii and Kenya, Kansas and Indonesia all at the same time, where you could jive talk like a street hustler and orate like a senator. What kind of a crazy place is that? But they underestimated how many people come from Dream City, how many Americans, in their daily lives, conjure contrasting voices and seek a synthesis between disparate things. Turns out, Dream City wasn't so strange to them.

Or did they never actually see it? We now know that Obama spoke of *Main Street* in Iowa and of *sweet potato pie* in Northwest Philly, and it could be argued that he succeeded because he so rarely misspoke, carefully tailoring his intonations to suit the sensibility of his listeners. Sometimes he did this within one speech, within one *line*: "We worship an *awesome* God in the blue states, and we don't like federal agents poking around our libraries in the red states." *Awesome God* comes to you straight from the pews of a Georgia church; *poking around* feels more at home at a kitchen table in South Bend, Indiana. The balance was perfect, cunningly counterpoised and never accidental. It's only now that it's over that we see him let his guard down a little, on *60 Minutes*, say, dropping in that culturally, casually black construction, "Hey, I'm not stupid, man, that's why I'm president," something it's hard to imagine him doing even three weeks earlier. To a certain kind of mind, it must have looked like the mask had slipped for a moment.

Which brings us to the single-voiced Obamanation crowd. They rage on in the blogs and on the radio, waiting obsessively for the mask to slip. They have a great fear of what they see as Obama's doubling ways. "He says one thing but he means another"—this is the essence of the fear campaign. He says he's a capitalist, but he'll spread your wealth. He says he's a Christian, but really he's going to empower the Muslims. And so on and so forth. These are fears that have their roots in an anxiety about voice. "Who is he?" people kept asking. I mean, who is this guy, really? He says "sweet potato pie" in Philly and "Main Street" in Iowa! When he talks to us, he sure sounds like us— but behind our backs he says we're clinging to our religion, to our guns. And when Jesse Jackson heard that Obama had lectured a black church congrega- tion about the epidemic of absent black fathers, he experienced this, too, as a tonal betrayal; Obama was "talking down to black people." In both cases, there was the sense of a double-dealer, of someone who tailors his speech to fit the audience, who is not of the people (because he is able to look at them objectively) but always above them.

The Jackson gaffe, with its Oedipal violence ("I want to cut his nuts out"), is especially poignant because it goes to the heart of a generational conflict in the black community, concerning what we will say in public and what we say in private. For it has been a point of honor, among the civil rights gen- eration, that any criticism or negative analysis of our community, expressed, as they often are by white politicians, without context, without real empa- thy or understanding, should not be repeated by a black politician when the white community is listening, even if (especially if) the criticism happens to be true (more than half of all black American children live in single-parent households). Our business is our business. Keep it in the family; don't wash your dirty linen in public; stay unified. (Of course, with his overheard gaffe, Jackson unwittingly broke his own rule.)

Until Obama, black politicians had always adhered to these unwritten rules. In this way, they defended themselves against those two bogeymen of black political life: the Uncle Tom and the House Nigger. The black politician who played up to, or even simply echoed, white fears, desires and hopes for the black community was in danger of earning these epithets—even Martin Luther King was not free from such suspicions. Then came Obama, and the new world he had supposedly ushered in, the postracial world, in which what mattered most was not blind racial allegiance but factual truth. It was felt that Jesse Jackson was sadly out of step with this new postracial world: even his own son felt moved to publicly repudiate his "ugly rhetoric." But Jackson's anger was not incomprehensible or his distrust unreasonable. Jackson lived through a bitter struggle, and bitter struggles deform their participants in subtle, complicated ways. The idea that one should speak one's cultural allegiance first and the truth second (and that this is a sign of authenticity) is precisely such a deformation.

Right up to the wire, Obama made many black men and women of Jackson's generation suspicious. How *can* the man who passes between culturally black and white voices with such flexibility, with such ease, be an honest man? How *will* the man from Dream City keep it real? Why won't he speak with a clear and unified voice? These were genuine questions for people born in real cities at a time when those cities were implacably divided, when the black movement had to yell with a clear and unified voice, or risk not being heard at all. And then he won. Watching Jesse Jackson in tears in Grant Park, pressed up against the varicolored American public, it seemed like he, at least, had received the answer he needed: only a many-voiced man could have spoken to that many people.

A clear and unified voice. In that context, this business of being biracial, of being half black and half white, is awkward. In his memoir, Obama takes care to ridicule a certain black girl called Joyce—a composite figure from his college days who happens also to be part Italian and part French and part Native American and is inordinately fond of mentioning these facts, and who likes to say:

I'm not black . . . I'm multiracial. . . . Why should I have to choose between them? . . . It's not white people who are making me choose. . . . No—it's black people who always have to make everything racial. They're the ones making me choose. They're the ones who are telling me I can't be who I am. . . .

He has her voice down pat and so condemns her out of her own mouth. For she's the third bogeyman of black life, the tragic mulatto, who secretly wishes she "passed," always keen to let you know about her white heritage. It's the fear of being mistaken for Joyce that has always ensured that I ignore the box marked "biracial" and tick the box marked "black" on any questionnaire I fill out, and call myself unequivocally a black writer and roll my eyes at anyone who insists that Obama is not the first black president but the first biracial one. But I also know in my heart that it's an equivocation; I know that Obama has a double consciousness, is black and, at the same time, white, as I am, unless we are suggesting that one side of a person's genetics and cultural heritage cancels out or trumps the other.

But to mention the double is to suggest shame at the singular. Joyce insists on her varied heritage because she fears and is ashamed of the singular black. I suppose it's possible that subconsciously I am also a tragic mulatto, torn between pride and shame. In my conscious life, though, I cannot honestly say I feel proud to be white and ashamed to be black or proud to be black and ashamed to be white. I find it impossible to experience either pride or shame over accidents of genetics in which I had no active part. I understand how those words got into the racial discourse, but I can't sign up to them. I'm not proud to be female either. I am not even proud to be human—I only love to be so. As I love to be female and I love to be black, and I love that I had a white father.

It's telling that Joyce is one of the few voices in *Dreams from My Father* that is truly left out in the cold, outside of the expansive sympathy of Obama's narrative. She is an entirely didactic being, a demon Obama has to raise up, if only for a page, so everyone can watch him slay her. I know the feeling. When I was in college I felt I'd rather run away with the Black Panthers than be associated with the Joyces I occasionally met. It's the Joyces of this world who "talk down to black people." And so to avoid being Joyce, or being seen to be Joyce, you unify, you speak with one voice. And the concept of a unified black voice is a potent one. It has filtered down, these past forty years, into the black community at all levels, settling itself in that impossible injunction "keep it real," the original intention of which was unification. We were going to unify the concept of Blackness in order to strengthen it. Instead we confined and restricted it. To me, the instruction "keep it real" is a sort of prison cell, two feet by five. The fact is, it's too narrow. I just can't live comfortably in there. "Keep it real" replaced the blessed and solid genetic fact of Blackness with a flimsy imperative. It made Blackness a quality each individual black person was constantly in danger of losing. And almost anything could trigger the loss of one's Blackness: attending certain universities, an impressive variety of jobs, a fondness for opera, a white girlfriend, an interest in golf. And of course, any change in the voice. There was a popular school of thought that maintained the voice was at the very heart of the thing; fail to keep it real there and you'd never see your Blackness again. How absurd that all seems now. And not because we live in a postracial world—we don't—but because the reality of race has diversified. Black reality has diversified. It's black people who talk like me, and black people who talk like Lil Wayne. It's black conservatives and black liberals, black sportsmen and black lawyers, black computer technicians and black ballet dancers and black truck drivers and black presidents. We're all black, and we all love to be black, and we all sing from our own hymn sheet. We're all surely black people, but we may be finally approaching a point of human history where you can't talk up or down to us anymore, but only *to* us. He's talking down to white people—how curious it sounds the other way round! In order to say such a thing, one would have to think collectively of white people, as a people of one mind who speak with one voice—a thought experiment in which we have no practice. But it's worth trying. It's only when you play the record backward that you hear the secret message.

3

For reasons that are obscure to me, those qualities we cherish in our artists we condemn in our politicians. In our artists we look for the many-colored voice, the multiple sensibility. The apogee of this is, of course, Shakespeare: even more than for his wordplay we cherish him for his lack of allegiance. Our Shakespeare sees always both sides of a thing; he is black and white, male and female—he is everyman. The giant lacunae in his biography are merely a convenience; if any new facts of religious or political affiliation were ever to arise, we would dismiss them in our hearts anyway. Was he, for example, a man of Rome or not? He has appeared, to generations of readers, not of one religion but of both, in truth, beyond both. Born into the middle of Britain's fierce Catholic-Protestant culture war, how could the bloody absurdity of those years not impress upon him a strong sense of cultural contingency?

It was a war of ideas that began for Will—as it began for Barack—in the dreams of his father. For we know that John Shakespeare, a civic officer in Protestant times, oversaw the repainting of medieval frescoes and the destruction of the rood loft and altar in Stratford's own fine Guild Chapel, but we also know that in the rafters of the Shakespeare home John hid a secret Catholic "Spiritual Testament," a signed profession of allegiance to the old faith. A strange experience, to watch one's own father thus divided, professing one thing in public while practicing another in private. John Shakespeare was a kind of equivocator: it's what you do when you're in a corner, when you can't be a Catholic and a loyal Englishman at the same time. When you can't be both black and white. Sometimes in a country ripped apart by dogma, those who wish to keep their heads—in both senses—must learn to split themselves in two. And this we still know, here, at a four-hundred-year distance. No one can hope to be president of these United States without professing a committed and straightforward belief in two things: the existence of God and the principle of American exceptionalism. But how many of them equivocated, and who, in their shoes, would not equivocate, too?

Fortunately, Shakespeare was an artist and so had an outlet his father didn't have—the many-voiced theater. Shakespeare's art, the very medium of it, allowed him to do what civic officers and politicians can't seem to: speak simultaneous truths. (Is it not, for example, experientially true that one can both believe and not believe in God?) In his plays he is woman, man, black, white, believer, heretic, Catholic, Protestant, Jew, Muslim. He grew up in an atmosphere of equivocation, but he lived in freedom. And he offers us freedom: to pin him down to a single identity would be an obvious diminishment, both for Shakespeare and for us. Generations of critics have insisted on this irreducible multiplicity, though they have each expressed it different ways, through the glass of their times. Here is Keats's famous attempt, in 1817, to give this quality a name:

At once it struck me, what quality went to form a Man of Achievement especially in Literature and which Shakespeare possessed so enormously— mean Negative Capability, that is when man is capable of being in uncertainties, Mysteries, doubts, without any irritable reaching after fact and reason.

And here is Stephen Greenblatt doing the same, in 2004:

There are many forms of heroism in Shakespeare, but ideological heroism— the fierce, self-immolating embrace of an idea or institution—is not one of them.

For Keats, Shakespeare's many voices are quasi-mystical, as suited the romantic thrust of Keats's age. For Greenblatt, Shakespeare's negative capability is sociopolitical at root. Will had seen too many wild-eyed martyrs, too many executed terrorists, too many wars on the Catholic terror. He had watched men rage absurdly at rood screens and write treatises in praise of tables. He had seen men disemboweled while still alive, their entrails burned before their eyes, and all for the preference of a Latin Mass over a common prayer or vice versa. He understood what fierce, singular certainty creates and what it destroys. In response, he made himself a diffuse, uncertain thing, a mass of contradictory, irresolvable voices that speak truth plurally. Through the glass of 2008, "negative capability" looks like the perfect antidote to "ideological heroism."

From our politicians, though, we still look for ideological heroism, despite everything. We consider pragmatists to be weak. We call men of balance naive fools. In England, we once had an insulting name for such people: trimmers. In the mid-1600s, a trimmer was any politician who attempted to straddle the reviled middle ground between Cavalier and Roundhead, Parliament and the Crown; to call a man a trimmer was to accuse him of being insufficiently committed to an ideology. But in telling us of these times, the nineteenth-century English historian Thomas Macaulay draws our attention to Halifax, great statesman of the Privy Council, set up to mediate between Parliament and Crown as London burned. Halifax proudly called himself a trimmer, assuming it, Macaulay explains, as

> a title of honour, and vindicat[ing], with great vivacity, the dignity of the appellation. Everything good, he said, trims between extremes. The temperate zone trims between the climate in which men are roasted and the climate in which they are frozen. The English Church trims between the Anabaptist madness and the Papist lethargy. The English constitution trims between the Turkish despotism and Polish anarchy. Virtue is nothing but a just temper between propensities any one of which, if indulged to excess, becomes vice.

Which all sounds eminently reasonable and Aristotelian. And Macaulay's description of Halifax's character is equally attractive:

> His intellect was fertile, subtle, and capacious. His polished, luminous, and animated eloquence . . . was the delight of the House of Lords. . . . His political tracts well deserve to be studied for their literary merit.

In fact, Halifax is familiar—he sounds like the man from Dream City. This makes Macaulay's caveat the more striking:

> Yet he was less successful in politics than many who enjoyed smaller advantages. Indeed, those intellectual peculiarities which make his writings valuable frequently impeded him in the contests of active life. For he always saw passing events, not in the point of view in which they commonly appear to one who bears a part in them, but in the point of view in which, after the lapse of many years, they appear to the philosophic historian.

To me, this is a doleful conclusion. It is exactly men with such intellectual peculiarities that I have always hoped to see in politics. But maybe Macaulay is correct: maybe the Halifaxes of this world make, in the end, better writers than politicians. A lot rests on how this president turns out—but that's a debate for the future. Here I want instead to hazard a little theory, concerning the evolution of a certain type of voice, typified by Halifax, by Shakespeare, and very possibly by the president. For the voice of what Macaulay called "the philosophic historian" is, to my mind, a valuable and particular one, and I think someone should make a proper study of it. It's a voice that develops in a man over time; my little theory sketches four developmental stages. The first stage in the evolution is contingent and cannot be contrived. In this first stage, the voice, by no fault of its own, finds itself trapped between two poles, two competing belief systems. And so this first stage necessitates the second: the voice learns to be flexible between these two fixed points, even to the point of equivocation. Then the third stage: this native flexibility leads to a sense of being able to "see a thing from both sides." And then the final stage, which I think of as the mark of a certain kind of genius: the voice relinquishes ownership of itself, develops a creative sense of disassociation in which the claims that are particular to it seem no stronger than anyone else's. There it is, my little theory—I'd rather call it a story. It is a story about a wonderful voice, occasionally used by citizens, rarely by men of power. Amid the din of the 2008 culture wars it proved especially hard to hear.

In this lecture I have been seeking to tentatively suggest that the voice that speaks with such freedom, thus unburdened by dogma and personal bias, thus flooded with empathy, might make a good president. It's only now that I realize that in all this utilitarianism I've left joyfulness out of the account, and thus neglected a key constituency of my own people, the poets! Being many voiced may be a complicated gift for a president, but in poets it is a pure delight in need of neither defense nor explanation. Plato banished them from his uptight and annoying republic so long ago that they have lost all their anxiety. They are fancy-free.

"I am a Hittite in love with a horse," writes Frank O'Hara.

I don't know what blood's

in me I feel like an African prince I am a girl walking downstairs

in a red pleated dress with heels I am a champion taking a fall

I am a jockey with a sprained ass-hole I am the light mist

    in which a face appears

and it is another face of blonde I am a baboon eating a banana

I am a dictator looking at his wife I am a doctor eating a child

and the child's mother smiling I am a Chinaman climbing a mountain

I am a child smelling his father's underwear I am an Indian

sleeping on a scalp

    and my pony is stamping in

    the birches,

and I've just caught sight of the

    Niña, the Pinta and the Santa

    Maria.

    What land is this, so free?

Frank O'Hara's republic is of the imagination, of course. It is the only land of perfect freedom. Presidents, as a breed, tend to dismiss this land, thinking it has nothing to teach them. If this new president turns out to be different, then writers will count their blessings, but with or without a president on board, writers should always count their blessings. A line of O'Hara's reminds us of this. It's carved on his gravestone. It reads: "Grace to be born and live as variously as possible."

But to live variously cannot simply be a gift, endowed by an accident of birth; it has to be a continual effort, continually renewed. I felt this with force the night of the election. I was at a lovely New York party, full of lovely people, almost all of whom were white, liberal, highly educated, and celebrating with one happy voice as the states turned blue. Just as they called Iowa, my phone rang and a strident German voice said: "Zadie! Come to Harlem! It's vild here. I'm in za middle of a crazy reggae bar—it's so vonderful! Vy not come now!"

I mention he was German only so we don't run away with the idea that flexibility comes only to the beige, or gay, or otherwise marginalized. Flexibility is a choice, always open to all of us. (He was a writer, however. Make of that what you will.)

But wait: all the way uptown? A crazy reggae bar? For a minute I hesitated, because I was at a lovely party having a lovely time. Or was that it? There was something else. In truth I thought: but I'll be ludicrous, in my silly dress, with this silly posh English voice, in a crowded bar of black New Yorkers celebrating. It's amazing how many of our cross-cultural and cross-class encounters are limited not by hate or pride or shame, but by another equally insidious, less-discussed, emotion: embarrassment. A few minutes later, I was in a taxi and heading uptown with my Northern Irish husband and our half-Indian, half-English friend, but that initial hesitation was ominous; the first step on a typical British journey. A hesitation in the face of difference, which leads to caution before difference and ends in fear of it. Before long, the only voice you recognize, the only life you can empathize with, is your own. You will think that a novelist's screwy leap of logic. Well, it's my novelist credo and I believe it. I believe that flexibility of voice leads to a flexibility in all things. My audacious hope in Obama is based, I'm afraid, on precisely such flimsy premises.

It's my audacious hope that a man born and raised between opposing dogmas, between cultures, between voices, could not help but be aware of the extreme contingency of culture. I further audaciously hope that such a man will not mistake the happy accident of his own cultural sensibilities for a set of natural laws, suitable for general application. I even hope that he will find himself in agreement with George Bernard Shaw when he declared, "Patriotism is, fundamentally, a conviction that a particular country is the best in the world because you were born in it." But that may be an audacious hope too far. We'll see if Obama's lifelong vocal flexibility will enable him to say proudly with one voice, "I love my country," while saying with another voice, "It is a country, like other countries." I hope so. He seems just the man to demonstrate that between those two voices there exists no contradiction and no equivocation, but rather a proper and decent human harmony.

SEEING

·

Ten

HEPBURN AND GARBO

1. THE NATURAL

Katharine Hepburn was the star of my favorite film, *The Philadelphia Story*. And she appeared in a large proportion of the other movies I can stand to watch without throwing something at the screen or falling asleep. The sheer scarcity, in cinema, of women who in any way resemble those unusual creatures we meet every day (our mothers, sisters, wives, lovers, daughters) has only intensified in the twenty years since Katharine Hepburn ceased making movies, and this has served to make her legacy more precious as time has passed.

From the earliest age I was devoted to her. My teenage bedroom, a shrine to the Golden Age of Hollywood, reserved a whole half wall for her alone. Amid the pictures of Cary Grant, Jimmy Stewart, Donald O'Connor, Ava Gardner and the rest, Ms. Hepburn—imperious, regal and redheaded (although this last was often disguised in the publicity shots)—sat high up by the cornice of the ceiling, like a Madonna looking over the lesser saints. I spent too much time worrying over her health and wanting assurance from my father (also a fan and only eighteen years her junior) that she would outlive us all. When she sailed through her late eighties without incident, I became partially convinced of her immortality. Possibly because she got to me so young, her effect is out of proportion with what any movie star should mean to anyone, but I am grateful for it. The kind of woman she played, the kind of woman she was, is still the kind of woman I should like to be, and an incidental line of hers, from the aforementioned *The Philadelphia Story*, remains my lodestar every time I pick up a pen to write anything all: "The time to make your mind up about people is never!"

In that film the question is class; Hepburn's Tracy Lord is trying to convince a class-conscious Jimmy Stewart that virtue is not restricted to the workingmen of the world, any more than honor rests solely with the rich. Similarly, it was Hepburn's unique real-life position in Hollywood to chip away at some of America's more banal and oppressive received ideas. Whenever Hollywood thought it knew what a woman was, or what a black man was, or what an intellectual might be, or what "sexiness" amounted to, Hepburn made a movie to turn the common thinking on its head, offering always something irreducibly singular. Sometimes they liked it, but more often than not—especially in the early days—they didn't. It was another trait of Hepburn's never to give an inch. When David O. Selznick told her she couldn't have the role of Scarlett O'Hara because he "couldn't see Rhett Butler chasing you for ten years," she told him snootily that "some people's idea of sex appeal is different from yours" and stormed out of his office. It was never a question of Hepburn changing to suit Hollywood; Hollywood had to change to suit Hepburn.

Her bullheadedness can be traced to her East Coast upbringing: Protestant, hardworking, sporty, intellectual, liberal, but severe. Cold showers were a staple of her childhood. Hepburn said that her family "gave [her] the impression that the bitterer the medicine, the better it was for you," and this strikes us as absolutely commensurate with her image on the big screen; never indulgent, always somehow utilitarian; only doing and using what was necessary. Ava Gardner you see in a big tub of bubbles, Hepburn in the Connecticut cold, standing in a bucket of ice water. Attributing to her childhood all her positive virtues, Hepburn always looked to her parents' lives and relationship as the model for her own. Her mother, Katharine Martha Houghton, known as Kit, was a committed feminist and an early graduate of Bryn Mawr College, one of the first institutions to offer women a PhD. She was good friends with Mrs. Pankhurst, became the president of the Connecticut Women's Suffrage Association and, in later years, was a vocal supporter of Planned Parenthood, despite giving birth to three boys and three girls. Her husband, Dr. Thomas Norval Hepburn, could trace his ancestry back to James Hepburn, Earl of Bothwell and third husband of Mary, Queen of Scots (whom Hepburn played in 1936, rather lumpenly. Later she recognized that fiery Elizabeth would have been more her bag). From him, Hepburn got her hair and her family nickname, Redtop, a great enthusiasm for all things physical and absolutely no understanding of feminine restriction. Dr. Hepburn made few distinctions between his sons and daughters. All of them played touch football, learned to wrestle, swim and sail and were encouraged in the idea that intellect and action are two sides of the same coin, for either sex. Her father was the kind of man Hepburn most admired: "There are men of action and men of thought, and if you ever get a combination of the two, well, that's the top— you've got someone like Dad." Born in 1907, two years after her parents' first child, Tom, Hepburn grew up as a very jolly, tree-climbing, trouser-wearing, straight-talking tomboy, devoted to her older brother and awkward with people outside her family circle. When she was twelve a tragedy occured, one that changed her life and seems to have gone some way to forming the actress she became. During a trip to New York, Katharine and Tom went to see the play *A Connecticut Yankee in King Arthur's Court*, in which there is a scene of a hanging. The next morning, when Katharine went into her brother's room to wake him, she found him hanging from the rafters by a bedsheet, already dead five hours. He was fifteen. There was a history of suicide on both sides of the family, but her father always believed it a stunt gone wrong. Either way, Hepburn was deeply affected by it. She began to attempt to take on many of her brother's traits, and in some way to replace him; she spoke of taking up medical studies at Yale, as he had intended to, and became involved in the sports he liked—golf and tennis and diving. Having no real academic ability, she never took that Yale place, but scraped through her exams sufficiently to follow her mother to Bryn Mawr. This college, often ridiculed for its supposed snobbery and bluestocking atmosphere, was where Hepburn began to act, and also—or so her later critics complained—where she picked up that unbelievable accent, that "Bryn Mawr twang," with its Anglified vowels that combine oddly with the sense that one is being spoken to from a pinnacle of high-Yankee condescension. Her class and ambivalent femininity were to become central to Hepburn's screen persona and were also the qualities that made her "box office poison" for the best part of a decade. Selznick's reluctance to let her play Scarlett referred pretty obviously to her body, and we should begin with that. Her great love, Spencer Tracy, put it this way: "There ain't much meat on her, but what there is, is choice." And so it was. Slender without being remotely skinny, Hepburn was pretty much one long muscle, devoid of bust, but surprisingly shapely if seen from the back. She could work a dress like any Hollywood starlet, but your heart stopped to see her in a pair of wide slacks and crisp, white shirt. Her face was feline without being flirty, her cheekbones sepulchral but her lips full and generous. Her eyes—and there isn't a movie star who doesn't come down to the eyes in the end—had that knack of looking intelligently and passionately into the middle distance, a gaze that presidents strive for and occasionally attain. Her nose was more problematic. It struck some people as noble and full of sprightly character, but for a great deal of others it was too refined, hoydenish and superior. There are certain of her early films where a good 70 percent of the acting is coming from the nose down, and the average 1930s Depression-era moviegoer was not in the mood to be looked down upon through quite so straight and severe an instrument. They didn't like her much as an aristocratic aviatrix in *Christopher Strong* (1933), and they liked her even less as an illiterate mountain girl in *Spitfire* (1934). But to really make them hate you, you might try spending an entire movie dressed as a boy and making Brian Aherne fall in love with you—*while you are still dressed as a boy*—and then have him say things like, "I don't know what it is that gives me a queer feeling when I look at you," as Hepburn did in the transvestite comedy flop *Sylvia Scarlett* (1935). The

Shakespearean references were pretty much lost on her Depression-era American audience, who had other worries and were unwilling to allow much brain space to the homoerotic possibilities of Katharine Hepburn dressed in green suede. *Time* magazine took the opportunity to point out, "Sylvia Scarlett reveals the interesting fact that Katharine Hepburn is better looking as a boy than a woman." There were hits during the 1930s, most notably *Little Women*, in which Hepburn played the greatest, most empathic and beautiful Jo March there ever has been or ever will be. But she was only playing good roles in hit movies—she could not yet carry a movie alone. Hepburn didn't help herself, either, with her on-set behavior, which was noted and commented upon by the usual L.A. gossip columnists sent by the magazines to investigate the potential starlet. They had been spun a red-haired, East Coast, high-society goddess by the studios and so were somewhat surprised to find a makeup-free woman striding around between takes in a pair of dungarees. The RKO publicity department asked her to stop wearing them. She refused. The next day, when she found them vanished from her dressing room, she walked around set in her knickers until they were returned to her. On another occasion, when denying to reporters that she was married (she was, but very briefly, to Ludlow Ogden Smith, a man she met at a college dance) and asked whether she had children, she replied: "Yes, two white and three colored."

It was around this time that Hepburn decided to return to the stage in a play called *The Lakes* and found herself on the receiving end of Dorothy Parker's poisonous little put-down: "Katharine Hepburn ran the gamut of emotion from A to B." In its way, this comment is true—Hepburn could not be stretched far beyond herself. But her triumph, like all the Golden Age actors, was to figure out that screen acting, in opposition to stage acting, has got nothing to do with range. The present-day enthusiasm for actors who can play anything from the severely disabled to the heroic to the romantic and so on, with their multiple accents and tedious gurning—this all meant nothing to Bogart or Grant or Stewart or, in the end, to Hepburn. It was by learning to play herself, and by continuing to do so, more or less, for the rest of her career, that Hepburn became a screen icon and a goddess.

Of *The Philadelphia Story*, *Life* magazine wrote, "When Katharine Hepburn sets out to play Katharine Hepburn, she is a sight to behold. Nobody is her equal," and I write now that if there is a greater pleasure in this world than watching her play drunk, while wearing a dressing gown, being carried by Jimmy Stewart and enjoying his loopy rendition of "Somewhere over the Rainbow," well, I don't know it. There is another line in that movie that seems key to Hepburn. George Kittredge (John Howard), her soon-to-be-jilted fiancé, complains that "a husband expects his wife to behave herself, naturally." To which C. K. Dexter Haven (Cary Grant), the ex-husband, offers a pointed correction: "To behave herself naturally." In this vanished comma and subsequent shift of emphasis, we find the womanly wonder of Hepburn's 1940s comedies.

She was thirty-six when she made her first comedy with Spencer Tracy, and to see her in *Woman of the Year* (1942) is to put a tongue to that great lie of our contemporary culture, that women are at their most beautiful between the ages of sixteen and twenty-five. To say she is in her prime doesn't begin to cover it. She is a woman behaving herself naturally, without fear, without shame and with the full confidence of her abilities. The battle and paradox of those Tracy/Hepburn vehicles is the same one they had to deal with in life: how to tame a great passion without either party submitting entirely to the other. This makes *Woman of the Year*, *Adam's Rib* (1949) and *Pat and Mike* (1952) sound like dry stuff—nothing could be less true. *Adam's Rib* is simultaneously so funny and so sharp—and I mean, to the bone—on the subject of the gender war that I have watched it with two different lovers and ended the night, on both occasions, in separate bedrooms. The question of competition in a marriage of equals is so accurately skewered you feel yourself writhing on the pin. You will recall that Hepburn and Tracy play two lawyers, who find themselves defending and prosecuting against each other on the same case. One evening, after a long day in court, a supposedly friendly smack on Hepburn's backside from Tracy (he is giving her a massage) results in this unbeatable snatch of dialogue:

Tracy: What, d'you don't want your rub now? What are you—sore about a little slap?

Hepburn: You meant that, didn't you?

Tracy: Why, no . . .

Hepburn: Yes you did, yes, I can tell a . . . a slap from a slug!

Tracy: Well, OK . . . OK . . .

Hepburn: No, I'm not so sure it is, I'm not so sure I care to . . . expose myself to typical, instinctive, masculine aggression!

Tracy: Oh, calm down . . .

Hepburn: And it felt not only as if you meant it but as if you felt you had a right to! I can tell!

Tracy: What've you got back there? Radar equipment?

Oh, just go out and rent it.

Although I am particularly susceptible to Kate in the 1940s, every decade of her career throws up humbling performances. She held the record for Oscar nominations until Meryl beat her, and any Hepburn devotee finds a place in his or her heart for the grand guignol of *Suddenly, Last Summer* (1959), despite the fact that she despised both the film and her treatment on the set—she spat in the director's face on the last day of filming. Also, the dynamite partnership with Humphrey Bogart in *The African Queen* (1951) is the equal of anything she did with Tracy. In Bogart, she found the action-man dimension of her father that she loved, and he found a woman with similar chutzpah to his own wife, Bacall, who followed them to the difficult, insect-ridden location, reportedly a little nervous of how good a match her husband and his costar looked on paper. She needn't have worried: Hepburn's romantic dedication to Tracy is now legendary, and I remember, again, as a child, hoping for the sort of relationship that seemed symbolized in the fact that even as he lay dying, Hepburn spent every day with him, lying on the floor beside his bed. They never married because he was already married, and as a Catholic and family man, he never divorced. One can only feel horror and pity for the kind of wife forced before the whole world to recognize the shimmering immortality of that adulterous relationship. Tracy claimed, "My wife and Kate like things just the way they are," and the truth or otherwise of this remained between the three of them, never publicly discussed. Tracy and Hepburn's last film together, *Guess Who's Coming to Dinner* (1967), was the first Hepburn movie I ever saw, aged about five, with a running commentary from my mother on the physical perfection of Sidney Poitier. The movie is sentimental, but the sentiment, both political and personal, is at least genuine; I struggle to think of another film of which this is so true. Tracy, a long-term alcoholic, was basically dying during filming, and when he delivers the last line, "If what they feel for each other is even half what we felt, then that is everything," Hepburn cries real tears. Six months later he was dead. They were both nominated for Oscars, and when she heard she had won again (Hepburn was not at the ceremony; she never picked up any of her four Oscars), her first and only question was "Did Spence get one too?" He did not, but she considered it a shared award.

So physical in her youth, always determined to perform her own stunts, old age struck Hepburn as one hell of a bore. She never hid like a starlet or felt destroyed by lost looks (she never really lost her looks), but she was frequently frustrated by not being able to do what had once come so easily. She once cried with frustration at having to employ a twenty-four-year-old stunt double to ride a bike for her in a film. At the time, Hepburn herself was seventy-two. Two days ago she died, aged ninety-six. I don't know why I should be surprised, but I was, and when I found out, I wept, and felt ridiculous for weeping. How can someone you have never met make you cry? Two years ago I went to see *The Philadelphia Story* play on a big screen in Bryant Park. It was July and so hot my brother and I had been spending the day in the penguin exhibit at the zoo (we had no air-conditioning), but then we heard about the film—my favorite film—playing outdoors and rushed downtown.

We were too late to get a seat. It was packed like I have never seen any New York open space since the Dalai Lama came to Central Park. We were disconsolately looking for a wall to sit on, when suddenly two unholy fools, two morons, changed their minds and gave up their second-row seats. Hard to describe how happy we were. And then over the loudspeakers came some news: Hepburn had been taken ill in the night—gasps, I mean, real gasps— but it was okay—happy sighs—she was back from the hospital and wished us all well. We roared! And then the film started, and I said all the lines before they came, and my brother asked me to shut up. But I wasn't the only one at it. When Katharine whispered to Jimmy Stewart, "Put me in your pocket, Mike!" a thousand people whispered with her. That was the best night at the movies I've ever had.

My teenage life was periodically dotted by melancholy little funerals, attended by me alone. I held one for Fred Astaire and one for Bette Davis and Cary Grant. On these occasions I would light candles in my room, cry a bit and mark the photo on the wall with a little cross in the right-hand corner. This time, less psychotically, I plan to spend the next few weeks watching every Hepburn movie and documentary that graces the television screen. I strongly recommend you watch as many as you can manage. She is the last of the great stars, the very last, and my God, I will miss the thrilling feeling of rewatching *Adam's Rib* and knowing her to be still on the planet, still in that East Forty-ninth Street brownstone, still fabulous. When people truly feel for a popular artist—when they follow in their thousands behind Dickens's coffin or Valentino's—it is only the dues returned for pleasure given, and it never feels like enough. Few artists in any medium have given me as much pleasure as Hepburn. In fact, the marvelous weight of the pleasure ennobles all clichés, and I hope to see the obituaries full of "the last of her kind," "the greatest star in the firmament" and the rest of that sort of guff because, for once, it is all true.

2. NATURE'S WORK OF ART

September 18, 2005, marks the centenary of the birth of Greta Garbo, an icon both resonant and remote to us. It feels a perilous centenary. In twenty years' time, no one will need to make an argument for the centenary of Marilyn Monroe, with her hourglass silhouette, her voluptuous blondness. It is different with Garbo: you have to make a case for Garbo. She resonates because hers was ultimately a career of photographs, and this we recognize. She is remote because the great photographs of Garbo are abstractions; they are not of a woman, they are of a face. Garbo's body was an irrelevance. From our twenty-first-century icons we demand bodies: bodies are to be admired, coveted and—if one works hard enough—gained. You can have something resembling Madonna's body, if you try. But you cannot have Garbo's face. It was hers alone, a gift she used for as long as she could make it signify and then, aged only thirty-six, withdrew from public view, keeping it hidden until she died.

This face was memorably described by the philosopher Roland Barthes, who identified it as a transition between two semiological epochs, two ways of seeing women. Garbo marked the passage from awe to charm, from concept to substance: "The face of Garbo is an idea, that of [Audrey] Hepburn an event." There was something essential, Platonic and unindividuated in Greta's face. She was Woman, as opposed to Audrey, who was *a* woman, whom we loved precisely because her beauty was so quirky, so particular. Garbo has no quirks at all. A close-up of her face appears to reveal fewer features than the rest of us have—such an expanse of white—punctuated by the minimum of detail, just enough to let you know that this is flesh, not spirit. Her vulnerable, change-able face is what comes prior to the emphatic mask of a beautiful woman—she is the ideal of beauty that those masks attempt to capture. Post-Garbo, we have taken what resonated in Garbo's fluid sexuality and mystery and hard-ened it, made it a commodity. Take Garbo's heavy, deep-set eyelids: these have become the mark of the diva, passing down through Marlene, to Marilyn and, more recently, to Madonna, in whom they have become ironic. Hers is the ultimate modern Garbo face, attached to a worked-out body, and also to the idea of female ambition, will and talent. The idea of Garbo is somehow more elevated than that—it doesn't even condescend itself to the pursuit and fulfillment of talent. It merely *is*. Garbo was not an actress in the way Bette Davis was an actress. Garbo was a presence. In fact, is it okay to say, a hundred years on, that Garbo was not a very good actress? That some of her best work was still and silent? It could be said that her best director was, in fact, a still photographer, MGM's famous Clarence Bull. He did not try to know her or "uncover" her, as her movie directors sometimes did, giving her those awk-ward, wordy speeches that revealed less than one raised eyebrow could man-age. Bull understood the attraction of her self-containment. Years later he recalled that where other photographers had tried to penetrate the mystery,

"I accepted it for what it was—nature's work of art. . . . She was the face and I was the camera. We each tried to get the best out of our equipment."

Garbo's equipment was not always so sublime. She grew up Greta Gustafsson, a lanky, overweight, big-footed girl from Sweden. Despite Hollywood's later intimations of an aristocratic lineage, she was poor, sharing a four-room, cold-water flat with her family in a Stockholm tenement. When her gardener father died of kidney failure, fourteen-year-old Greta dropped out of school and began work in the millinery department at the Paul Bergstrom department store. She wanted to be an actress, always. Discovered by her manager modeling hats in the mirror, she was asked to appear in a commercial film to promote millinery, *How Not to Dress*. This led to other commercial shorts. In her capacity as shopgirl, she would look out for famous Swedish actresses in the store and make sure she waited on them.

It was through a connection she made here that she secured an audition for the state-sponsored Dramatic Theatre Academy, where she was accepted at age seventeen. There she met director Mauritz Stiller, the first of many Garbo mentors. He changed her name and told her to lose twenty pounds. He cast her in *The Saga of Gosta Berling* (1924), which was a success in Sweden and Germany and brought Stiller to the attention of Louis B. Mayer at MGM. They met in Germany. Mayer's original interest was Stiller, who had directed more than forty-five films, but he saw something in Garbo. He invited them both to America, although not before a word in Stiller's ear: "In America, we don't like fat women." Garbo went on a diet of spinach for three weeks, was terribly sick, lost the weight and replaced it with no muscle. She stayed that way—slender, shapeless, suggestive of a dangerous lack of physical vitality— throughout her movie career. With her newly revealed cheekbones and wispy frame, she embarked upon her first photo shoots in New York. Any other hopeful starlet would have posed for cheesecake shots, swimsuits, "come hither" glances—the whole Hollywood routine. Garbo's shots, lit with the "Rembrandt lighting" that would make her famous, are sculptural portraits, more Rodin than raunch. The Garbo image is yet unformed, but the beginnings of an iconic persona are here. She had a relationship with light like no other actress; wherever you directed it on her face, it created luminosity. She needed no soft or diffuse lighting to disguise defects. There were no defects. And then there is that sense of European ennui, of weltschmerz, that no MGM player had projected before. They had vamps, they had sex bombs, but they'd never had existential depression. "In America you are all so happy," she told a reporter. "Why are you all so happy all the time? I am not always happy. Sometimes yes, sometimes no. When I am angry, I am very bad. I shut my door and do not speak."

Once she reached Hollywood, the fan magazines responded enthusiastically, not as much to the fiery sexuality she was asked to play in those early silents, but to the sadness that seemed to lie behind it. A typical headline: "What is wrong with Greta Garbo?" Whatever it was, she was unable to articulate it. She refused all interviews, and her few private letters are banal—she often complained about the vulgarity of American film but had few ideas of her own to bring to the table. To the director of *Queen Christina* (the story of the abdication of the Swedish queen, a pet project that Garbo was very anxious about), she could only offer the suggestion that there should be a scene with trousers. She put herself in others' hands. First Stiller, then the actor John Gilbert, the lesbian clique of Mercedes de Acosta, and the producer Irving Thalberg. Louis B. Mayer was driven mad by all these advisers and intercessors; he thought she was too easily influenced. And yet what comes across on film is a resolute, inviolable selfhood, ultimately impenetrable by other people. The public felt it, and expressed it in their popular nicknames: "The Swedish Sphinx" and "The Divine."

Flesh and the Devil (1926) was her smash hit, creating a Garbo model that the studio exploited for the next fifteen years. It is silent and possibly her best film. She was only twenty-one, but her world-weariness on-screen suggests an older woman, longed for and chased after by the puppyish John Gilbert, who was to become her real-life lover. This romance, as it was rendered on-screen, scandalized America: a young man lying underneath a more experienced woman who seemed to literally feed from his mouth as she kissed him. It was a ravishment—female moviegoers loved it. This was a new kind of woman. For this reason she was punished in the movies (in *Flesh and the Devil* she drowns in ice water; in *Camille* it's tuberculosis; in *Anna Karenina* it's that pesky train), but she was free in life. It was Gilbert who suffered when she refused to marry him; it was Mayer who went crazy when she went on strike rather than make a corny movie (*Women Love Diamonds*) that she didn't like the look of.

What was the matter with Garbo? Mayer couldn't understand it. Why wasn't she thankful? But after *Flesh and the Devil*, the power had changed hands: Garbo was an MGM gold mine. Garbo's imperial aloofness appealed to Depression-era women on a scale that even Mayer could not have predicted. They were dependent; she was beyond dependence. Whatever made her happy or sad, it came from within. Film critics often mention her unusual responses: where another actress would laugh, she cries, when they would be serious, she plays it light. She seems to respond to something deep inside herself, not to the actor she plays opposite. It was a world of her own she was in, and it was wonderful to watch.

There are two halves of Garbo's career: before and after sound. She made the transition as late as she possibly could, in 1930. "GARBO TALKS!" announced the publicity, and luckily for MGM, the voice matched the face. Her first line ("Gimme me a visky, ginger ale on the side—and don't be stingy, baby!") was delivered in that deep, miserable, sexy baritone that delighted her fans because they had, subconsciously, expected it. But a talking Garbo also revealed less fortunate traits. Her line readings are offbeat, bizarre; she had an unsteady grasp of the English language. She is a terrible reactor to spoken dialogue. If someone else is speaking, she simply looks bored. For the next ten years, her success in talkies depended on how much she was allowed to use her real strengths: her face, her eyes. This is why the silent final scene of *Queen Christina* (1933) is justly famous. Her lover, for whom she has renounced the throne, has just been killed by a jealous rival; she walks to the prow of the ship she is on and becomes a part of its helm—you may remember the image from *Titanic*. Where DiCaprio announces himself to the world, Garbo does nothing. Says nothing. Moves nothing on her face. It is a Swedish mix of cold water and private thoughts. The camera gets closer and closer. What you see there is humanized stoicism; she is going through what she is going through, deeply, personally and without public expression. She is resolutely herself.

This kind of interiority was soon to be under threat from a new breed of actress, women such as Joan Crawford, who projected everything they had outward to the public, leaving nothing in reserve. Crawford admired Garbo greatly but was already preparing to supplant her as the queen of MGM. She described an encounter on a staircase during the filming of *Grand Hotel* (1932): "She stopped and cupped my face in her hands and said, 'What a pity. Our first picture together, and we won't work with each other. I am so sorry. You have a marvelous face.' If there was ever a time in my life I might have become a lesbian that was it."

Crawford did not succumb, but many others did, including Marlene Dietrich, the playwright Mercedes de Acosta and Louise Brooks, who described Garbo as a "completely masculine dyke." Closer friends thought of her androgyny as more complicated, nearer to the character of Queen Christina, who, disguised as a man, shares a bed with John Gilbert. Gore Vidal, an acquaintance from the last twenty years of her life, claims: "She thought of herself as a boy with another boy, that was her sexual fantasy." She habitually referred to herself in the masculine, as a "bachelor"; at parties she would ask: "Where's the little boy's room?"

In the movies they were still determined to make a lady of her. In *Ninotchka* (1939), playing a Soviet apparatchik, she goes from macho, humorless Russian to glamorous Parisian party girl. Famously, she laughs. She can't laugh. When she satirizes her own European dolor, she is hilarious. ("The show trials were a great success," she deadpans. "We are going to have fewer but better Russians.") But when she becomes gay and carefree, the movie dies. *Ninotchka* was a huge success (mostly thanks to an ingenious marketing campaign), but the studio picked up on the wrong trait, the newfound gaiety. *Two-Faced Woman* (1941), in which a newly happy Garbo does the rumba and goes swimming, was a disaster. You don't put the sphinx in a swimsuit.

It was to be her last movie. The uniformly bad reviews for *Two-Faced Woman* were terribly wounding to her, but more than this, she had spotted something in the mirror. Two faint lines on either side of her mouth, connecting her nose to her chin. The face was no longer eternal, ethereal. It was over. Garbo after 1941 is simply a tale of withdrawal. She stands high in the roll call of twentieth-century recluses. But it would be more accurate, her biographer Barry Paris suggests, to call her a "hermit-about-town." She walked for miles through New York every day, window-shopping. In the 1960s, almost every Manhattanite had a Garbo-spotting story to tell. She described herself at this time as "a mollusc. I don't move, I don't do anything. I just am." This is not quite true: she had friends, walking partners. She went to auctions and bought paintings and antiques for her lavish apartment (when she died she left a $32 million estate, which included two Renoirs). It is no story of tragedy. She wished to live, only not publicly. She dressed as she liked, did as she liked. In her own later years, Crawford told a journalist: "I never go out unless I look like Joan Crawford the movie star. If you want to see the girl next door, go next door." Garbo didn't even look as good as the girl next door. Her face (though she refused to believe it) was still beautiful, her wardrobe less so: sweaters, hats, scarves, slacks, raincoats. She kept a screwed-up piece of Kleenex in her left hand to cover her face should anyone try to photograph her. If she saw a fan approaching, she would say to her walking companion, "We've got a customer," and change direction. She wanted to be alone. Garbo, the icon, was over. Age made of Greta a person, and the personhood of Garbo was never for sale. She would be myth or nothing at all.

Eleven

NOTES ON VISCONTI'S *BELLISSIMA*

"Please don't retouch my wrinkles. It took me so long to earn them."

—Anna Magnani

PREFACE

In the Piazza della Madonna dei Monti, in the *ombra di colosseo*, expats gather to complain. Not about the piazza itself, generally agreed to be among the prettiest in Rome. The central café, shrouded in pink bougainvillea, looks out upon a two-tiered fountain, mercifully cherub free. The thin white column of a Ukrainian orthodox church is discreet, unexpected. Depending on the hour, we watch mighty-calved American kids drink cheap hock straight from the bottle; tanned Roman girls, chain-smoking, dressed in the sunset silks they bought in Mumbai; hipster gays en route to Testaccio; three boxer dogs; delighted German tourists who think themselves the first to discover the place; very old Italians of suspicious vitality; two boys who use the church door as a goal mouth; and a beautiful young man who has been sleeping rough here for six months after a disagreement with his girlfriend. The young man is much appreciated—he is the sort of local color for which we came to Rome in the first place. His stench is monitored: sweet in the first month, eye watering in the fourth, café clearing in the sixth. And we enjoy Sundays, when the Ukrainian church congregation spills outside, bringing with it a close-harmony praise song. Everything else is complaint. Italian bureaucracy is impossible, the TV unwatchable, the government unbelievable, and the newspapers impenetrable. Expats in Rome are somehow able to consistently maintain their sense of outraged wonder, despite all reading *The Dark Heart of Italy* two years earlier on the plane over. Italian Women is a subject to stretch from morning coffee to midday ravioli. "The land that feminism forgot!" And on cue it all rolls out like an index: the degrading sexualization of, the nightly televisual humiliation of, Berlusconi's condescending opinion of, perilous abortion rights of, low wages of, minimal parliamentary presence of, invisibility within the church of, et cetera. Yet there exist confusing countersigns. The new mothers with tiny babes-in-arm, welcome at any gathering. The four women chatting at the next table, a frank, practical conversation about sexual pleasure. The handsome lady grocer with her giant biceps and third-trimester belly, unpacking boxes of beer from the delivery truck, separating street fights, bullying her menfolk, lecturing the local drunks, overcharging the tourists, strategizing with the priests, running this piazza and everyone in it. Respected, desired, feared.

Such countersigns are not unified: they do not all point in one direction, and so as expats we find it difficult to process them—which may be the difference between a Catholic and a Protestant sensibility. The strongest countersign of all is Anna's face. It follows you everywhere, staring out from restaurants, pub bathrooms, private houses, lined up on the display table of the *edicolas*, and writ large on the walls of the city itself, for this summer marks her centenary. *Nannarella*. Mamma Roma. La Magnani. Anna is a confusing countersign, in the land that feminism forgot.

1

A chorus of women sing in a radio studio. Plain women, not actresses, of early middle age, and dressed in black, with simple strands of pearls around their necks. The credits identify them as the RAI choir.[1] The lead soprano has a light but discernible mustache. The song is "Saria possibile?" (Could it be possible?) from Donizetti's *L'elisir d'amore*, a silly opera about a peasant who, in his desperation to woo a beautiful, unattainable woman, buys a love potion from a mountebank. (The potion turns out to be red wine.) Visconti pans through this choir dispassionately, even a little cruelly, as it responds with minute precision to the baton of a dashing male conductor. A chorus of Italian women, eager to please. The song ends; we move to a smaller studio. A young man at a desk speaks into the microphone, to announce the premise of the film:

We are looking for a girl between six and eight years. A pretty Italian girl. Take your girls to Stella Films in Cinecittà, Via Tuscolana, km 9. It could be your and her lucky day!

The next shot is unexpected. A great waste ground: what would seem to be the ruins of a city, with the blown-out frames of buildings and a mass of women and girl children, their best clothes on their backs (being transported? fleeing some disaster?). Another beat reveals its true, benign aspect: the outskirts of a movie studio. The frames are for set facades, as yet unfinished. The women are here to audition their girl children. But still men yell at them through megaphones. ("Keep quiet and stay calm!") The camera stays very high. This is a pared-down, unfamiliar Visconti, a decade before the opulence of *Il gattopardo*. The borrowed severity of *neorealismo* is not quite natural to him. His instinctive tendency toward the fantastic has only been transferred from style to content, to the hopes of this great female chorus, who now push as one toward a narrow doorway.

A woman. A woman both like and not like the rest, in a black skirt suit, nipped waspishly at the waist, spilling out at both extremes, with black shoes and wild black hair and black pouches under her eyes, wailing like a heroine of the Greeks. She has lost her child! But the camera remains aloof, a gesture we might mistake for Visconti's familiar misogyny, if it were not for what Magnani makes of the angle. Think of it as a gift from director to actress. We are so far from Magnani she is practically inaudible, yet this is no obstacle

---

1. RAI is the Italian state broadcasting corporation.

to comprehending her. We see her anger, panic, and desperation—and even that these emotions are both sincere and a little overdone, *un po' esagerato*, in a calculated manner, in case the sympathy thus roused might help her case later. All this is put across with her hands (the natural advantage of Italian actors) but also in the stamp of her little foot, the way her hair flies from its bun, the way her hips bend forward and back in pantomime outrage. What a silent star Magnani would have been! Now she leaves the chorus and runs alone, across this desolate city, as she did in *Roma, città aperta*. The chorus passes through opportunity's door without her.

•

Bellissima as a series of formal, ancient gestures, in which an all-female chorus threatens to swallow a single female actor, and from which that actor determinedly separates herself first, and then—by force of will—also a second actor, her child. A cinematic rerun of Aeschylus's revolutionary innovation.

•

The chorus pushes forward toward a makeshift stage. The name of the fictional film is on the wall behind them—*Oggi domani mai*—but so is the name of the real film: *Bellissima*. The character of Director is also both fictional and real, Alessandro Blasetti.[2] He walks through the crowd (taking great care over his acting, wanting to get the playing of himself right) to the tune of Donizetti's "Charlatan's Theme," although he did not know this at the time. (Visconti: "One day somebody told him about it. He wrote me an indignant letter: "Really, I'd never have believed you capable of such a thing," and so on: and I replied: "Why? We're all charlatans, us directors. It is we who put illusions into the heads of mothers and little girls. . . . We're selling a love potion which isn't really a magic elixir: it's simply a glass of Bordeaux.") The director, the assistants, the producers, the hangers-on—powerful men with their powerful boredom—climb the elevated stage and prepare to judge, positioning

2. Alessandro Blasetti (July 3, 1900–February 1, 1987) was the director of more than twenty films including *Quattro passi fra le nuvole* (1942) and *La fortuna di essere donna* (1956).

themselves in attitudes of jolly contempt. In Italy, a woman is always the looked-at-thing, always appraised by that measure. Today, tomorrow—this beauty contest is as old as the judgment of Paris. The descendants of these men still audition *veline*[3] each Roman summer. As any expat will tell you, the queues run for miles. Now, here, in postwar Italy, the first little girl lifts her skirts, gyrates, pouts and rolls her eyes, doing "an impression of Betty Grable." The men smile. "You're starting early!" cries Blasetti.

2

Bellissima, in its initial conception (a story by Cesare Zavattini), was intended as a riff on the hypocrisy of cinema. Maddalena Cecconi (Magnani), a working-class woman from Rome's urban suburbs, wants her daughter, Maria (Tina Apicella), to be a star. She will use whatever she has—her savings, her own sympathetic sex appeal—in the attempt to secure for her daughter what Italians call a *raccomandazione di ferro*.[4] In the end, she gets what she wants but, in the same moment, turns from it: too much of the empty, cruel, and capitalistic world of Cinecittà has been revealed to her. But though the cruelty of Cinecittà was Zavattini's neorealistic focus, it did not prove to be Visconti's. "The story really was a pretext," he admitted later. "The whole subject was Magnani: I wanted to create a portrait of a woman out of her, a contemporary woman, a mother, and I think we pretty well succeeded because Magnani lent me her enormous talent, her personality." This is the same as saying Magnani's personality overwhelmed Zavattini's concept. To allow Zavattini's moral tale to function, one would have to feel Magnani's soul was *actually in the hazard*. Which is not possible. Magnani as a personality being too self-reliant, too confident, with too constant an access to joy. Even when she is being blackmailed, she laughs. Her character—played by anyone else—is a tragic woman pursuing the dreams of her youth through her child. But no hint of the female zombie, no trace of Norma Desmond, clings to Magnani. Everything she wants—

---

3. The bikini-clad showgirls on Italian television.
4. Literally a recommendation of iron. A good word that will secure an applicant in a position.

certainly a little money, possibly a little reflected fame—she wants directly, in a straight and open manner, as men are said to want things. Her dream is strategic, not delusional. And in her mind, the child remains only a child, *come tutte*: "Well, at that age they're *all* pretty." This is her sensible reply to a calculated compliment from the slick young stranger, Annovazzi (Walter Chiari), a production assistant low down in the Cinecittà food chain who is willing to do certain favors in exchange for certain favors—the oldest of Italian stories. "Yes, that's true," he agrees. "But I prefer their mothers." Annovazzi is younger than Maddalena, skinnier, and in a bland cinematic sense, better looking. But she knows as we know: he is the shadow of her shadow. On the other hand, he has access to the director, Blasetti. All this passes through Magnani's face in a mannerist instant: a sharp glance in which she responds at once to the cheek of the boy and the perfect civility and necessity of the compliment. (It would be rude of him not to notice that she is a goddess!) Few actresses are so directly appreciative of their own earthy, natural attractions. On-screen, Magnani is the opposite of neurotic.

3

The complicated cinematic partnership between straight women and gay men (Irving Rapper and Bette Davis, George Cukor and Joan Crawford) does not usually result in this easy, playful relation between woman and world. For Davis and Crawford the roles came laced with Grand Guignol, campy tragedy, the arch appreciation of female artifice. Both actresses traded what was transient and human in their work for the waxwork grandeur of eternal iconicity. *I made her what she is today* may be the ultimate Hollywood sentence. Laced always with a little bitterness, perhaps because the woman-muse of the gay Svengali is a double agent. Loving the same impossible men, living in the same impossible patriarchy, but always able to apply for the love and acceptance of the public. (She can become a national treasure.) Magnani—the sexy-maternal, working-class Roman—is Italy as it dreams of itself. Visconti represents a different Italy entirely: gay, aristocratic, Milanese. Inevitably the partnership had its poisonous side. Visconti on Magnani: "Left completely to her own devices, I have to say, she would never have achieved a happy result." Hard to believe—her own devices seem to be all she has. Hyperanimate, frankly scheming, playing the odds, rolling the eyes, huffing, puffing, bursting the binds of script and taking her costars with her. *Mi raccomando, eh?—uffa!—per carità!—abbia pazienza!—O dio mio!—come no?—meno male!* Italian is a language packed with verbal *fillers*. Magnani makes musical use of them. No gap between sentences survives without an exclamation of one sort or another. And witness her making her way back through that chorus, Maria in hand, convincing each pushy mother she pushes past that it really can be no other way; giving each woman just what they need—smile or insult—in order to let her pass. In front of Blasetti at last, Maddalena turns on the charm but with a blatant Roman cunning that no one could mistake for coquetry. Blasetti: "But I said the child has to be six or seven years old, not less . . . she looks a bit small." Maddalena: "Really? No, it must be the dress that makes her short." The legends of Davis and Crawford are built on a camp proposition, equal parts adoration and contempt. *All women are artificial. All women are, in the end, actresses. Womanhood itself is an act!* But Magnani turns the proposition on its head. She is the incarnation of that paradoxical imperative: *act natural.* She is always and everywhere apparently without artifice, spontaneous, just another Roman woman *come tutte.* Which leads to a strange conclusion: the actor isn't acting—the *character* is acting. For isn't it *Maddalena,* and not Magnani, who puts on a bit of an act now and then, when circumstances call for it?

One morning an eccentric acting teacher approaches the family. She wants to give little Maria lessons that Maddalena can't afford. Alone in her bedroom, Maddalena considers the offer, combing her unruly hair and addressing her own reflection in the mirror: "To act . . . after all, what is acting? If I imagined to be somebody else . . . if I pretended to be somebody else . . . I'd be acting. . . . But *you* can act. . . . You're my daughter and you can become an actress. You really can. I could have, too, if I had wanted to."

With Magnani, womanhood is utterly real—it simply does what it must to get by.

4

Much Italian cinema revolves around the classic Italian philosophical problem: blonde or brunette? For Fellini, the answer was, usually, both. Antonioni solved the dilemma on an abstract intellectual plane by discovering Monica Vitti, the blonde with the face of a brunette. In Visconti's *Bellissima* no counterweight is put up against black-haired Anna Magnani, for what counterweight could there possibly be? Her husband Spartaco (Gastone Renzelli) has the elemental, hulking beauty his name implies (a nonactor, he was picked out by the director's assistant, a young Zeffirelli, from a crowd of bone merchants in a Roman slaughterhouse). But in character, in *personality*, he is no match for her. He is left to plot weakly with his mother against her ("Mamma, I won't even bother with her. She always does what she likes anyway!"), though only for the length of a lunchtime, as he eats the meals his mother still cooks for him. He seeks no real alternative to Magnani.

Bellissima is that rare thing in Italian cinema: a film in which the woman is not a question posed to a man. Even more rare: she is not in question to herself. She finds herself perfectly satisfactory, or at least, her flaws cause her no more than the normal amount of discomfort. A less common trait in a female movie star can hardly be imagined.

In the *parrucchiere* where little Maria is taken for a haircut:

Hairdresser: (*to Maddalena*) I could give you a good style, too.
Maddalena: Don't even try, no one has managed that.
Hairdresser: I could manage.
Maddalena: (*laughing*) You'd waste your time!

Like Davis and Crawford, Magnani is an unconventional beauty. Unlike them, she is beautiful without any cosmetic effort whatsoever, and moreover, without any interest in the cosmetic. Cosmetic beauty is not the type that attracts her.

To wit: in the courtyard of her grim *casa popolare*,[5] projected on a giant makeshift screen, a Hollywood blockbuster plays. Maddalena watches, enraptured. Spartaco comes to retrieve her:

> **Spartaco:** Maddalena, leave the cinema alone.
> **Maddalena:** Oh, Spartaco, you don't understand me. Look at those beautiful things, look at where we live. When I see these things . . .
> **Spartaco:** Maddalena, it's a fantasy.
> **Maddalena:** It's not!

We might expect to see up there Rita Hayworth in *Gilda*, peeling off those silk elbow-length gloves. But it is Howard Hawks's *Red River*, a wild open plain, two cowboys on their horses. The object of Maddalena's desire, a herd of bulls crossing a creek.

5

The chorus of mothers gossip among themselves. The rumor is that so-and-so has a recommendation of iron ("He was saying how pretty the girl was . . . but he was looking at her mother!" "Ah, now I understand!" "That's how it is these days!"); the fix is in; the auditions are worthless—it has all already been decided. A typical Roman inside job. Something must be done: they'll unite to complain, it's a *vergogna*, they'll confront the producer! However, upon consideration, a more attractive, less violent, solution is found: each woman will look to her own recommendation. For one lady's husband knows the director of the phone company ("What does that matter?" asks Maddalena. The reply: "He's *important*"); someone else's husband has a friend on set; yet another has a Cinecittà waiter in her family.

And Maddalena knows Annovazzi. They meet in the Borghese gardens, dappled in leafy light, the scene of a Shakespearean comedy. "I never come

5. Urban Italian mass housing, the equivalent of England's housing estates and America's projects.

here!" she says, for there exists a Roman life that does not include and never comes near the expats of Monti, or the Forum, the Pantheon, or even the Colosseum. The pair walk to a tree and lean against it like lovers. Annovazzi plays the cynic: "We're so used to recommendations, both to making and receiving them. . . . In Italy we rely on recommendations: 'Please don't forget.' 'I assure you.' 'I promise you.' . . . But who are we supposed to remember and why?" The only safe thing, he concludes, is to "put the person who needs your help in a position to *ask* for that help."

He strokes her arm, offering her the possibility of the sexual favor instead of the financial. She removes his hand, laughing. "No, this way is much better." He takes her fifty thousand lire, supposedly to smooth the ground for Maria, in the form of small favors ("A bunch of flowers to the producer of the film, a bottle of perfume for the lover of the producer"). In the event he will spend it on a Lambretta for himself.

"How shrewd you are!"

"It's a practical way of getting through life."

Even as she hands over her pocketbook, she knows he can't be trusted. Later, when she discovers the deception, she only laughs her big laugh. It is a plot point hard to understand if you are not Italian. She pays him for a favor. He buys a bike. She finds out. But she is not angry, *because he will still remember her, especially.*

6

"The big mistake of *neorealismo*," claimed Visconti, "to my way of thinking, is its unrelenting and sometimes dour concentration on social reality. What *neorealismo* needs . . . 'dangerous' mixture of reality and romanticism."

He found the perfect objective correlative in the summer life of the Roman projects: reality on the inside, cinema in the outside (courtyard). Inside, Maddalena's reality is stark: she earns the little lire she has going door to door, giving injections to invalids and hypochondriac ladies, a business that survives more on Maddalena's charm than the efficacy of her "medicines." Otherwise, alliances with other women prove hard to forge. In Italy, your mother-in-law (*suocera*, a perfectly vile-sounding word) is your nemesis, the other mothers are your competitors and the gossiping neighbors in the stairwell, your daily tormentors. But there is also a practical, strategic sisterhood, which makes itself visible in times of crisis. When Spartaco physically attacks Maddalena (she has spent money they don't have on a dress for Maria's screen test), the women of the housing estate invade the Cecconi apartment, another chorus, heavyset and loud-mouthed, outnumbering Spartaco, who has Maria in his arms and is trying to take her away, as his paternal property. Maddalena is hysterical: she screams and weeps. It is, as far as an expat is concerned, a scene of horrific domestic terror. A raging Spartaco calls the women *balene*, whales (the English translation—one of many poor examples—renders it "cows"), and they sing a whale song of overlapping accusation. Visconti, an opera buff, choreographs the scene as an echo of the RAI choir.

"You only do it because I'm weaker!" cries Maddalena.

"Spartaco, today you really crossed the line!" cry the whales.

"I want my daughter to be somebody. . . . Am I entitled to feel this way or not? . . . She mustn't depend on anyone or get beaten like me!"

"Spartaco, she went all the way to Piazza Vittorio to a man with diabetes!"

"I'm full of bruises! I'm all swollen!"

"Spartaco, she's made so many sacrifices!"

"Maddalena, stop *acting*," yells Spartaco, to the outrage of the whales, as Maddalena collapses into a chair. Frightened he may have gone too far, he releases the child to the protection of one of them, and runs from the house.

"Women like me," said the actress Anna Magnani, "can only submit to men capable of dominating them, and I have never found anyone capable of dominating me." It is the sort of statement to make an expat sigh. What is this mysterious deflected Italian feminism that can only take power discreetly, without ever saying that this is what it is doing? And what is an expat to make of the sudden evaporation of Maddalena's tears (Spartaco was right!) as her face creases into a coy smile? The whales, nodding appreciatively at the art of the thing, pass the child, hand to hand, back to its mother. The crisis is averted.

Congratulations are due. Italy is truly the land of the sign and countersign, incomprehensible to outsiders. Maddalena begins to laugh.

"We've won, darling. If we didn't do that, we wouldn't get an audition. My
dear, do you think I'm working for nothing?"

●

The director Vittorio De Sica called Magnani's laugh "loud, overwhelming and tragic." Tragic is a word men will reach for if called upon to describe
women outside of their relation to men. In American cinema, a woman's
laugh is almost always flirtatious, a response to a male call. The unexpected
thing about Magnani is that she makes herself laugh.

7

In Italy, the right recommendation will get you through the door, to the
top of the class, and behind the scenes. Maddalena's has got her this far, into
the editing room ("Mr. Annovazzi told me to come and see you"), where a
beautiful young girl lines up the screen tests, ready to take downstairs to Blasetti and the producers. Maddalena, in the process of pleading for one more
favor (she wants to be hidden in the projection room to watch her daughter's
test) recognizes the girl. Wasn't she in that courtyard summer movie? *Sotto
il sole di Roma?* The girl's face contorts, a mix of pride and dejection. In Italy,
a woman is the looked-at-thing, until people tire of looking at her, at which
point she is cut loose:

"I don't make films anymore. . . . I'm not an actress. They only hired me
once or twice. . . . as I was the type they needed. I even got my hopes up.
And I lost my boyfriend and my job. . . . I convinced myself I was so beautiful
and so great, and yet I'm stuck here, doing the editing. Nobody called me, so
I'm here."

Maddalena is shocked, then calms herself. For Maddalena, the dream is
the truth: "Surely it can't be that way for everyone." In the projection room,
she watches, hidden in a corner. Maria's film rolls. Her tiny face is elaborately
painted. She wears the dress for which Maddalena received her bruises. Here

are the men again, slouching in their chairs, making their decisions. But on the screen, Maria, stumbling over her words, begins to cry, then scream. A scream of real distress, of protest. The men, finding it very funny, set each other off in rounds of cruel laughter ("What a disaster!" "She's a dwarf. Look!"), Annovazzi first among them.

A little later there is the sentimental neorealist ending: Maddalena nobly refuses the contract that is eventually offered to Maria ("I didn't bring her into this world to amuse anyone. To her father and me she's beautiful!"), an impossibility given her situation and the money involved. It would be pleasant to give oneself fully to this conclusion, and to the marital, erotic frisson that seems to spring up between Spartaco and Maddalena in the final frames, but a dusting of political idealism covers it. For he does not blame her and she needn't explain herself, and as the moneymen go off with their tails between their legs, these two Romans collapse on the bed together ("This crazy wife of mine," murmurs Spartaco as his hand reaches out, not to hit her this time, but to caress her) and hold on to each other for dear life. The vitality and mystery of a working-class marriage (hearing the voice of Burt Lancaster through the window, Maddalena, forgetting her worries for a moment, murmurs: "How *simpatico* he is!" Spartaco: "Now Maddalena, you really deserve a slap!" Maddalena: "What? Can't I joke now?") is not natural territory for Visconti, and the implied Marxist sentiment (They have nothing! But they need nothing!) is too smoothly sold.

Really the movie ends fifteen minutes earlier. Here where Maddalena covers her child's eyes with a palm like a priest over the face of a dead man. Lowering Maria down to floor, she removes her entirely from view, out of that little chink of reflected illumination cast in this dark room by the light of the screen. There is still the power of refusal. There is still the possibility of removing the looked-at-thing from the gaze of those who care for nothing but its surface. *Today? Tomorrow? Never!* But Magnani's own face stays where it is, oppressively close to us and to the camera, makeup free, wrinkled, bagged under the eyes, shadowed round the mouth, masculine and feminine in equal parts, a hawk nose splitting it down the middle, a different kind of challenge to the male gaze. How beautiful she is! Then she, too, turns away.

Twelve

AT THE MULTIPLEX, 2006

For a single season I reviewed movies. Each week the section editor gave me a couple of the mainstream releases to choose from. Occasionally, if there was space, I got to squeeze in a second title. No fancy stuff, no art movies, no foreign films and only one documentary. I wish this explained some of the enthusiasms recorded below but I don't think it does. All I can say in my defense is if you've ever seen Date Movie, V for Vendetta *starts to look like a masterpiece.*

MEMOIRS OF A GEISHA

The opening scenes of Rob Marshall's *Memoirs of a Geisha* are washed in a gray blue light, the same light that is to be found in *Million Dollar Baby, Mystic River* and the city shots of Marshall's own *Chicago*. Back in the 1970s, Oscar hopefuls had a yellowy glow to their film stock; now the color of Oscar is mineral blue. Serendipitously, this is the exact same shade as the unusual eyes of our hero, young Chiyo (Suzuka Ohgo), a nine-year-old Japanese girl from a poor fishing village. Chiyo's mother is dying. In Japan, all is tumult:

it is raining, the sea is crashing, the camera wobbles. A strange man arrives. Chiyo's father is crying. He weeps for Chiyo and her elder sister, both of whom he has decided to sell to the strange man. He weeps for the 150 pages of the original novel now crowbarred into this four-minute sequence. A panpipe plays its melancholy tune of longing. This pipe was also in *Titanic*.

Soon, sooner than anyone could imagine, the girls are dropped off at an *okiya*, a house of repute (depending on whom you ask) where girls are taught to be geisha. The owners, Mother (Kaori Momoi) and Auntie (Tsai Chin), examine the sisters. One girl has lovely gray blue eyes. She can stay. The other does not. She must go and become a common prostitute on the other side of town. Chiyo, who is to become an uncommon prostitute, is therefore the fortunate one, and is shown her brand-new world by fellow trainee Pumpkin (Zoe Weizenbaum), as they climb up onto the roof and look out across miles of handsome gray blue CGI rooftops. These rooftops were also in *Crouching Tiger, Hidden Dragon*.

In a musical, the form in which Rob Marshall, originally a choreographer, was trained, this would be the moment for a song. But there's no time: five hundred pages of plot remain. So: downstairs in the *okiya* lurks the evil Hatsumomo (Gong Li), a violent, imperious, gorgeous young harridan who is here to make Chiyo's life hell. She teaches our heroine an important lesson: old geisha, like Mother, are Japanese. Young geisha, like Hatsumomo, are Chinese and do not look like geisha but rather like willowy Vivienne Westwood models.

To escape the wrath of Hatsumomo, Chiyo wanders into the first of many ravishing street scenes, staged with all the indoor artifice of a Vincente Minnelli production. On a bridge, she comes across a dashing man in his forties called Chairman (Ken Watanabe). He is Japanese, as all men are. The nine-year-old Chiyo conceives a passion for Chairman that will outlast the film itself. Why she feels this way is unclear. Perhaps it is because he buys her an ice cone. She is decided: one day she will become a geisha so that she might be bought by the Chairman himself (thus becoming, in the coy terminology, her *danna*) and they can be together forever.

Sadly, things are not so easy: being Japanese, it is Chiyo's fate to be a maid. Only after a number of vicious beatings at the hands of Hatsumomo does Chiyo finally get the message and grow up to be a bewitching Chinese actress (Ziyi Zhang). She is also in *Crouching Tiger*. Chiyo's name is changed to Sayuri and she is taken under the wing of a successful geisha from another *okiya* called Mameha (Michelle Yeoh), who is neither Chinese nor Japanese but rather Malaysian. She is also in *Crouching Tiger*.

There has been a hoo-ha in Japan regarding the racial origins of these three geisha, much of which seemed to me a case of oversensitivity, until I found lurking within me the conviction that I, as an Englishwoman, can tell the difference between an Irishman and a Welshman at forty paces. I see how it must be galling, if you are Japanese, to look at three long-faced, high-cheekboned, patently not Japanese women and be told that they are Japanese. Although the Chinese, too, have cause for complaint: Ziyi Zhang, to Western eyes, is only slightly Chinese in the way that Lena Horne was slightly black.

This is no fault of the actress herself, whose comeliness is as self-evident and insistent as the wafting cherry blossom and the orange lanterns floating on pellucid water, the sumptuous silk of the kimono and the trimmed perfection of the formal gardens—all of which we are repeatedly encouraged to appreciate until you begin to feel that if something ugly does not appear on-screen soon you might go quite out of your mind. Japanese sliding screens neatly reveal the various beauties, opening on one action and closing on another as formally as the red velvet curtains in a musical revue. But inauthenticity of this kind, so well placed in *Chicago*, is all to naught here. Without songs, without pleasure, without humor, all the artifice in the world goes to waste.

At times the film suffers from a lack of sufficient artifice: there is more white powder in *Dangerous Liaisons* than there is here, with each actress apparently following her own personal taste in the matter of geisha stylings. You can imagine the debate on set ("Oh, Rob . . . do we have to . . . ?"). Ziyi Zhang is a good sport–*ish*; she'll wear quite a bit of white paint but won't black her eyebrows; Gong Li will wear a little, but she's not having her hair in that ludicrous bouffant; Michelle Yeoh eschews the entire conceit and goes about

in much the same makeup she wore for *The World is Not Enough*. Yet the
merest Google search reveals that real geisha are square-jawed, ghost-faced,
stocky women swathed in shapeless fabric and wearing six-inch clogs. In
Geisha only the clogs remain. The kimono is nipped in at the waist and
hugs the abdomen, the mad bud lip is gone, the big hair has been made
small. Everything that makes geisha truly alien (and alienating) has been
removed.

The plot pushes on: war arrives. The gray blue is back, and so is the wobbly
camera. The *okiya* closes and we find Sayuri reduced to dyeing kimonos in a
village far, far away that still does not look like Japan. An old client arrives.
He wants to help her recreate the geisha glory days. An American general is in
town who wants entertaining. They hatch a plan: "We'll show the Americans
just how hospitable we can be!" As a battle cry this lacks something, even as a
substitute for "We'll put the show on right here!" But so begins that conven-
tion beloved of the movies, especially movie musicals: the comeback. The
plot turns one part *42nd Street* to three parts *Lethal Weapon*, except this time
the lethal weapon is a kimono. Mameha is dug up; she's running a guesthouse
and wants no part of it. She left all that behind, long ago. She's given away all
her kimonos. All except one . . .

In the end, it is poor plotting and not cultural inauthenticity that is the
true problem here. Authenticity is not everything in cinema. (Who cared
about the authenticity of culture and locale in *Yentl?* In *Meet Me in St.
Louis?*) *Memoirs of a Geisha* hurts the heart and the brain with its crushing
monotony, inert, subhuman dialogue (made more ridiculous by being spoken
in English with a faux Japanese accent) and Marshall's calculated attempt
to sell us another Hollywood fairy tale of prostitution. This tale was also in
Pretty Woman.

Marshall manages only one scene that dispenses with the fantasy. Sayuri
is welcomed back to the *okiya* by Mother, having sold her virginity to the
highest bidder. "Now you are a geisha!" crows Mother, but her eyes are wet.
Sayuri's gray blue eyes are dead. A noxious tradition continues. It is a beautiful scene. It makes the endless blossom look like scrub.

SHOPGIRL *AND* GET RICH OR DIE TRYIN'

Mirabelle is not your average L.A. girl. She works in the glove department of Saks selling a product that nobody buys anymore. Actually, gloves are Mirabelle's day job: she is an artist. However, due to a hefty student-loan debt, and a productivity rate of three etchings a year, Mirabelle has had to seek other employment. To her right, the disembodied arm of a mannequin is on display, seeming to reach for somebody who is not there. Mirabelle is lonely. She drives a beat-up truck. She is from Vermont. She has a cat she never sees. She takes antidepressants. She is unassuming, clever, innocent, kind. She would like to be in love. Most important, in *Shopgirl*, she is played by Claire Danes. Ms. Danes is not your average actress. She has a graceful, natural body. She is in possession of a frankly enormous and unexpected nose, which she has never fixed and for which we thank the Lord. Her elastic face is kind, beautiful and expressive. Danes is to this movie what Mirabelle is to L.A.—a diamond in the rough. The rough first manifests itself in the form of her new lover Jeremy (Jason Schwartzman), a rock groupie loser whom she met in a launderette. His dream—which he has fulfilled—is to stencil logos onto amplifiers. When he can't find a condom he suggests using a plastic bag. Yet Mirabelle is optimistic about Jeremy, as she is about all things. "Are you one of those people," she asks, "who, if you get to know them, turns out to be . . . fantastic?" Alas, with Schwartzman, familiarity breeds contempt. He was spectacular in the hipster classic *Rushmore*, but the emotional autism played for laughs there now reveals itself as a tic of the actor himself: he cannot say a line without mentally enclosing it in quotation marks. Anyway, the end result is the same: we are meant to despair for lovely Mirabelle, and we do. Where is her white knight?

Nothing can prepare you for what comes next, not even reading the original Steve Martin novel: Ray Porter (Steve Martin himself) walks up to the glove counter and asks Mirabelle for a date. Steve Martin's face. I can't explain it. You have to see it. But whatever he has done to it, he does not look one day younger than he is. He has, however, succeeded in leaving himself only one facial expression: smug. No, that's not fair. He also looks creepy. And yet the creepy, intrusive voice-over (also voiced by Martin) assures us: "Mirabelle sizes him up and no alarm bells ring." Really? Not even the one that tolls: "He's forty years older than me"? The voice-over continues: "She doesn't ask the question foremost in her mind: why me?" Good point. Why would a successful man like Ray Porter wish to date twenty-four-year-old, exquisite, milky-skinned Mirabelle? We are at the mercy of a delusional voice-over.

This film is not entirely delusional. It is selectively truthful. As far as May-to-December love stories are concerned, Steve Martin has made a quantum leap in male self-awareness. He understands that what happens between Ray and Mirabelle is fundamentally an exchange of services. Ray Porter wants an innocent girl with whom to have a short affair. Mirabelle is vulnerable and depressed, enjoys receiving expensive gifts and is thankful when her student loan is paid off. Jeremy could do none of these things for her. So: older rich man helps young poor girl out of a rut (while sleeping with her) and then mercifully ends the relationship so both parties can go on to date someone who is their true "peer": a redeemed Jeremy for Mirabelle, and some classy older woman for Ray. In the (very good) novel, Martin's writing is so sparse and elegant you can almost excuse the concept. But here on film Ray Porter's unmoving, waxy face is on top of hers, he is running his crepe fingers (one place where Botox will not work) over the perfection of Mirabelle's backside—it is intolerable.

So we turn to Jeremy as Mirabelle's only escape route, but the script has overwhelmingly stacked the odds against him. His lines are moronic, his clothes are foul. He is four or five inches shorter than Mirabelle. His late redemption (he reads a self-help book called *How to Love a Woman* and buys a white suit) cannot obscure these facts, and as the inappropriate swirling violins crescendo and Ray graciously allows Mirabelle to leave him for her "peer," too much has already been set against Jeremy. What is styled as a happy ending looks more like the exchange of a rock for a hard place. "How do you turn yourself into a person capable of loving another person?" muses the voice-over, as if this were the universal problem. But it is only Ray's problem. It is Ray who thinks it appropriate—nay, educational—to use a person for pleasure without giving any piece of yourself apart from your credit card. Mirabelle doesn't have that problem. Mirabelle loves Ray. She accepts his gifts without guilt or neurosis because she needs them. When Jeremy is redeemed, she loves him. In her last scene she made me cry as she said good-bye to Ray's inert face and walked away, unsullied by the vanity project that surrounds her. It's hard to act your way out of so much bad faith, but somehow she manages it. In conclusion, here's that bad faith in full: (1) Ray Porter tells Mirabelle he is "past fifty." The actor who plays him was born on the August 14, 1945; (2) Steve Martin's script sneers at the vanity of fake L.A. girls and their plastic surgery; he is in no position to sneer; (3) The line that precipitates Mirabelle and Ray's breakup is this: "I'm looking for a three-bedroom place, in case I want to have a serious relationship, have some kids." Mirabelle dissolves into tears. This is meant to reveal that Ray is not serious about her. The truth is, this film is not serious. Ray Porter does not want a relationship with a peer. His real peer would be too old to have a child. He wants someone young, but not so young as to make him look foolish. Sure enough, at the end of the movie, Ray Porter turns up with a well-preserved woman in her early forties. If he'd turned up with a real peer, then this would not be a self-satisfied little indie drama. It would be a comedy.

Curtis "50 Cent" Jackson. My brain is giving you one star, but my heart wants to give five. I want you to know that *Get Rich or Die Tryin'* is to ghetto movies what *Stop! Or My Mom Will Shoot* was to Mafia movies, and I love, love, love it. I love that there are more naked men in this movie than in *Brokeback*. I love that you keep getting your fellow gangsters to admit that they love you. Really loudly. In the middle of robberies. I love the Beckettian dialogue: "I'm in it for the money." "For what?" "Sneakers." "Anything else?" "A gun." "What you need that for?" "I don't know." I love that you watched *GoodFellas* and *Scarface*, like, a million times and decided to ditch all that narrative arc crap and get straight to the point with a minimalist voice-over: "Crack meant money. Money meant power. Power meant war." I love how your acting style makes Bogart look animated. I love that the boss of your gang is dressed like Brando and is doing the voice from *The Godfather*. And then there is this: "So that was the crew. Four niggas dedicated to one thing and one thing only: getting paid and getting laid." Tupac, you can sleep easy. Richard Pryor, watch out.

MUNICH

Steven Spielberg is sometimes condescendingly described as a "family filmmaker," as if family were not one of the more profound aspects of our experience. His instinct for the family dynamic has offered intimacy to many a big-budget premise—the struggling single mother in *E.T.*, the couple teetering on divorce in *Close Encounters*, Indiana Jones's Oedipal struggles. In the 1990s there seemed to come a tipping point: family was no longer a metaphor for the action, it *was* the action. This became explicit as Spielberg grew ambitious for larger clans—the African slaves of *Amistad*, the six million Jews memorialized in *Schindler's List*, the lost generation of American men in *Saving Private Ryan*. Depending on whom you talk to, this was either an extension of his emotional reach or a grandiose exercise in cinematic grandstanding.

I should lay my cards on the table: I think Spielberg is one of the great popular artists of our time, and I base this upon the stupidity/pleasure axis I apply to popular artists: how much pleasure they give versus how stupid one has to become to receive said pleasure. The answer with Spielberg is usually: "not that stupid." His films bring pleasure where they most engage. Of course, when reviewing *Munich*, the cards the critic lays down are expected to be of another kind. As it happens, the film itself is neither "pro-Israeli" nor "pro-Palestinian," but this is precisely why, in the opinion of many American reviewers, it is inherently aggressive toward Israel, under the logic that anything that isn't pro is, by definition, anti. There is no way out of that intellectual cul-de-sac, which is why Tony Kushner's and Eric Roth's script does its best to avoid that road.

Munich is a film about a truly horrific terrorist attack and the response to that terrorist attack. It is not about moral equivalence. It is about what people will do for their families, for their clans, in order to protect and define them. It is about how far we will go in the service of the people we come from and the narratives we tell ourselves to justify what we have done. Those who have sympathies with either side will go away retaining their sympathies: that is the nature of the argument. And it is exactly this, the nature of the argument—what it does to those who are involved in it—and not the argument itself that *Munich* is interested in. Crucially, it is billed as "historical fiction," which will permit those who cling to their separate, mutually exclusive and antagonistic set of facts to call the film a "fantasy." This film has made groups on both sides uncomfortable because the truths it tells are of a kind that transcend facticity. Whichever family you belong to, national or personal, these truths are recognizable and difficult to dismiss.

Munich is an imagined reconstruction of a program of assassination that Mossad implemented against the organizers and surviving participants of the 1972 Munich massacre. If you are too young to remember that massacre, rent the documentary *One Day in September*, because *Munich* wastes no time setting up context. Unusually for Spielberg, he treats us as historical grown-ups (though not, as we shall see, geographical ones). At the heart of the movie is Avner (Eric Bana), a young Israeli who loves his families, both small—his pregnant wife, Daphna (a wonderful English-language debut from Ayelet Zurer)—and large: Israel itself. He is an inexperienced but dedicated soldier chosen by Mossad agent Ephraim (Geoffrey Rush) to head up a ragtag team of four operatives: a brash, South African–born getaway driver called Steve (Daniel Craig), a Belgian toy maker turned explosives expert (Mathieu Kassovitz), a German-Jewish document forger (Hanns Zischler) and a "cleanup" guy (Ciarán Hinds). Together they roam through a series of 1970s European cities meticulously re-created, although too laboriously symbolized (in Spielberg's Paris, wherever you are, you can always see the Eiffel Tower), doing unto their enemies as their enemies have done unto them.

In the process we begin to understand the biblical imperative "an eye for an eye" as something more deadly than simple revenge: it is of the body. It permits us the indulgence of thinking with our blood. And Spielberg understands the blood thinkers in his audience: for every assassination of an Arab, we return—lest we forget—to a grim flashback of that day in September, when eleven innocent Israeli athletes met their deaths in brutal and disgusting fashion. Flashbacks repeatedly punctuate the film's (slightly overlong) running time. We are not allowed to forget. But neither can we ignore what is happening to Avner as he progresses through his mission. Eric Bana gives a convincing portrayal of a man traveling far from who he is in order to defend who he is. His great asset is a subtle face that is not histrionic when conveying competing emotions. The scene where Avner is offered a double mazel tov— once for the arrival of his new baby, and once for the death of a target—is a startling example of this. Through Avner, Spielberg makes a reluctant audience recognize a natural and dangerous imperative in the blood, a fury we all share. "I did it for my family" is the most repeated line in this film. Its echo is silent, yet you can't help hearing it: what would you do for yours? The perverse nullity of the cycle of violence is made clear. Death is handed out to those who handed out death and from whose ashes new death dealers will rise. Children repeatedly wander into the line of fire. Normal human relations are warped or discarded. When Black September launches a letter-bomb campaign in response to Avner's assassinations, there is a twisted satisfaction. "Now we're in dialogue," says one Mossad agent. Thirty years later we are familiar with this kind of dialogue and where it leads.

The technical achievements of the film are many. Most notable is Janusz Kaminski's photography, which gives a subtle color palette to each city while lighting the whole like *The Third Man*, with bleached-out windows and skies that the actors shy away from, preferring the darker corners of the frame. The play of shadow and light looks like a church, a synagogue, a mosque. In the shadows, the cast debates the ethics of their situation and offer as many answers as there are speakers. If the audience recoils from South African Steve's assessment, "The only blood that matters to me is Jewish blood!" it understands Avner when he says, "I'm not comfortable with confusion." It is easier to think with the blood. It is easier to be certain.

But how many of us know what to do with these two competing, equally true facts we hear exchanged between Ephraim and Avner: "Israelis will die if these men live. You know this is true!" says Ephraim. Avner replies, "There is no peace at the end of this. You know this is true!"

WALK THE LINE *AND* GRIZZLY MAN

Arkansas, 1944. Two brothers walk the long, flat corridor of earth between one cornfield and another. Jack Cash, the elder, is memorizing the Bible. His little brother prefers the music of the hymnals; he worries that Jack's talent for stories is the nobler enterprise. Jack wants to be a preacher. "You can't help nobody," he explains, "if you don't tell them the right story." Yet we already know it is his little brother, Johnny, who will grow up to tell the memorable stories, the kind you sing, the kind that matter most.

In their own generic way, musical biopics are always the right story: the struggle toward self-actualization. With songs. They are as predictable and joyful as Bible stories: the Passion of Tina Turner, the Ascension of Billie Holiday. It is a very hard-hearted atheist indeed who does not believe that Music Saves. *Walk the Line*—although conspicuously well acted—is really no different from previous efforts, and that's a good thing. It shares the charm of the genre. It has Cash abandoning the music of the church for the devil's tunes. It has Cash falling down drunk onstage and smashing up a dressing room. It has the low times ("Didn't you used to be . . . ?") and the times when Cash's name rode high on the hit parade.

It has the greatest of all musical biopic tropes: the instrument endangered by a parent. One begins to suspect a reverse psychology ploy: parents ambitious of turning a daughter into a future Jacqueline du Pré would do well to smash up a cello in front of her. In Cash's case, he has a hick father who wants to hock the family piano and buy whatever hicks buy with piano money— chewing tobacco, maybe. It's Johnny's downtrodden mother who saves it, but worse is to come: beloved brother Jack is killed in a farming accident for which Johnny feels responsible. Daddy Cash reckons the devil took the wrong son. Next time we see those cornfields, the boy Johnny has turned into Joaquin Phoenix, walking that line alone.

Joaquin alone is, for many women, the reason to see this film. For this reviewer, his elemental masculinity strays rather too far into Victor Mature territory—still, I respect the majority opinion. Certainly when he is covered in water or sweat (which he frequently is) and filling the screen with his ungainly bulk, he possesses a certain Old Testament style. He looks as if he's struggling with himself—he'd make a good Abraham. For Johnny Cash, he's perfect. On those early tours, when we see Cash playing alongside Elvis (Tyler Hilton) and Jerry Lee Lewis (Waylon Payne), Phoenix works the difference between those two coltish, flamboyant stars and the bullish man in black whose sole piece of stagecraft was his no-frills introduction: "Hello, I'm Johnny Cash." It's fun to see three musical pilgrims at the beginning of their journey, before their places in history were settled. "How about that Johnny Cash, everybody?" cries Elvis, with the magnanimous generosity of a man confident that he himself has the greater talent. While Elvis launches into "Hound Dog," Cash watches from the wings with a face that encapsulates Bing Crosby's sentiment re Sinatra: "I know one great singer is born into every generation, but why'd *he* have to be born into *mine*?"

But Cash has bigger problems than Elvis. In a recent interview, Woody Allen put the trouble well: "The thing standing between me and genius is me." The bad guy in every musician's biopic is the musician himself. Cash is stuck in a bad marriage, he drinks and he never got over Jack's death. One night he is offered amphetamines on the assurance that "Elvis takes them," surely one of the worst celebrity health tips ever recorded. Once the addiction takes hold, Phoenix is free to give us what he does best: a very dark night of the soul.

It is presumptuous to speak of the parallels between Phoenix's biography and Cash's, but there is no doubt that whenever the plot returns to the trauma of the missing brother, Phoenix's game raises and the audience grows tense. Several scenes are of an emotional intensity out of all proportion to the humdrum musical biopic one expects.

And then, at just the right moment, Reese Witherspoon takes over and brings the film home. Witherspoon has the kind of maniacal feminine perkiness that people of a Woosterish temperament cannot abide. I like her. I like her triangular chin and her head-girl, can-do attitude. Here she plays Cash's savior and eventual second wife, June Carter, and it's a great piece of casting: Witherspoon is a twelve-step program in and of herself. She's so capable, so hardworking, so upright and practical—underrated virtues among actresses. Physically, and in all other ways, Witherspoon makes the best of what she has. She has June's steely self-sufficiency down pat. "Marry me, June," begs Cash, not for the first time. "Oh, please, get up off your knees; you look pathetic" is the sensible response.

There is in this film the serious notion that nothing is as existentially fatal as a miserable relationship. And no redemption like a good one. But to get the good one, you've got to work harder than Job. Before the successful prison concerts and the comeback and the hagiography of the very movie we're watching, we see Cash taken low. Real low. Drugs, poverty, despair, violence. Each biopic digs its own way out of this hole. Black soul singers are redeemed differently from white punks—everyone's got their own groove—but the principle is the same: keep it real, get back on track. Here's Johnny at his lowest ebb, just before the turnaround, begging his bank for money: "I need this, see? To get my phone on . . . cos I got a woman . . . and I need to speak to her." That's country music logic, and it's really quite beautiful.

After the cultural violence of much nineteenth-century anthropology, there came a twentieth-century emphasis on reticence—we should no longer seek to explain people definitively, but rather observe them, respecting their otherness. Fortunately, no one told Werner Herzog, and that is why his *Grizzly Man* is so damn cool. Herzog (whose voice-over perfectly matches *The Simpsons's* hard man, Rainier Wolfcastle) is an infamous egomaniacal, auteur nutjob (i.e., a great European director) with a bent for the Germanically literal. (To pay off a bet he once made a movie called *Werner Herzog Eats His Shoe*. It did not disappoint.) Herzog is hard-core. He's not interested in your interpretation of why American nutjob Timothy Treadwell lived among bears. Who cares what you think? Herzog has his documentary in hand, explaining

that what we have here "iz on astone-ishing story of beauty and depth." He's
not wrong. The footage itself is mostly Treadwell's, but the film is a discord-
ant duet of two voices: Herzog's old-world Schopenhaurian pessimism versus Treadwell's new-world optimism (which, Herzog believes, masks a deep
despair).

Herzog calls bears a "primordial encounter." Timothy calls them Mr. Chocolate and Aunt Melissa. Herzog believes Timothy was "fighing against the civi-
lization that cast Thoreau out of Walden." According to Timothy's parents,
the motivation was more prosaic. Not to give the specifics away, but "failed TV
actor" is at the root of the crisis. Still, Herzog is determined to spin grandeur
out of poor Timmy. And fabulous though it is to hear Herzog shouting about
the "ooltimatt indifference of nature," it's Timothy saying to a fox, "I love you.
Thanks for being my friend. I like this—do you like this?" that brings real joy.
All you need to know about indifference is right there in that fox's face.

BRIEF ENCOUNTER *AND* PROOF

In the spring of 1945, when David Lean's *Brief Encounter* was first released,
my father was nineteen. I envy him that vintage year of cinema and all opening weekends between, say, 1933 and 1955. Instead of *Memoirs of a Geisha*,
he saw *Woman of the Year*. Instead of *Shopgirl*, he got *Top Hat*. The first film
he ever saw was *King Kong*, and it was a merciful hour and a half shorter than
the beast I slept through in January. In New York and Paris, we can revisit the
films of our fathers any night of the week in dozens of fine revival cinemas;
in London we rely on the occasional largesse of film festivals and the BFI. To
those who love them, any rerelease of a 1940s film is a draught of sunshine. I
have never seen a movie of this period in which there was not something to
like, just as I have never come across a cheese I wouldn't eat. *Brief Encounter*
is a Wensleydale: a lovely slice of English fare, familiar, inadvertently comic. It
has become its own parody. The English are slightly ashamed of it, as the Aus-
trians are annoyed by *The Sound of Music*. In fact, its reputation as a period
piece is unfair. It is not all cut-glass diction and antediluvian good manners.
The film is really about the dream life of the English, those secret parts of

us that are most important and to which we have least access. It's a shame to go to the cinema only to laugh (as modern audiences laugh at the supposed camp excess of another sincere movie, Now, Voyager). If you pass over the superficial culture shocks of sixty years passed (A lending library in Boots the chemist! A string quartet in a railway café!), it is as astute about the English character as it ever was.

The story is easily paraphrased: Laura Jesson (Celia Johnson) and Dr. Alec Harvey (Trevor Howard) meet in a railway station and fall in love. Unfortunately, they are married to other people. Laura has a stolid, suburban husband, Fred, whose only connection to the Keatsian strain in English life is via the Times crossword, the clue in question being "When I behold, upon the night's starr'd face, Huge cloudy symbols of a high . . . (seven letters)." Laura suggests "romance." It's right—but it doesn't fit with the other answers. In this moment the entire film is contained. There are many things that the English want and dream and believe. But they do not fit in with our other answers.

Lean's sad, buttoned-up account of unconsummated love is about all of us and our cautious natures. It's not that the English don't want true love or self-knowledge. Rather, unlike our European cousins, we will not easily give up the real for the dream. We remain skeptical about throwing away a concrete asset like Fred in favor of "the faery power of unreflecting love," no matter how much Keats may recommend it. Laura, a Midlands mother of two, is certainly not a fairy by temperament, despite her pixie face. She will not give up the reality of Fred for the dream of Alec. Alec, gentleman that he is, quite agrees. An Italian (or indeed, the modern English viewer of this film) will diagnose Laura and Alec as morbidly repressed. The film offers a different hypothesis: that the possibility of two people's pleasure cannot override the certainty of other people's pain. Primum non nocere is the principle upon which the film operates. As a national motto we could do a lot worse.

These days, carpe diem is more popular, and self-sacrifice invites sniggers. But the impulse behind Laura's and Alec's sacrifice seems to me neither smug, religious nor self-satisfied. Brief Encounter is not about English sexual repression or Christian values. It's about personal grandeur. By the end of the film, Alec and Laura are truly grand; they are their best selves. And if there is a moral lesson, it is not about the sin of sexual infidelity but the secular sin of being unfaithful to oneself.

In the last few minutes of their good-bye, they are interrupted by Dolly, a silly woman whom Laura knows. She sits down uninvited and starts to talk about train timetables. She represents all the petty horror of English life, the inconsequential stuff and nonsense that gets in the way of our real lives and separates us from that "high romance" Keats knew the English have within them. It is sad that Alec and Laura must part, but what makes this an English tragedy is that they will politely listen to Dolly as they do it. They should be showing their souls. Instead they discuss the weather.

Hollywood recycles its actresses. Ava Gardner turned into Angelina Jolie. Claudette Colbert reincarnated as Reese Witherspoon. Cate Blanchett may one day prove worthy of the Katharine Hepburn echoes she evokes. Gwyneth Paltrow, star of the depressing misfire *Proof*, is Grace Kelly's replacement, and that's a poisoned chalice if ever there was one. The qualities of Grace and Gwyneth, as I see them, are as follows: a sense of entitlement, a glacial physical beauty and an apparently genuine submissive attitude to the opposite sex. They worship the men they play opposite and don't so much act as react to them. It is this talent for silent reaction that won Paltrow an Oscar for *Shakespeare in Love*, one of the least verbal Oscar-winning performances in recent memory. Her face flushes, her eyes flood. If you hold her in your arms, she trembles. It's all good old-fashioned movie actress stuff. If you were a male moviegoer looking for someone to love you, to just love you, and not drive you crazy with questions and smart talk like Bette Davis or Renée Zellweger, then Gwyneth's your girl. Classy as she is, she'll love you even if you're completely unsuitable, even if you're Ripley or Ted Hughes. But just as Grace did, Gwyneth has grown tired of the princess gig. She wants to be an actress. *Proof* sees her acting and acting and acting. I'm sure it's true that on stage she made this role her own, wowing audiences with her portrayal of Catherine, the emotionally and mentally vulnerable daughter of a math genius who has lost his mind.

Did the father write the mathematical proof posthumously found in a desk drawer—or did the daughter? The theatrical script uses the word *proof* as a metaphorical launchpad for discussions of work and love and life, as plays will. It's that kind of verbal swordplay that so impresses onstage while seeming so redundant and brittle on-screen. Everyone involved tries really hard, and Jake Gyllenhaal is puppyishly excited by the whole project, but dominating it all is Paltrow's voice, with its hipsterish high-rising terminals that sound as if she is saying only one thing, over and over: "Like, I can act, right?" She has something to prove, but it has nothing to do with math.

The best course of action for Paltrow is to remember her antecedent and follow her example. There is a way out of the princess gig. Grace Kelly cracked it in *High Society* and *Rear Window*. Paltrow glimpsed it in *Emma*, which was, in truth, the role that deserved an Oscar. Keep the vulnerability, but don't be coy about the self-possession that is so obviously there. He goes down on his knees because you have something of value—and you know it. And if he left, you'd survive. Grace Kelly proved that princesses have power, too.

GOOD NIGHT, AND GOOD LUCK *AND* CASANOVA

First, a disclaimer. With regard to *Good Night, and Good Luck*, George Clooney's strident political docudrama, I find myself in a difficult position. I watched it and liked it. Then I spent two hours on the Internet and changed my mind.

What remains is still the review I intended, but it is qualified by the obvious fact that liberal films like this are made to please liberals like me. In terms of historical content, the film is neither quite honest nor quite true. That's a shame, because it's a good film. I don't have space to discuss the several disappointing inaccuracies, elisions of fact and deliberate obfuscations. All I can do is direct you to the Internet and to Joseph E. Persico's 1988 biography *Edward R. Murrow: An American Original*. What follows, then, is a glowing review of a fine piece of agitprop leftist cinema, which I very much enjoyed in the same spirit a person of the opposite sensibility will enjoy Ann Coulter's recent celebratory defense of McCarthyism, *Treason*, not because it is entirely true but because she's fighting in your corner. Clooney's fighting in mine, and doing it in style.

And how. This is a beautifully made, superficially coherent, effective movie, and you have to pinch yourself to believe an actor directed it, wrote it and produced it. The generosity of the ensemble casting, the control of the heavily verbal material, the expert pacing—it is a mature work. Clooney understands that style is what you leave out, and in its taut ninety minutes he leaves out so much of what we have come to expect that Warner refused to fund the film. He left out the color. He left out the subplots. He left out the love interest. He sidelined historical reenactments in favor of the real thing: archive footage.

What remains is strongly reminiscent of *Citizen Kane*, not simply for its loquacious, crusading journalists, but because it is both visually luscious and aurally self-sufficient. You could close your eyes and understand everything. But don't close your eyes. Here in sumptuous black and white is a perfectly recreated Capraesque newsroom. Here are quick-fire conversations à la Preston Sturges. The period detail is given a kick in the pants by the witty camera work (borrowed from Soderbergh and the Coen brothers), shooting faces from below, zooming in on a finger worrying a shirt button.

Clooney himself avoids the camera, slinking through the film as unobtrusively as a star can. In a film that is about editorializing and is itself heavily editorialized, Clooney edits himself out for the sake of the material. Into the Clooney-shaped hole slips an accomplished ensemble cast—Tate Donovan, Reed Diamond, Jeff Daniels, Robert Downey Jr., Patricia Clarkson—all of whom back up David Strathairn's pitch-perfect Murrow impersonation by being entirely convincing newshounds. Well, all but one. I think you know who I'm talking about. Mr. Downey remains the most aggressive scene stealer in Hollywood. He's barely restrained here, but if someone doesn't give him free rein soon, there's a danger of auto-combustion.

I digress. Like Murrow—the campaigning television broadcaster who squared off against Senator McCarthy in the mid-1950s—Clooney uses the "wires and lights" of his medium to make simple, forceful arguments. His case against McCarthy is familiar and correct: the paranoid fervor of

McCarthyism placed the right to fair trial and the rights of the First Amendment under serious threat. Today, these rights are endangered once more. "We cannot defend freedom abroad by deserting it at home," argues Murrow in 1956, foreshadowing our present concerns. Clooney doesn't have to push hard for analogies like this—they're everywhere. In fact, they're a little too easy, and so admiring is he of Murrow that he follows his hero's editorial style to the letter. (Clooney has always seemed boyishly prone to masculine hero worship, from his consecration of his own newscaster father to the re-creation—both on- and offscreen—of Sinatra's rat-pack heyday.) Just as Murrow gave McCarthy enough rope to hang himself by allowing him "right to reply" on Murrow's own prime-time show, *See It Now*, so Clooney refrains from casting an actor as McCarthy and simply replays the archive film. The edited archive film. He chooses all the same shots as Murrow did for his TV show: the off-guard, twitching, sweating, hysterical McCarthy, asking pointless questions, chasing phantoms that were not there.

Clooney clearly believes, like Murrow, that his editorializing has truth on its side. He has a case. Sometimes there is no "other side of the argument." Nazis have no right of reply. Ed Murrow made a bet that what was pinko liberal thinking in 1956 would prove to be a condition of basic humanity fifty years later. He was wrong. The basic human rights he defended are once again assailed. Clooney is angry about that.

This must be why he cuts into his movie Murrow's selectively edited footage of McCarthy's interrogation of Annie Moss, an elderly, uneducated black woman whose Communist connections—McCarthy believed—had led her to seek a job inside the Pentagon. We see this meek woman verbally bullied and cheated of her right to see the evidence put against her. We are led to believe she knows nothing of the charges. One senator tries to help her. McCarthy leaves the hearing. Bobby Kennedy sits at the end of the table of senators, failing to come to her aid.

What evil breeds where good men stay silent! So we are meant to think. And this is a true liberal principle, as is the principle that no one should be tried without seeing the evidence held against them. Yet it remains disappointing to go on the Internet, in a shameful state of historical innocence, and discover that Bobby Kennedy was a good friend of Senator McCarthy and that Annie Moss was, as it happens, a member of the Communist Party. Clooney could have included gray areas such as this and still have made a fine liberal argument. It's a sure sign that things are bad when the Left, like the Right, wants its history black and white.

•

Casanova is a silly film. Half *Carry On*, half Shakespearean comedy, everyone in it is perfectly nice and should reassemble to make a lively *Twelfth Night*. The trouble here is that the words are not by Shakespeare but rather by one Kimberly Simi, who worked as an attorney before selling this script. It has Heath Ledger sounding like James Mason with a soupçon of Peter O'Toole. It has tights and bosoms. It has mistaken identity, gender switching, girls wearing mustaches, a shrew tamed, hearts sundered then reattached and finally a journey by sea. Some of the best writing is in the program notes: "Sienna Miller . . . catapulted into the public eye when she appeared in the BBC comedy *Bedtime*." Strange. That's not how I remember it. Speaking of the young actress, she might ask hair and makeup how it is possible to make a preternaturally pretty twenty-two-year-old look like a dull matron. In the film, Francesca Bruni, for that is the character's name, is secretly writing a feminist tract called "The Subjugation of Women" under a nom de plume—maybe that was the reasoning. Feminists can't be blond and must have big eyebrows. I would love it if Miss Miller was secretly the author of the works of Elaine Showalter. I fear it is not so.

CAPOTE *AND* DATE MOVIE

Some cinematic seasons throw up abstract questions. In the early 1990s a clutch of movies asked: What is adulthood? Children found themselves in the bodies of adults, and vice versa. Adults left children home alone. Children were shrunk by careless fathers. Babies started talking with the voice of John Travolta. It may be vocational myopia on my part, but this year I hear the question "What is a writer?" In *Hidden* (released in the United States as

Caché) the answer is painful: writers are petty bourgeois. In *Good Night, and Good Luck* it's the writer as hero, noble champion of the people. In *Casanova* she's a harmless firebrand, in *Memoirs of a Geisha*, a naïf who simply records events as they happen. In both *Get Rich or Die Tryin'* and *Walk the Line* the writer is an alchemist, turning pain into gold.

Why all the sudden concern with scribblers? Writers like to flatter themselves that in times of communal trauma people turn to the written word for comfort and direction. Maybe once. But in the noughties we've begun to legislate against language itself: writers are not to be trusted. They are double-dealers. For this reason, *Capote*, despite its 1950s setting, is timely. When people rail against the "media," the bogeymen they have in mind owe not a little to the specter of Truman Capote. What is a writer? He knocks on your door with a smile, a pen and a shard of ice in his heart. Around that shard Philip Seymour Hoffman molds his tremendous Capote impersonation, by turns fey, friendly, oleaginous, deadly. He is Janus-faced. In New York, he's a quixotic queen laughing in smoky nightclubs at the stupidity of his own readers; in Holcomb, Kansas, he does a damn good impression of being the boy next door. He'll turn up at the sheriff's house early in the morning with doughnuts and coffee, find the sheriff's wife alone and explain he came on a whim to eat breakfast with her. She wanders off to get plates. Slowly the camera and Hoffman slink to the left into a side room where little Perry Smith, multiple murderer, is locked up in a cell.

The sea change that comes over Hoffman's face during this pan shot is as close as silence comes to narrative. His Capote coolly dissembles, yet he is impassioned; he lied to get into the house, and yet he came to uncover truths. He is a writer: a man who tells the truth by lying. An actor of Hoffman's caliber, who also tells the truth that way, can't help but have a deep understanding of writerly psychology. "When I think of how good it could be," wrote Capote of his unwritten book, "I can hardly breathe." When Hoffman says these lines—sexually, venally, desperately—you fear him and yourself. How far will he go for a good story? How far will you go with him to hear it?

Hoffman has been vocal in his praise of the writer, Dan Futterman, and director, Bennett Miller, but this is an actor's traditional demurral: the lion's

share of the praise belongs to Hoffman. Everything looks lovely and period
and prestige, but shots linger ponderously, keen that we should fully appreciate them, as predictable a tic of a first-time director as the first-time novelist
compulsively inserting adjectives. It's the acting that sings, especially when
Hoffman duets with luminous Catherine Keener (playing another writer,
Harper Lee), the lady with the loveliest laugh in cinema. Hoffman's writer is a
self-serving egoist; Keener's a restrained, wise soul. But just as in life, cinema's
Capote trumps Harper Lee. We admire those who refrain, but we make movies about personae. Capote's persona was enormous and, unusually, his talent
was almost its equal. Yet we still tell Capote's story with pity and use his life as
a parable: talent can't buy you morals. The film implies Truman couldn't finish another book after *In Cold Blood* because he never got over his betrayal of
Perry Smith and Dick Hickock. To my mind, the problem was less moral and
more writerly: stage fright. Capote stumbled across a true story that suited
him perfectly and dressed himself up in it to fabulous effect. Without it, he
felt naked.

●

I could have seen a lot of good films this week. I chose *Date Movie,* and
actually I'm thankful because it allows me to say with certainty something I
had not decided until this moment: *Date Movie* is the worst movie I have ever
seen. I really mean that. Forty minutes in, I fled the cinema feeling dazed,
aggrieved and strangely weepy, as if a stranger had just physically threatened
me. I took *Date Movie* personally. The actress who stars in it means a lot to
me. She is Alyson Hannigan, a petite redhead with goofy good looks, who cos-
tarred in *Buffy the Vampire Slayer,* the only TV show I have truly loved. I have
tried to convince people that she is one of the finest tragicomic actresses in
L.A. I have persisted in this despite *American Pie* and its sequels. At the very
least, I expected her to step effortlessly into the shoes Meg Ryan left empty.
Ms. Hannigan shares Ms. Ryan's triumvirate of talents—quick wit, deep soul
and gummy smile—and is happily free of the emotional neediness with which
Ms. Ryan occasionally oppresses the audience. When I dared to dream, I pictured Alyson at a podium, thanking her parents. But there will be no prizes

for *Date Movie*. The very fact of its existence forces a wedge between Alyson and anything resembling mainstream or indie Hollywood. And for that she has Jason Friedberg and Aaron Seltzer to thank, two "filmmakers" whom I can only name and shame in the full knowledge it will not stop them.

In the first forty minutes of *Date Movie*, Hannigan beats up a homeless man for sport, wears a grotesque fat suit, watches a cat eat a dead woman's face, has a carpet of ginger hair waxed from her backside and takes part in a parody of *The Bachelor*, in which women the bachelor "doesn't want to bang" are "eliminated" by submachine gun. The humor is so broad it's less than human—it's the laughter of monkeys as they fall out of trees. To imagine the audience for this film, one has to envision new levels of adolescent nullity. Who *are* these kids? Why are they evolving *backward*? *American Pie* was an amusing gross-out. *Scary Movie* was a gross-out, funny piece of nothing. *Date Movie* is less than nothing. It's a new concept in crap: a film that is in itself an absence of film. For Hannigan, it's cinema suicide. The worst humiliation comes when she sits opposite her date as he laboriously spoofs the orgasm scene from *When Harry Met Sally*. Eventually he finishes. Hannigan says: "I'll have what he's having." As a metacomment on Hannigan's career, it's the cruelest joke of all. And yes, I know this movie wasn't meant for me, but I'm repulsed by the children it's meant for and dread the adults they will become. On the Internet the little darlings are legion, defending *Date Movie* against all attackers. I reproduce one such review: "OK I'm a 13-year-old girl and I thought the movie was hillarious [sic]. That kind of stuff is what kids joke about and talk about now a days [sic]. Its [sic] a comedy so stop acting like a 50-year-old spinster with a stick up your ass and get on with your life."

SYRIANA *AND* THE WEATHER MAN

What is Clooney saying? A sentence he began sparklingly with *Ocean's Eleven* (2001), which stumbled at *Intolerable Cruelty* (2003), grew lamentable at *Ocean's Twelve* (2004), having seemed almost to make sense with *Confessions of a Dangerous Mind* (2002), now reaches its conclusion with the impressive *Good Night, and Good Luck* and the rigorous *Syriana*. I judged too quickly, thinking him one of those actors who prides himself on making the big bad movies in order to fund the small good ones—a kind of vanity tax upon the audience, whereby the pointless shoot-'em-up is the price we supposedly pay for the chilly little chamber piece about divorce.

Clooney is not that actor. He doesn't make sterile, unlovable vanity projects. In a cultural climate that ridicules and is repulsed by intellectual and moral commitment, in his way he pursues both. With his role as executive producer and front-of-shop "face" of *Syriana*, he has now created an unprecedented scenario: the most popular actor in Hollywood is also the man who wants to agitate us most. Something like this has happened only once before, with Marlon Brando, an actor whose personal failings and self-regard overran all his most serious ambitions. Clooney appears to have no such tragic flaw. He is making real American films instead of American products; he is helping real American films to get made. At a time when most people with half a brain cell have long given up on the products of the American multiplex, Clooney gives us a reason to put our foot back through the door and cautiously buy some popcorn. Rarely in the history of Hollywood has so much personal charm been put to such good use.

Syriana is the first film this season that demands and deserves to be rewatched as soon as it has concluded. Unless your mind naturally turns to the economic and political intrigues of the global oil industry, much of this film will remain obscure to you upon first viewing. Writer/director Stephen Gaghan has followed the same narrative policy as he did in *Traffic* (2000), connecting the dots between the alienating anonymity of great power and its human cost. But where *Traffic* was neat and pleasingly didactic, *Syriana* is as murky and multifaceted as our present historical moment. The story revolves around a Justice Department investigation into the merger of two giant oil companies, an investigation that is for appearances only ("We're looking for the illusion of due diligence"), for the merger will ultimately benefit the American consumer. Gaghan's talent is for Marxist explication, demonstrating how one transaction contains within it elements of the entire system it supports. He knows one drug deal on the streets of Brooklyn can be traced back to the rich dealers in Florida, to the desperate backstreets of Mexico City, to the peasants who slave in the cocaine fields of Colombia. So it is in *Syriana*, where a dull piece of political stagecraft is shown to contain multitudes: Arab princes, CIA agents, Texas oil barons, energy analysts, Washington attorneys and two young Pakistani boys who lose their pitifully paid jobs in the oil fields when the merger causes huge layoffs. Guerrilla camera work and bravura acting fuse to create a realism not unlike the edgy, off-kilter work of Cassavetes, a particularly striking achievement when one considers the fame of many of the actors involved. Playing an all-American, square-chinned energy analyst, Matt Damon joins Clooney, here fat, bearded and sluggish as a U.S. agent with a conscience, and both appear to be just what they claim to be—real players in this dark world.

My complaint is clarity: it is evident that the sociopolitical contexts of this film have been closely observed, so much so that at times it feels like an overresearched novel, the writer having forgotten that we have not shared in his research. This film treats its audience not merely as adults but as experts. I was frequently thrown into scenes on the back foot; only understanding what had passed when it was almost over. You don't walk out of *Syriana* outraged and decided, as from *Traffic*, but this is part of its sophistication. It prompts you to begin thinking, not to finish. Ultimately, what is most impressive about *Syriana* is the scrupulousness of its production: the genuinely multicultural casting; the sensitivity and nuance of its use of languages, accents, vocabulary; the clothes people wear in each city; the respectful attention to the smallest cultural details.

Syriana is an American movie that reaches out beyond itself. Watching it made me feel hopeful—a rare sensation in a multiplex. Of course, no one film or book will make of us a reasonable, decent people, and what we are living through is not simply a war of ideas; but ideas are no small part of our troubles, and the American film industry is, for better or worse, among the largest engines and disseminators of ideas on the planet. Films like *Syriana* are not revolutions, but they are contributions. And if this film reaches the countries of which it speaks—on illegal DVDs or in backroom cinemas—a novel message will be passed to the people who live there: we believe you exist and are human, as we are. "When I grew up the only time you would see Arabs on-screen would be in something like *Sinbad*, where they're climbing over the side of the ship with a saber in their mouth," says Alexander Siddig, who plays the character of Prince Nasir, a young, reform-minded emir-in-waiting who has an idea about halting the sale of cheap oil to Americans and getting a better deal for the people of his country. To deal fairly with other humans one must first see them as human. American movies disseminate more images of humans than any other medium. Here Hollywood has something approaching a responsibility; *Syriana* goes some way to honoring that.

•

The Sunday Telegraph does not hold with the idea of half stars. I understand the thinking, but it makes it difficult for this reviewer to rate a certain kind of "quirky" American film set in the suburbs, of which half a dozen are released each year and for which two and a half stars is precisely the correct denomination. *The Weather Man* is one of those films; in fact, it might be the ür-quirky film, for it is an exact splicing of two mild giants of the genre: *American Beauty* and *About Schmidt*.

I think I found this film palatable because I read it perversely. As I see it, this film's central concept is the aversion most right thinking people have to the actor Nicolas Cage. And he accepts this mantle so honorably and humbly in this film that I think maybe now I quite like him. It's an honest and comic performance and seems filled with all the genuine humiliations that one imagines Cage himself has suffered in the past ten years. I don't want to tell you any more about it—it's best stumbled upon without expectations but with my reading kept in mind. One recommendation, though: Nicholas Hoult (the kid from *About a Boy*) is almost grown and is possibly on the cusp of becoming better looking than the original teenage Leo DiCaprio. Oh, and one warning: Michael Caine's American accent will make your eyes bleed. Again.

V FOR VENDETTA *AND* TSOTSI

As a rule, film critics fondly place themselves at a slight remove from the passive mass of cinema audiences. The fortunate among us have pens with lights on them and, while you let the medium of film simply wash over you, we are making notes on such aesthetic minutiae as the Aryan Band-Aid on the big black head of Marsellus Wallace, or the Damoclean slice of light that falls over Harry Lime in a gloomy alleyway.

Cinema—the most pleasurable of mediums—is made to jump through the same hoops of theme, argument and "imagery" as its more resistant cousin, the novel; necessarily so—otherwise there would be little to critique. No one is asked to review roller coasters. And yet the truth is some films affect you so viscerally and with such fluidity that a pen with a light on it is no match for them. I barely made a note during V for Vendetta, unless "Wow!" and "Awesome!" and "This is so fucking cool!" count as notes.

In the face of this film something adolescent in me surged to the surface, and I mean that as a great compliment: adolescence is a state I hold in high regard. After the fact, I saw what other critics have seen—portentousness, absurdity, misogyny, political naïveté—but the truth is during the film I was utterly engaged, somewhat radicalized and very excited. To me, the film, like the original graphic novel from which it comes, is about personal integrity and, more important, about how that notion might be parlayed into our political lives.

It pursues this idea violently, without humor, and with a bald Natalie Portman onboard. It's easy to ridicule. Personal integrity is always ridiculed by adults and worshipped by adolescents, because principles are the only thing adolescents, unlike adults, really own. I first read V for Vendetta, by the writer Alan Moore and illustrator David Lloyd, when I was an adolescent myself, back when pieces of its dialogue, rendered faithfully in this film, were of great personal importance to me: "Our integrity sells for so little, but it is all we ever have—it is the last inch of us. The only inch that matters!"

It is clear that Moore, who has removed his name from the credits, feels his own integrity has been damaged by the streamlining Andy and Larry Wachowski (of the Matrix trilogy) have made to his crowded narrative. The brothers have ditched the supporting cast that tends to proliferate in graphic novels and moved Moore's English dystopia from its original post-Thatcher, postnuclear era to a world not long after Blair and Bush. Eighty thousand

Londoners have died in an act of germ warfare for which terrorists have been blamed. The state has turned from "nanny" to monolithic; the media show a Goebbelsian respect for the truth and a zeal for censorship; homosexuals, "ethnics" and dissidents are mysteriously "vanished"; the people are in the long sleep of fear and lethargy.

Into this bleak world comes V, a man in a white clown mask who takes as his model a long-forgotten English terrorist: Guy Fawkes. The original novel's respect for Fawkes is one of its sillier aspects—Fawkes was no truth-loving anarchist destroying in order to create, but a Catholic with a grudge against the Protestant majority. And Che Guevara was no prince among men either, but then, adolescents aren't sticklers for history.

What they are, however, is impassioned. They believe, like V, that "everything is connected," that "a revolution without dancing isn't worth having" and that "truth, freedom and justice are more than mere words—they are perspectives." They find it quite reasonable that V should alight upon tiny, porcelain beauty Evey Hammond (Natalie Portman), lock her up, torture her and allow her to believe she will be executed if she doesn't give the state a piece of information—all in order to set her (existentially speaking) free.

Without spoiling anything, I think I can tell you that during her incarceration, Evey is sent pieces of a story, pushed through a hole in the prison wall, and this story gives her the strength to resist her torture, to find an integrity she didn't know she had, and radicalizes her in a manner that you either believe or you don't. The story she reads is a gift (the person who wrote it is about to die and can expect nothing in exchange) and therefore also an act of love. Acts of love, because they are unattached to the world of commodities, are radical propositions. The complaint that a girl is put through a sadomasochistic experience by a man in a mask misses a key element of the story that is in both book and film: the man in the mask was radicalized in the exact same way. The gender is irrelevant; the gift is everything.

And that's not even factoring in the pleasure of the massive explosions, Buffyesque fight scenes, a sharp cast of British talent (John Hurt, Sinéad Cusack, Stephen Rea) and the pleasantly subversive fact that the adolescent son of our present prime minister, Euan Blair, was a runner for a film that

takes great pleasure in blowing up the Houses of Parliament. The letdown—
and I am sad to say it—is Portman herself, who continues to suffer under the
weight of a beauty so great it makes Audrey Hepburn look dowdy. Even her
bald-headed mug shot looks like a *Vogue* shoot. Compounding the problem is
the kind of English accent only ever found in Swiss finishing schools and the
offices of dialect coaches in Hollywood—and Long Island lingers in it still.
There is a film for this beautiful girl out there somewhere. I'm just not sure
what it is.

In the meantime, she throws a wrench in the works of V *for Vendetta* by
being both too feminine and too mild for a story that in book form was an
act of fury and lit a fire under the Thatcher-era kids who read it. Its message
was not "Blow up the Houses of Parliament" or "Wear a white mask and knife
people," for kids are not morons and understand what an allegory is. The message of V *for Vendetta* is "Change is possible." In its film form this is a truly
radical notion to be filed in the adolescent brain right next to the message of
the first *Matrix* movie: the world is other than it seems. If this film makes kids
think that way again, that'll be, like, totally awesome.

•

The premise of *Tsotsi* is terrific. A young thug from a South African township shoots a middle-class black woman in the stomach and drives off in
her car. A mile down the road he hears a baby crying in the backseat. The
audience gasps in that odd mixture of surprise and recognition that great
storytelling affords. Everything flows from this point with the inevitability
and moral didacticism of the Moses story. But the setting is fascinating; everything is news: the township shacks, the glamorous black middle class, the
tube station, the concrete rings in which orphaned children sleep out in the
open air. At the center is Tsotsi himself (Presley Chweneyagae), who needs no
mask to commit his acts of terror—his face is a mask. In a scene so menacing
it outpaces the deadliest moments of *Scarface* itself, he stalks a crippled man
through a train station, a beast on the hunt. Frantic local hip-hop, *kwaito*,
choreographs his frenetic impulse to violence; gospel swells as we glimpse
the possibility of redemption in a boy who seemed lost to all pity. I wept

throughout the last fifteen minutes. Unfortunately, unlike the woeful 50 Cent movie, this film—from which young black men could genuinely profit—will be seen by Ekow Eshun and nobody else. It will not sell for five quid on the Kilburn High Road, and no one will pass it around a playground.

TRANSAMERICA *AND* ROMANCE & CIGARETTES

Sometimes it's the little things that matter. Just before Humbert Humbert meets Mrs. Haze, the mother of the girl who will go on to obsess and destroy him, his gaze falls on "an old gray tennis ball that lay on an oak chest." This tennis ball has nothing whatsoever to do with the grand themes of *Lolita*—it "just is," and in this is beautiful. Many films attempt to master the art of the little moment, the unnecessary aside, the "just is" that makes the work human, and not merely a contrivance of art.

Transamerica is almost entirely contrived, desperately panting after the Oscars it did not, in the end, win—but hidden within its improbable plot and grotesqueries dressed up as humans, there is a policeman looking at the duty roster of the previous night and finding the crime for which a seventeen-year-old drug-using hustler has been locked up overnight: "This is a new one: apparently he shoplifted a frog." Neither the frog nor the incident is mentioned again, but I gift a whole extra star to this film for that line alone: it is a piece of human business that will stay with me long after many of the season's films have passed from my mind.

And what else? Well, like *Lolita*, *Transamerica* spends much of its time on the road traveling from East Coast to West in a beat-up car, passing tourist joints and freshwater lakes and pausing in roadside bars and motels. Two people who don't much like each other in New York get closer in Kentucky and learn to love each other in L.A. That one of these people is a pre-op male-to-female transsexual and the other is her son does not, in and of itself, rescue this film from an intense overfamiliarity. To watch this film go through its paces is a reminder that all cultures, no matter how alternative, petrify into cliché in the end. Part of this is in their desire for mainstream affirmation, which requires that they develop a "line" about their "issue" and not deviate from it.

From this film we divine that the present line on transgendered people is that they have a genetic disorder and not a psychological one, and therefore neither the script nor the audience is allowed even momentarily to consider the possibility that the operation Bree (Felicity Huffman) is about to undertake is anything other than a necessary and correct procedure. Nor are we allowed to wonder why, if transsexuality is (as a character puts it) "a radically evolved state of being," Bree wants to take this radical male/female doubleness and reduce it into a singularity. What if the "problem" is neither genetic nor psychological, but social? For what did "women trapped in a male body" do three hundred years ago? Maybe they expanded the social category of what it is to be male so that it was expansive enough to include the "female" traits they longed for.

Well, so I think privately—but I'd never say it in front of Bree, who is a film character in need of near-constant affirmation. For this she has an extraordinary therapist—possibly unique to American shores—whom she is encouraged to phone whenever she needs the equivalent of a therapeutic cheerleading session. "It hurts," says Bree. "That's what hearts do," says her therapist. "Let it out—this is good, this is so good."

But is it? It's finely acted by Felicity Huffman, who has exactly the careful, overstylized physical movements used by those who aspire to the feminine and feel they do not naturally possess it. She has her icky wardrobe of light pink separates and chiffon neckerchiefs, a Harry Belafonte basso and the prickly vulnerability of the permanently self-conscious. But around a bold performance shelter cardboard cutouts: a sassy old black woman and a wise Native American, an unsupportive Suburban Mom in an electric blue shell suit and a street-kid son (Kevin Zegers) who has gone off the rails.

When this son, Toby, attempts to make the road trip go faster by explaining how the subtext of *The Lord of the Rings* is "totally gay," I felt we were driving dangerously close to contemporary cliché land. When Bree took him to task for using the word *like* in every sentence, we'd made a camp in cliché land and bedded down for the night. The film thinks it brings cultural news, with its talk of "stealth" transsexuals who "walk amongst us," but really none of these characters walks among us—they haven't the imaginative breadth to survive in our world. They walk in another land, a mirror land through which Charlize Theron and Hilary Swank (two actresses the official publicity notes shamelessly compare to Huffman) have walked before, a place where the fact that the central female role is "unflattering" is considered a daring artistic act in and of itself.

If you are one of those people who, like me, found Hilary Swank better looking in *Boys Don't Cry* than she ever is on the red carpet, you too might find it surprising that we are meant to think Felicity Huffman's brown hair and lack of backless Versace dress a terrible deprivation. She has a handsome beauty that is not obscured in this film and a gift for characterization that deserves a better script. But Bree's journey was never intended to genuinely challenge ideas of female beauty or femininity itself or gender dysmorphia or the surgery now regularly practiced to "correct" it. It was meant to be a nice hook to hang a movie on. And so it is.

•

Romance & Cigarettes is the last film I am to review for this paper, and I had hopes that it would be the best. It is a musical—a form shamefully close to my heart—and has the most remarkable cast: James Gandolfini, Kate Winslet, Susan Sarandon, Christopher Walken and Steve Buscemi, to name half. When a respected actor-turned-writer-director such as John Turturro cashes in fifteen years' worth of art-house chips, the result is stellar. And so I can say nothing against any performance in this film—who could object to Winslet's luscious, humorous, genuinely sexy naturalism! Or malign Gandolfini's side glance of self-loathing that makes watching Tony Soprano as penetrating an emotional experience as watching Othello and King Lear combined! Christopher Walken is a madman and an anarchic delight, Susan Sarandon is still an obscenely attractive and intelligent performer and Steve Buscemi is the greatest addition to the character actor's art since Peter Lorre—fact is, he's better. But the play's the thing. John Turturro conceived this script while sitting at Barton Fink's desk pretending to be a writer. It is a real-life role he should have left alone. Turturro is, however, a very talented actor, and maybe this is why he has faith that actors alone can transform lines such as "You made your bed; now lie in it" and "I love you—maybe I don't know how to show it" and "Life doesn't give you second chances" and "His lips fill my dreams." And then there is the fact that a musical is an act of pure chutzpah. You can't do a half-assed musical, with people half singing, half lip-syncing, sort of dancing but sort of not. Good dancing is never shameful—it's awe inspiring. To watch Astaire is to gasp. It's bad, uncertain dancing that makes us cringe. No American musical in the past ten years (with the exception of *Chicago*) has had the courage of its convictions, and that's the whole problem. Ditch the irony and you're right back with awe, as Christopher Walken proved in that wonderful Spike Jonze music video of a few years back that revived the true spirit of the musical. Anyway, enough.

Thirteen

TEN NOTES ON OSCAR WEEKEND

1

Hollywood is vulgar. Every Englishman knows that. He knows it as he knows there is no comedy in Germany, as he knows that the Italians "get it right," if "it" includes food, marriage, weather and landscape but excludes governance, work, driving and God. David Hockney's aquamarine L.A. swimming pools strike the correct English attitude to Los Angeles: affectionate contempt for sparkling surfaces. La La Land! Red carpets; semisacred actors in an exclusive Valhalla; parties beyond imagination; jewels beyond price. Over Oscar weekend, an automatic journalism rehashes these eternal ideas, the accounts in newspapers precisely matching the tall tales of the cab driver who brings you in from the airport.

It's oddly oppressive to set off on a journey into a place so thoroughly imagined by other people. I have already in my dress bag the very picture of someone else's Hollywood dream, having made the mistake of telling the women in Bond Street that I am on a journalistic assignment to the Oscars. It is single strapped and red; a huge bow sits on its hip; it has a bustle, a train.

It is a dress that misunderstands Hollywood, its complex tiers of power and display, its careful politics and manners, which feel at times as intricate as any eighteenth-century France had to offer. On the plane my airplane steward approves, folding the bag carefully over his arm ("I can tell by the weight—it's fabulous") and hanging it reverentially in the little closet for which it is too long by a foot and a half.

2

A *New Yorker* cartoon: a delighted man in a bathtub is proclaiming "It's Oscar time—there's that special tingle in the air!" Meanwhile his wife is ironing in the kitchen, surrounded by cats. As you land in Hollywood, a strange inverse relation takes hold between involvement and anticipation: the more degrees removed a person is from the Oscars themselves, the more excited he or she is. Oscar-nominated directors sigh and speak wistfully of going instead to a ball game. The boys who valet park are putting bets on best actor. In the cab to the hotel the driver has this to say: "You gotta understand: when you can imagine that everyone around you has the same goal, one focus, that's a shared spirituality. It's beautiful!" My driver, like many in Hollywood, is a screenwriter. He has two scripts at the moment. The first is described as "a shoot-'em-up for the Xbox generation." The second concerns itself with a hypothetical meeting between the comedian Harpo Marx and the millionaire Armand Hammer. He has done his research and can prove that both men were in Hamburg in September of 1933.

"And you? You here for work?" Well, I'm assigned to write this piece and there is some, mild, talk of turning a book of mine into a screenplay. This is dismissed out of hand, correctly—the article is not yet written, the film is not made. This is not work. My driver can speak with real pity of some of the most famous actors in Hollywood for the simple reason that he or she has had no film releases so far this year. Success is success and is not mistaken for anything else. The town is bigger than any individual, even the superstars, and in that it is the exact opposite of vulgarity.

3

Friday afternoon at the Mondrian Hotel on Sunset Boulevard. The Mondrian is a true fantasy Hollywood hotel and this is evinced by the fact that few people in the industry choose to stay there. The front door crawls with photographers; the pool is surrounded by bougainvillea and blond bathing beauties; just below my room in the hotel's precipitous "sky bar"—from which you can look out over the whole of Hollywood—a DJ starts the party at six and keeps on going till three in the morning. The music is gangsta rap, played for a mostly white crowd who see in the "pimp" the model of smart business practice. The rooms are white, as are all the fittings; every sheet and chair and table and pillowcase, every vase, every flower in each vase. Actors screw up their faces in displeasure at the mention of the Mondrian: "It's a little bit too . . . *much* somehow."

Hollywood has many tiers. Sitting by the pool are hot girls in bikinis and their jock guys, ordering twenty-dollar cocktails and lobster maki rolls, watching the dreamy water of the Hockney pool lap at the edges of the terra-cotta tile surround. Nobody swims. A young black couple, dressed in the Versace knockoffs they believe appropriate to this scene, pose in a lounger and get a waitress to photograph them, living the dream. This is repeated several times that afternoon, by Italians, English, Australians. Everybody speaks of the Oscars, loudly. It's the only conversation in town. The hot girls check their watches and turn over. These girls create a Hollywood frisson by the pool, but they are quite different from actresses. Hot girls are perfect—actresses are not. Actresses are too short; their faces are lopsided, their noses askew. Actresses are charming. They are not tanned to a brown crisp; they do not wear sarongs with Gucci symbols on them. Their breasts are real, or else the work they have had done is of a tremendous subtlety. There is a depressing disconnect between these girls who wish to be actresses and what a successful Hollywood actress actually is. It is the strangest thing to sit by a fabulous L.A. pool in a fabulous hotel and understand that as far as Hollywood is concerned, these are the have-nots.

4

Friday night brings a private party in the hills. The house is in the prairie style of Frank Lloyd Wright; wide, low and elegantly extended. At the end of a wide vista of lawn lies a dimly lit swimming pool, a long thin rectangle cut out of plain white stone. Steam rises off the water. The many connecting doors are wide open: you can stand outside the bathroom and see right through the building to the garden, two hundred feet away. Freshly cut purple poppies are in their simple stone vases. Saul Steinberg is on the walls. Everyone is cold—even for the desert, this is a chilly night. People gather under heat lamps and squeeze four to a bench, keeping close for warmth. It is an effort to be continually amazed; these are humans, after all, and in a celebrity party without any press, the celebrity aspect fades, having nothing to contrast with. After passing through the shock of their normal human scale and all that Photoshop obscures—smallness, wrinkles, slightly smeared mascara—you are left with something like a golden wedding anniversary party at which no one can identify the happy couple. The young actors goof off, tease their elders, threaten to play the piano. Elder statesmen greet one another with respectful formality, listing one another's achievements, discussing future projects. The nominees are, by now, battle-scarred companions—they've been through half a dozen award shows since January. People drink little and eat less. Music plays and an infamous wild-child starlet tries to encourage dancing but gets no takers. The atmosphere is civilized to the point of suffocation. In two aspects it is reminiscent of a party in a university town. First, it is entirely self-referential. People talk about Hollywood in Hollywood as they speak of Harvard at Harvard. Second, there is a great fear of the ridiculous. People take care not to say anything that might make them look foolish. This fear manifests itself in a strange impulse to narrate events as they happen and thereby hold fast to a shared understanding of their meaning. Jokes are met not with laughter but with the statement "That's hilarious. That is *so* funny." Interesting or risqué anecdotes are neutralized by saying "That is darling. She's *completely* darling." People are friendly, polite, but never frivolous. Joan Didion, a West Coast believer but a Hollywood skeptic, has the last word on such events: "Flirtations between men and women, like drinks after dinner, remain largely the luxury of character actors out from New York, one-shot-writers . . . and others who do not understand the *mise* of the local *scene*."

5

At about one in the morning, the young waiters, who have worked discreetly all night, now begin to approach: "I just wanted to say, I really dig your work. I think you're totally amazing. Good luck on Sunday!" The actors, caught midway through conversations about their families, their dogs, a book they've read, a good restaurant in New York, now have to put their game face back on and become whoever it is the waiter thinks they are. They do this, for the most part, graciously. Confronted with such an embarrassment of riches, each waiter has chosen his virtual intimate to harass—that special actor who made him cry in the cinema, the singer whose tunes he plays when he clocks off work.

Outside the party the paparazzi have arrived. They do not have to chase anybody—there is nowhere to run. We are on a dark hillside in the middle of night. "And what would happen," asks a rueful young director, "if an actor just stood out there all night? Took a photo from every possible angle, naked, told them every last thing they wanted to know. Would that be it? Would they be finished then?" It's a long process; the huddle under heat lamps, the wait for cars. The actors themselves are relaxed about both the wait and the photographers outside; it's their drivers who are anxious and defensive, projecting desires onto their charges that don't seem to be there: "Can I get this guy out of the way for you? Shall I move him out of your face?" An actor goes out into the scrum and then comes back a minute later. "They don't recognize me—I got fat for a role and now they don't recognize me. I'm fasting now. Eight days so far." To which comes the reply, "Me too! I just did five. Isn't it *great!*"

6

A few of the nominees adjourn to Canter's, a sprawling Jewish diner where you can get good chicken soup at two in the morning. I order one such soup with a matzo ball the size of my fist swimming in the center. The nominees order a plate of pickles and corned beef sandwiches; they drink beer and joke with a gang of teenage girls behind them. They talk about an actor's distant family connection to the poet Wordsworth, about Hollywood, the house prices in Brooklyn and who has the largest fry on their plate. How to explain the fact that the same kinds of kids who on Sunday will scream their lungs out on the bleachers outside the Kodak Theatre are, right now, at two in the morning in Canter's, sitting perfectly calmly while several globally famous actors eat home fries in the booth right next to them?

7

On morning TV, some of the human beings from the night before are being described in Olympian terms by a pretty girl with a microphone. The detail is obsessive and alienating: what they might wear, eat and drink this coming Sunday is carefully itemized and salivated over; how they exercise, what they think about, whom they kiss, how they speak, where they go. The answers to these questions are all different, but one truth reigns: they are other. In relation to them, the only correct position is incomprehending awe. One cannot imagine their world, their ways.

I take my laptop out in an attempt to work by the water. A hot girl is loudly telling another hot girl that "*Brokeback* is so fucking awesome," which is the consensus of the town, though little satisfaction can be drawn from this. That *Brokeback*, *Capote* and *Crash* are fucking awesome is neither here nor there for Hollywood: these films were all privately funded. This pool, like every pool in town, is now more frequently visited by excited young writers with laptops who have been cheered by the year's "maverick" wave. This is the time for telling the world how Harpo Marx met Armand Hammer. Up in the hills the mood is less joyous. Strung up all over town are giant posters for Paramount's new romantic comedy *Failure To Launch*, which is exactly the kind of underperforming, studio-made film that is causing the problem. These posters, with their airbrushed, smiling stars, flutter above the highway like the standards of a king who has been deposed, at least for this weekend.

8

Brunch with the nominated writers. Like everybody else, I have my Hollywood fantasy, and this it: a 1920s Spanish-style villa with original Mexican red and blue tiles in the fountain, with a living room Jimmy Stewart may have sat in once. It's next to a golf course; every few years a ball breaks a window. The weather is darling: eggs and bacon and omelets are served in the courtyard. Being with writers instead of actors is like sitting in the pits instead of in the gods—one can speak freely, without fear. This is not their lives, but only an interlude. They make sure to tell you how they have kept their Manhattan apartments. Occasionally you meet a delusional Hollywood screenwriter who believes that without people like him there would be no movie business at all. Factually, of course, this is true—but it is delusional to draw any real conclusions from it. Scripts will be written, if need be, by fifteen people and the producer, or one million monkeys and a typewriter. Most screenwriters understand this and are wry about their Hollywood interludes. They are full of warnings and horror stories. "Do a first draft, but don't touch it after that—unless you want your heart broken." Or, alternatively, "Do the final polish, but that's it. You'll never write another novel if you get in too deep." One writer nods and smiles encouragingly as some structural plans are outlined. "That's very nice. But it doesn't mean shit once an actor gets hold of it." There is a campy relish for the Hollywood experience among the writers that is inaccessible to the "front-of-house" actors, who must live every day with the fantasies that are pressed upon them. "I weigh myself four times daily!" a man screeches, laughing as he says it. His companion wants to know if he has ever found that he weighs something different by the end of the day than he did at the start.

"Frequently!"

9

Oscar morning arrives and it is impossible not to succumb to the thrill of the thing. A man comes to do my makeup. Here is his assessment of my dress: "If you were collecting the all-time queen of Hollywood lifetime achievement award, you would be overdressed." A cocktail dress is substituted. At four o'clock in the afternoon, I get in a car and pick up two writers who are writing a film that actually has a shot at getting made. We are going to the *Vanity Fair* dinner at Morton's to watch the ceremony on video screens, eat some great tuna and then wait for everybody to leave the Kodak Theatre and join us. The Oscar ceremony most resembles Christmas in its sense of anticlimax. Everyone was so excited earlier; now they are subdued, and grow more subdued as prizes are won and the potential web of alternative futures gets smaller and smaller, until there are only the people who won and everyone else who didn't. There is a chorus of "Well, that's just *hilarious*" from every table as the Oscar host makes his jokes, although few people actually laugh, and everyone is made tense by occasional jibes against individuals, studios or Hollywood itself. When it is over people seem relieved. The consensus is that it wasn't as bad as it might have been. One girl text messages through the entire event.

And then they come. We are told to vacate our tables and walk forward, where we will find Morton's magically extended by the addition of a huge tarpaulin tent. At the mouth of the tent, the same TV girl with the microphone interviews the stars as they appear. Her MO is extreme naïveté: "What goes *on* in there?" she keeps asking, although she is as famous as many of the people inside and will soon join the party. "Can you just give us *some idea* of what kind of thing happens at a party like this?" Most of the invitees are at a loss to answer this question. An action star thinks about it and then indulges her: "It's like Vegas: what goes on in there stays in there." But "in there" there is only a charming, if tame, cocktail party, with a good deal of free booze and stilted conversation and a Porta-Potty. Everywhere people are trying to get introduced to other people, and feel glad when they are. These are melancholy victories, though. At a normal party we befriend people with the hope of seeing them again, of having a friendship, even a love affair. A "celebrity" encounter is more like a badge to be collected and then shown to other people. A whole night of collecting such badges grows demoralizing. You begin to understand the angry people you meet in Hollywood, who by choice or necessity regularly submit themselves to these one-way charm offensives, speaking with other human beings whom the world believes to be more than that. Yet there are people who seem to enjoy it; who work the room collecting all the badges and have no time to waste. At this party, a very short man who had been talking to a star and then, through a subtle shift in the circle, got stuck with me, actually asked to be released from his bondage. "Is it okay if I talk to someone else over there?"

This party is fun, all are beautiful, except for the old men who are powerful. People are drinking, finally, and the room is full of indiscreet conversation, much of it about where people will go next. Are you following the rappers with the thirty-thousand-dollar grills on their teeth and their newest accessory—a gold statuette in the palm? Or are you following the Frenchmen holding plush toy penguins above their heads? Committed badge collectors follow the whisper of the hope of an invitation up into the Hollywood Hills, in someone else's car, with no clear idea of how they will get home.

Outside Morton's, waiting for my car back to the hotel, I meet an old actor, a favorite of the late John Cassavetes, smoking a cigar and explaining how things are with him. "He chose me, you see?" he says of Cassavetes. "Me. It was a thing to be chosen by him, I can tell you that." He is full of soul, and his eyes are rheumy and beautiful. "This town's treated me well. I was never a star, no one knows my name, but I always worked, and now it's given me a retirement plan. I'm the old dude in any movie you care to mention. Make nine or ten a year." He smiled joyfully. We stood together on the forecourt with a lot of other people less joyful: losing nominees, yesterday's news, TV stars, hungry models and people so famous they couldn't get to their car without causing a riot. Of all the fantasies and dreams people have of a life in Hollywood, it seemed odd that no one had thought to dream a career like the one just described.

10

The next day I woke at eight. In the name of research I watched an hour of fantasy television about the Oscars that in no way described the evening I had just had. I went back to sleep and woke at eleven. I checked out and dragged my hangover and my laptop down to the pool. It was empty. I ordered a quesadilla, but the speedy service that had been in place only yesterday had vanished. It took half an hour to get some Tabasco sauce. And then it began to rain, softly at first and then dramatically. I moved in under the glass roof and thought of nearby San Fernando Valley, where the American porn industry—a fantasy industry even larger and more remunerative than Hollywood—is located. The pool boys packed up the loungers around me. The rain drummed the surface of the pool and forced water over its edge, soaking the feet of the waitresses as they cleared the tables.

I packed up myself and went outside to wait for a cab. Three New York hipster kids ran into the hotel with their coats above their heads, one of them complaining: "It's not supposed to *rain!*" The dream persists, even as reality asserts itself. I looked to my right and for the first time that weekend spotted someone I actually knew: Bret Easton Ellis. He asked what I was doing in L.A. and I told him. I asked what he was doing, and he looked at me with a kind of beatific insanity, as if he didn't quite believe what he was about to say: "I'm moving back to L.A.!" I wanted to a share a novelist's joke with him: what if you got assigned to write about the Oscars and you didn't mention a single actor? You know, as a kind of demystifying strategy? How about that? But he had to get in his car. Anyway, Bret's been there, done that: his own *Glamorama* tried another demystifying strategy, with fifty celebrities name-dropped in the first five pages. But the fantasies of fame cannot be dislodged by anyone's pen. It'll have to be a collective effort; we'll have to wake from this dream together. It'll be darling.

FEELING

Fourteen

SMITH FAMILY CHRISTMAS

This is a picture of my father and me, Christmas 1980 or thereabouts.
Across his chest and my bottom there is the faint pink, inverted water-
mark of postal instructions—something about a card, and then "stamp here."
Hanging from the tree like a decoration more mirror writing, this time from
my own pen. Does it say *Nothing?* Or maybe *Letting?* I've ruined this photo. I
don't understand why I can't take better care of things like this. It's an original, I have no negative, yet I allowed it to sit for months in a pile of mail on
my open windowsill. Finally the photo got soaked, imprinted with the text
of phone bills and Post-it notes. I felt sick wedging it inside my *OED* to stop
the curling. But I also felt the weird relief that comes from knowing that the

inevitable destruction of precious things, though done in your house, was not done by your hand. Christmas, childhood, the past, families, fathers, regret of all kinds—no one wants to be the grinch who steals these things, but you leave the door open with the hope he might come in and relieve you of your heavy stuff. Christmas is heavy.

Anyway, it's done now. And this is me and my dad one Christmas past. I'm five and he's too old to have a five-year-old. At the time, the Smiths lived in London in a half-English, half-Irish council estate called Athelstan Gardens, one black family squished between two tribes at war. It was confusing. I didn't understand why certain football games made people pour into Biddy Mulligan's pub and hit other people over the head with chairs and bottles, and I didn't get the thing about people pouring into the Prince Charles the next day and repeating the procedure. I didn't get the men who came around collecting for the IRA on Christmas Eve, and I didn't have to give them anything either—once they saw my mum, with her exotic shift dress and her cornrows, they respectfully withdrew, thinking we had nothing to do with their particular argument. In fact, my parents were friends with an Irishman who gave us a homemade fruit bowl this same Christmas and then the following winter betrayed the spirit of Christmas by making a different kind of homemade gift with which he tried to blow up No. 11 Downing Street. We knew nothing about the bomb until years later, but we all knew about the ugly fruit bowl, ceramic and swirly and unable to stand straight on a table-top. This was filled with nuts and laid on the carpet to limit the wobble. It's out of the frame in this photo, on the floor by Dad's feet. My brother Ben, a little fat thing back then, has it between his legs like Buddha with his lotus flower. Ben was always on food detail in the war that is Christmas. I did, or overdid, the decorations (as you will note, the tree is bending to the left under the weight of manga-eyed reindeer, chocolate Santas, swollen baubles, tin-sel, three sets of lights and the presents I tastefully nestled in the branches). Dad cooked. Mum marked out television schedules with a pen. Ben ate the food. Just as Joseph tended to the Virgin Mary, we tended to Ben, making his comfort our first priority. He ate what he needed, and whatever was left we ate. I think it's Carole King's *Tapestry* on the record player. But which song? "It's Too Late" would make thematic sense—my dad's smile has the let's-just-get-through-this tension of a code-red marriage. As for the "Natural Woman" Christmas or the "You've Got a Friend" Christmas—these predate my consciousness. But they must have existed, what with Ben being a September baby and me October. Those were the sexy Noels, delivering babies like presents nine months later. By contrast, Luke, my youngest brother, came in July and is still unborn in this photo. I've always assumed he was the result of a we-haven't-had-sex-in-five-years birthday treat (Dad's birthday is in late September), and by the time he turned up, *Blood on the Tracks* had replaced *Tapestry* as the family Christmas soundtrack. Maybe you wonder about the black man in the pink hat. I wonder about him, too. I think he's an uncle of mine by the name of Denzil (spelling uncertain). My mother claims an uncertain number of siblings, certainly more than twenty, most of them—in the Jamaican parlance—"outdoor children," meaning same father, different mother. Denzil must have been one of these, because he was six foot seven, whereas my mother is five foot five and shrinking, as I'm sure I will, and as my grandmother did before us.

This Christmas was the only time we ever met each other, Denzil and I. He was the gift that kept on giving, with his strange patois and his huge feet and the piggyback rides he conducted out on the balcony because the ceilings were too low. Outside was where he wanted to be anyway—you can tell that much from the look of infinite weariness he's giving my dad's left elbow. Poor Denzil; off the plane from Jamaica into bitter England, and stuck in the most cultish, insular day in the nuclear-family calendar. Families speak in semaphore at Christmas; the falcons are the only ones to understand the falconer, and something dismal is slouching toward Bethlehem. It's called *The Truth About What Happens to Your Family When No Member Is Allowed to Leave the House.* Outsiders do best if they seeketh neither enlightenment nor the remote control.

Denzil found this out when he attempted, on this most sacred of days, to do the things we could not do because we'd always done them another way, our way—a way we all hated, to be sure, but could not change. Denzil wants to open a present on Christmas Eve—don't do that, Denzil. Denzil wants to go for a walk—I'm so sorry, Denzil, that's impossible. We'd like to, but we just can't swing it. Why not? Because, Denzil. Just because. Because like the two parts of Ireland, because like the Holy Trinity, because like nuclear proliferation, like men not wearing skirts, because like brandy butter.

Because that's the way we do things around here, Denzil. We don't eat till four o'clock, we open the smallest presents first, we have to watch two MGM musicals when we wake up, followed by a Jimmy Stewart movie, and then settle down in front of a feted sitcom's "Christmas special," which is also the time—read my lips—when we begin the search for batteries to go into the many things we have bought that require batteries we forgot to buy. Don't mess with us on this, Denzil. The Smiths are not for turning. It's our way or the highway. We want Christmas, dead or alive.

I make it sound bad. In truth, we had great times. As great as anybody's. Certainly better than Denzil's the year he got his own place and phoned us to say he'd killed a partridge in the backyard with a slingshot and just finished eating it like a proper English gentleman (it was a London pigeon, of course). Oh, we Smiths are ardent seekers after the spirit of Christmas, and we do not listen to Iris Murdoch's sensible analogical advice: "Good represents the reality of which God is the dream." We're chasing the dream, baby.

But we do sense the more difficult truth: that Family represents the reality of which Christmas is the dream. It is, of course, Family (messy, complex, miserable, happy, so many gradations of those last two words) that is the real gift, beneath the wrapping. Family is the daily miracle, and Christmas is the enforcement of ideals that, in truth, do not matter. It would be tempting therefore to say, "Well, then ditch Christmas!" the same way people say "Ditch God" or "Ditch marriage," but people find it hard to do these things because they feel that there is more than a ghost in these machines; there is an animating spirit.

Santa help me, but I believe this, too. You know you believe it when you start your own little family with some person you met four years ago in a bar, and then he tries to open the presents on Christmas Eve because that's what he did in his family and you have the strong urge to run screaming from the building holding your banner about the end and how it is nigh. It is a moving

and comic thing—a Murdochian scuffle between the Real and the Dream—
to watch a young couple as they teeter around the Idea of Christmas, trying
to avoid internecine festive warfare.

Of course, sometimes the angel of history gets the better of you; one part
of your family simply secedes from the other. When my parents divorced,
seven years after this photo, the Christmas war became briefly more violent
(which day, which house, which parent) and then grew subdued, because
peace is what you want, in the end, at Christmas. On that one day you value
it more than your life. Nowadays, we all get into a car with presents in the
trunk, quietly drive to my father's in Felixstowe, where two people divorced
fifteen years ago rediscover that cycle whereby "It's Too Late" doubles back
onto itself and becomes "You've Got a Friend." It's called a cease-fire.

Then, last year, out of nowhere hostilities resumed. Not with my dad, who
is beyond such things now, but between mother and brood. That ancient
battle poor Denzil couldn't understand, the one about not bloody leaving the
house on Christmas Eve, which is the one day you're meant to spend with
your bloody family, the one day your mother asks for a little quality time, et
cetera, hit the house like a grenade, and everybody yelled a lot and walked out
and I spent Christmas Eve sleeping in my friend Adam's bath.

I see now the mistake we made. We thought that because we'd reached
adulthood, Mum wouldn't mind if we ditched Christmas—the ritual, the
dream, the animating spirit, the whole shebang—and just paraded around
town at nightclubs and other people's dinner parties as if we were individuals
living in the free world. Don't ever think that. Where women are concerned
(mothers especially), Zora Neale Hurston had it right: the dream is the truth.
After all, for 364 days of the year you live in the Real. Your mother is asking
you only for this one day. It's nothing, it says on my photo, nothing but letting; it's about letting Christmas in, letting go of that Kantian will of yours,
getting freaky like Iris, giving it up to a beautiful, insane, mystical idea. So
you damaged the photo of Christmas Past—well, let's try it again: Christmas
Present, Christmas Future. "War is over, if you want it," sang John and Yoko.
So let it happen.

Fifteen

ACCIDENTAL HERO

On the sixtieth anniversary of the end of World War II, the BBC asked members of the public to submit their personal war stories. These were to be placed online as a historical resource. I helped my father to write his account and then, using the material I had gathered, expanded it into a newspaper article, of which this is a revised version.

I knew my father had "stormed the beach at Normandy." I knew nobody else's father had—that job had been wisely left to their grandfathers. That's all I knew. As a child, the mildewed war came to me piecemeal through the usual sources, very rarely from him. Harvey never spoke about it as a personal reality, and the truth was I didn't think of it as a reality, but only as one of many fictional details woven into the fabric of my childhood: Jane Eyre was sent to the red room, Lucy Pevensie met Mr. Tumnus, Harvey Smith stormed the beach at Normandy. Later, in my twenties, small facts escaped, mostly concerning his year spent in Germany helping with the reconstruction. But Normandy stayed as fictional to me as Narnia. "Stormed!"—this made no sense. A sentimental man, physically gentle, pacifistic in all things and possessed of a liberal heart that does not so much bleed as hemorrhage. It is perfectly normal to phone my father around 6:30 in the evening and find him distraught, reduced to tears by watching the news.

Then one recent adult summer, I happened to find myself in Normandy, visiting an American poet. She was writing a verse sequence about the layers of social history in the area and took me on a day trip to the beach, where we swam and sat in the sun. It was stupidly late into my swim before it occurred to me that this might be the beach Harvey had landed upon, fifty-nine years earlier. I mentioned it to the poet, and she asked after details I was shamed to admit I didn't have. Our day turned historical. She showed me Juno Beach, the cliffs in which the snipers crouched, the maze of hedgerows that proved so lethal. Finally, the American cemetery. Thousands upon thousands of squat white crosses, punctuated by the Star of David, line up in rows on the manicured grass. You can't see the end of it. I'm my father's daughter: I burst into tears.

I returned home, full of journalistic zeal. I bought a Dictaphone. This seemed like half the job done already. I was the gutsy truth seeker, uncovering the poignant war story of a man who found it all too painful to talk about. Except I found my father not especially resistant to the idea. True, he had never really spoken about it—then again, I had never really asked. He laid out a fish lunch in his garden in Felixstowe and carefully set up the microphone on its little stand.

"It's funny you mention it, actually." Why was it funny? "Well, I've been thinking a bit about it, what with the anniversary. It's only now that I've started thinking: I would like my lost service medals back . . . you know, for next year. Just be nice, wouldn't it." But why didn't you ask for them back, years ago? "Well . . . they charge you for them, don't they," said Harvey doubtfully, and returned to filleting his grilled sole.

A struggle my father has always had: between hating war and having been in one, between being committed to, as he puts it, the future, and at the same time not wanting to be entirely forgotten. I think he was surprised, at this late hour, to find he wanted his medals back. I was surprised I wanted to see them. A kindly veteran who lives opposite helped us send off the necessary paperwork. When the medals arrived, I came up to Felixstowe and we sat about staring at them. These moon rocks laid out on the kitchen table.

●

I was a bad journalist to my father, short-tempered, bullying. He never said what I wanted him to. Each week we struggled as I tried to force his story into my mold—territory previously covered by *Saving Private Ryan* or *The Great Escape*—and he tried to stop me. He only wanted to explain what had happened to him. And his war, as he sees it, was an accidental thing, ambivalent, unplanned, an ordinary man's experience of extremity. It's not Private Ryan's war or Steve McQueen's war or Bert Scaife's war (of whom more later). It's Harvey Smith's war. If it embodies anything (Harvey's not much into things embodying other things), it is the fact that when wars are fought, perfectly normal people fight them. Alongside the heroes and martyrs, sergeants and generals, there are the millions of average young people who simply tumble into it, their childhood barely behind them. Harvey was one of those. A working-class lad from East Croydon at a loose end. At seventeen, he was still too young to be drafted, but when he passed the recruiting office on the high street, he went inside. They took his details and told him he'd be called up when he was seventeen and six months. "Made me feel a little bit special— and when you're a teenager, that's what you want, isn't it?" In November 1943 initial training was completed. They moved to Suffolk, where Harvey joined the 6th Assault Regiment RE and was mobilized the week after Christmas. "That meant our unit were officially at war. I think that's right. It meant that they could shoot you if you deserted, or something."

There followed six months of regimental training and tank training, how to ride in one, how to sleep under one, how to service it when it broke down. Harvey was still not expecting to see action before 1945. You had to be nineteen. When the rest of the unit moved to Calshott, he went to Felixstowe. (He ended up there once again, in the late 1990s, after his second divorce. Sometimes he refers to his life's journey as "the round-trip.")

"I was with the old buggers, like Dad's army. But I was only there three weeks. The law changed; suddenly you could be eighteen. So that was me."

Harvey's war was on. He spent that last month hiding in the Fawley woods with his regiment. You can't see the stars like that in Croydon. On June 3, he listened to the final briefing with the rest of his regiment. "That's when they told us the truth, where we were going, King Beach, and when. I was hoping to be in one of the tanks. But last minute, I was assigned to be the radio man for the CO's truck. All the boys thought that was pretty funny. Me stuck alone with the CO."

On the fifth of June at about 11 P.M., they set off. They were meant to land on the morning of the fifth, but the conditions had been too dreadful. They were still dreadful—everybody was sick. In the middle of the crossing, Harvey saw his first British warship, a huge shadowed beast, moving through the water. As he watched, it shot off a broadside from its sixteen-inch guns, rocking sideways in the recoil. "I knew then. I hadn't known before. I knew this was serious."

It was not to be as serious for Harvey as it had already been for thousands. He didn't land at 6 A.M., he didn't land in a tank (many of these had grenades thrown into them and "brewed up," exploding from the inside) and he didn't land as an American at Omaha. Though he didn't know it, already he was steeped in luck. He approached the relatively quiet King Beach at midday and waited while his CO argued with an American general onboard who was convinced it was too dangerous to land. It was two hours before he drove onto the beach. So much experience that should be parceled out, tenderly, over years, came to my father that day, concertinaed into twenty-four hours. First time he'd left England. First time he'd been at sea. First time he'd seen a dead body.

"I was looking out from the back of the truck. Young dead Germans were everywhere. They looked like us; they could have *been* us. It was gruesome. And we'd heard by then that Major Elphinstone, our major, had died the minute he hit the beach. He stuck his head out of the tank to look about and—pop—a sniper shot him in the face. But you must write that I had an easy day. I had absolutely an easy day. The work had been done, you see. It'd been done. I wasn't like Bert Scaife."

Who?

"He was this bloke, he was a legend by the end of the day—caught so many men, shot all these mortars off—he got decorated later. I was no Bert Scaife. Not by a long way."

Harvey's truck rode up the lanes, unharmed. There were dugouts everywhere and people shooting at him, but with the help of the radio and excellent information, they made it safely through the worst. They stopped at a monastery that had been commandeered by the Nazis and now stood abandoned. There was a dead man in Nazi uniform lying in the hallway. My father bent down to turn him over and would have joined him in oblivion if it hadn't been for his CO stopping his hand just in time. The body was booby-trapped. Coiled within it, my future, and that of my brothers, and the future of our future children, and so on, into unthinkability.

He slept that night in a fragrant orchard. And what else? "Well, I stopped in Bayeux a bit after that. Bought a pen." At this point, my patience with my father bottomed out. He looked at me helplessly. "It's so hard to remember. . . . I only remember the obscure stuff."

So now I started playing hardball; now I picked the Dictaphone up and demanded to know about the shrapnel, for Harvey has some shrapnel in his groin, I know he does, and he knows I know. A doctor found it in a routine X-ray in 1991, forty-seven years after Harvey thought it had been removed. I was sixteen at the time, EMF had a hit with "Unbelievable" and I was wearing harem pants. If he'd come home and told me he'd been a waiter on the *Titanic* it couldn't have seemed more fantastical.

"Oh, that was different. That was just after I bought the pen."

●

A few days after the pen incident, then, my father was again in an orchard in the middle of the night. He decided to make tea, the way you did during the war, by filling a biscuit tin full of sand and a little petrol and setting that alight. He shouldn't have done that. The flames were spotted and a mortar bomb sent over. He doesn't know how many men died. Maybe two, maybe three. I leaned forward and turned up the volume. For hadn't I brought this little contraption here for my own purposes? Not to record my father's history, and not even to write this article, but *precisely for this revelation*, for this very moment or another like it; in the hope of catching a painful war secret, in the queer belief that such a thing would lead to some epiphanic shift in my relationship with my father. There is such a vanity in each succeeding generation—we think we can free our parents from experience, that we will be their talking cure, that we are the catharsis they need. I said, But, Dad, it was a simple mistake. We all make so many at the same age, but in a normal situation, they can't lead to anybody's dying. I put my hand on his hand. "But it was my fault." "Of course it wasn't. It was a mistake." "Yes, yes," said Harvey, humoring me, crying quietly, "if that's how you want to say it."

He woke up on a stretcher in a truck, two dead Germans either side of him, picked up from some other incident. That was the end of his war for a few weeks while he recuperated in England. When he went back, in the final months of the war, he did some remarkable things. He caught a senior Nazi, an episode I turned into idiotic comedy for a novel. He helped liberate Belsen. But it's those weeks in Normandy that are most significant to him. The mistakes he made, the things he didn't do, how lucky he was. To finish up, I asked him if he thought he was brave in Normandy.

"I wasn't brave! I wasn't asked to be brave. . . . I wasn't Bert Scaife! I wasn't *individually* brave; that's how you should say it for the paper." Is that why he never spoke about it? "Not really. . . . I s'pose when you realized you were playing your part in killing ordinary people, well, it's an awful thing to think about . . . and then, well, I spent a year in Germany after the war, you see, working for the army and making friends with ordinary Germans. I almost married a German girl, from the country, with a strong jaw. Lovely girl. And in her house there was a photo of her brother, in a Nazi uniform, about eighteen. He wasn't coming home. And my mate who came to visit her with me, he turned the photo to the wall. But I said no. These were just country people. There was so much evil in that war. And then they were just people like that, simple people."

That's the end of our interview on the tape. Afterward, he phoned me up several times to reiterate one point. He wasn't brave. I said, okay, Dad, yes, I've got that bit.

During one of these conversations, I revised my earlier question to him. If he wasn't brave, is he at least proud? "Not really. If I'd been one of the medicos on beach. Or done something like Bert Scaife did, then I'd be proud, I suppose. But I didn't."

Harvey Smith is not Bert Scaife—he wants me to make that very clear to you. When he caught that senior Nazi, his fellow soldiers wanted to kill the man. It was my father who persuaded them to settle for a lesser punishment: he set the Nazi walking in front of their tank for five miles before handing him over to the authorities. It is characteristic of Harvey that he was somewhat ashamed to tell me that story. He feels he behaved cruelly.

In sum, Harvey thinks pride a pale virtue. To his mind, an individual act either helps a little or it does not, and to be proud of it afterward helps nobody much, changes nothing. Still, I am proud of him. In the first version of this article, I wrote here: "He was a man able to retain his humanity in the most inhumane of circumstances." Later I scratched it out because *humanity* is these days a vainglorious, much debased word and *inhumanity* is a deceitful one. My generation was raised with the idea that those who pride themselves on their humanity are perfectly capable of atrocity. I think I'll put instead: he didn't lose himself in horror. Which is a special way of being brave, of being courageous, and a quality my father shares with millions of ordinary men and women who fought that miserable war.

Sixteen

DEAD MAN LAUGHING

My father had few enthusiasms, but he loved comedy. He was a comedy nerd, though this is so common a condition in Britain as to be almost not worth mentioning. Like most Britons, Harvey gathered his family around the defunct hearth each night to watch the same half-hour comic situations repeatedly, in reruns and on video. We knew the "Dead Parrot" sketch by heart. We had the usual religious feeling for *Monty Python's Life of Brian*. If we were notable in any way, it was not in kind but in extent. In our wood-cabinet music center, comedy records outnumbered the Beatles. The Goons' "I'm Walking Backwards for Christmas" got an airing all year long. We liked to think of ourselves as particular, on guard against slapstick's easy laughs—Benny Hill was beneath our collective consideration. I suppose the more precise term is "comedy snobs."

Left unchecked, comedy snobbery can squeeze the joy out of the enterprise. You end up thinking of comedy as Hemingway thought of narrative: structured like an iceberg, with all the greater satisfactions fathoms underwater, while the surface pleasure of the joke is somehow the least of it. In my father, this tendency was especially pronounced. He objected to joke merchants. He was wary

of the revue-style bonhomie of the popular TV double act Morecambe and
Wise and disapproved of the cheery bawdiness of their rivals, the Two Ronnies. He was allergic to racial and sexual humor, to a far greater degree than
any of the actual black people or women in his immediate family. Harvey's
idea of a good time was the BBC sitcom *Steptoe and Son*, the grim tale of two
mutually antagonistic "rag-and-bone" men who pass their days in a Beckettian
pile of rubbish, tearing psychological strips off each other. Each episode ends
with the son (a philosopher manqué, who considers himself trapped in the
filthy family business) submitting to a funk of existential despair. The sadder
and more desolate the comedy, the better Harvey liked it.

His favorite was Tony Hancock, a comic wedded to despair, in his life as
much as in his work. (Hancock died of an overdose in 1968.) Harvey had him
on vinyl: a pristine, twenty-year-old set of LPs. The series was *Hancock's Half
Hour*, a situation comedy in which Hancock plays a broad version of himself
and, to my mind, of my father: a quintessentially English, poorly educated,
working-class war veteran with social and intellectual aspirations, whose fictional address—23 Railway Cuttings, East Cheam—perfectly conjures the
aspirant bleakness of London's suburbs (as if Cheam were significant enough
a spot to have an East). Harvey, meanwhile, could be found in 24 Athelstan
Gardens, Willesden Green (a poky housing estate named after the ancient
king of England), also by a railway. Hancock's heartbreaking inability to pass
as a middle-class beatnik or otherwise pull himself out of the hole he was
born in was a source of great mirth to Harvey, despite the fact that this was
precisely his own situation. He loved Hancock's hopefulness, and loved the
way he was always disappointed. He passed this love on to his children, with
the result that we inherited the comic tastes of a previous generation. (Born
in 1925, Harvey was old enough to be our grandfather.) Occasionally, I'd lure
friends to my room and make them listen to "The Blood Donor" or "The
Radio Ham." This never went well. I demanded complete silence, was in the
habit of lifting the stylus and replaying a section if any incidental noise should
muffle a line and generally leached all potential pleasure from the exercise
with laborious explanations of the humor and said humor's possible obfus-

cation by period details: ration books, shillings and farthings, coins for the meter, and so on. It was a hard sell in the brave new comedic world of *The Jerk* and *Beverly Hills Cop* and *Ghostbusters*.

Hancock wasn't such an anachronism, as it turns out. Genealogically speaking, Harvey had his finger on the pulse of British comedy, for Hancock begot Basil Fawlty, and Fawlty begot Alan Partridge, and Partridge begot the immortal David Brent. And Hancock and his descendants served as a constant source of conversation between my father and me, a vital link between us when, classwise, and in every other wise, each year placed us further apart. As in many British families, it was university wot dunnit. When I returned home from my first term at Cambridge, we couldn't discuss the things I'd learned; about *Anna Karenina*, or G. E. Moore, or Gawain and his staggeringly boring Green Knight, because Harvey had never learned them—but we could always speak of Basil. It was a conversation that lasted decades, well beyond the twelve episodes in which Basil himself is contained. The episodes were merely jumping-off points; we carried on compulsively creating Basil long after his authors had stopped. Great situation comedy expands in the imagination. For my generation, never having seen David Brent's apartment in *The Office* is no obstacle to conjuring up his interior decoration: the risqué Athena poster, the gigantic entertainment system, the comical fridge magnets. Similarly, for my father, imagining Basil Fawlty's school career was a creative exercise. "He would have failed his eleven-plus," Harvey once explained to me. "And that would've been the start of the trouble." When meditating on the sitcom, you extrapolate from the details, which in Britain are almost always signifiers of social class: Hancock's battered homburg, Fawlty's cravat, Partridge's driving gloves, Brent's fake Italian suits. It's a relief to be able to laugh at these things. In British comedy, the painful class dividers of real life are neutralized and exposed. In my family, at least, it was a way of talking about things we didn't want to talk about.

When Harvey was very ill, in the autumn of 2006, I went to visit him at a nursing home in the seaside town of Felixstowe, armed with the DVD boxed set of *Fawlty Towers*. By this point, he was long divorced from my mother, his second divorce, and was living alone on the gray East Anglian coast, far from his children. On dialysis for a decade (he lost his first kidney to stones, the second to cancer), his body now began to give up. I had meant to leave the DVDs with him, something for the empty hours alone, but when I got there, with nothing to talk about, we ended up watching them together for the umpteenth time, he on the single chair, me on the floor, cramped in that grim little nursing-home bedroom, surely the least funny place he'd ever found himself in—with the possible exception of the 1944 Normandy landings. We watched several episodes, back to back. We laughed. Never more than when Basil thrashed an Austin 1100 with the branch of a tree, an act of inspired pointlessness that seemed analogous to our own situation. And then we watched the DVD extras, in which we found an illuminating little depth charge hidden among the nostalgia and the bloopers:

> It was probably—may have been—my idea that she should be a bit less posh than him, because we couldn't see otherwise what would have attracted them to each other. I have a sort of vision of her family being in catering on the south coast, you know, and her working behind a bar somewhere, he being demobbed from his national service and getting his gratuity, you know, and going in for a drink and this . . . barmaid behind the bar and she fancied him because he was so posh. And they sort of thought they'd get married and run a hotel together and it was all a bit sort of romantic and idealistic, and the grim reality then caught up with them.

That is the actress Prunella Scales answering a question of comic (and class) motivation that had troubled my father for twenty years: why on earth did they marry each other? A question that—given his own late, failed marriage to a Jamaican girl less than half his age—must have had a resonance beyond the laugh track. On finally hearing an answer, he gave a sigh of comedy-snob satisfaction. Not long after my visit, Harvey died, at the age of eighty-one. He had told me that he wanted "It's All Over Now, Baby Blue" played at his funeral. When the day came, I managed to remember that.

I forgot which version, though (sweet, melodic Baez). What he got instead was jeering, postbreakup Dylan, which made it seem as if my mild-mannered father had gathered his friends and family with the particular aim of telling them all to fuck off from beyond the grave. As comedy, this would have raised a half smile out of Harvey, not much more. It was a little broad for his tastes.

In birth, two people go into a room and three come out. In death, one person goes in and none come out. This is a cosmic joke told by Martin Amis. I like the metaphysical absurdity it draws out of the death event, the sense that death doesn't happen at all—that it is, in fact, the opposite of a happening. There are philosophers who take this joke seriously. To their way of thinking, the only option in the face of death—in facing death's absurd nonface—is to laugh. This is not the bold, humorless laugh of the triumphant atheist, who conquers what he calls death and his own fear of it. No: this is more unhinged. It comes from the powerless, despairing realization that death cannot be conquered, defied, contemplated or even approached, because it's not there; it's only a word, signifying nothing. It's a truly funny laugh, of the laugh-or-you'll-cry variety. There is "plenty of hope, an infinite amount of hope—but not for us!" This is a cosmic joke told by Franz Kafka, a wisecrack projected into a void. When I first put the partial cremains of my father in a Tupperware sandwich box and placed it on my writing desk, that was the joke I felt like telling.

Conversely, the death we speak of and deal with every day, the death that is full of meaning, the nonabsurd death, this is a place marker, a fake, a convenient substitute. It was this sort of death that I was determined to press upon my father, as he did his dying. In my version, Harvey was dying meaningfully, in linear fashion, within a scenario stage-managed and scripted by the people around him. Neatly crafted, like an American sitcom: "The One in Which My Father Dies." It was to conclude with a real event called Death, which he would *experience* and for which he would be ready. I did all the usual, banal things. I brought a Dictaphone to his bedside, in order to collect the narrative of his life (this perplexed him—he couldn't see the through line). I grew furious with overworked nurses. I refused to countenance any morbidity from my father, or any despair. The funniest thing about dying is how much we, the living, ask of the dying; how we beg them to make it easy on us. At the hospital, I ingratiated myself with the doctors and threw what the British call "new money" at the situation. Harvey watched me go about my business with a puzzled half smile. To all my eager suggestions he said, "Yes, dear—if you like," for he knew well that we were dealing with the National Health Service, into which all Smiths are born and die, and my new money would mean only that exactly the same staff, in the same hospital, would administer the same treatments, though in a slightly nicer room, with a window and possibly a television. He left me to my own devices, sensing that these things made a difference to me, though they made none to him: "Yes, dear—if you like." I was still thrashing an Austin 1100 with a tree branch; he was some way beyond that. And then, when he was truly beyond it, far out on the other side of nowhere, a nurse offered me the opportunity to see the body, which I refused. That was a mistake. It left me suspended in a bad joke in which a living man inexplicably becomes two pints of dust and everyone acts as if this were not a joke at all but, rather, the most reasonable thing in the world. A body would have been usefully, concretely absurd. I would have known—or so people say—that the thing lying there on the slab wasn't my father. As it was, I missed the death, I missed the body, I got the dust and from these facts I tried to extrapolate a story, as writers will, but found myself, instead, in a kind of stasis. A moment in which nothing happened, and keeps not happening, forever. Later, I was informed, by way of comfort, that Harvey had also missed his death: he was in the middle of a sentence, joking with his nurse. "He didn't even know what hit him!" the head matron said, which was funny, too, because who the hell does?

Proximity to death inspired the manic spirit of carpe diem in the Smiths. After Harvey died, my mother met a younger man in Africa and married him. The younger of my two brothers, Luke, went to Atlanta to pursue dreams of rap stardom. Both decisions sounded like promising pilot episodes for new sitcoms. And then I tried to ring in the changes by moving to Italy. In my empty kitchen, on the eve of leaving the country, I put my finger in the dust of my father and put the dust into my mouth and swallowed it, and there was something very funny about that—I laughed as I did it. After that, it felt as if I didn't laugh again for a long time. Or do much of anything. Imagined worlds moved quite out of my reach, seemed utterly pointless, not to mention a colossal human presumption: "Yes, dear—if you like." For two years in Rome, I looked from blank computer screen to handful of dust and back again—a scenario that no one, even in Britain, could turn into a sitcom. Then, as I was preparing to leave Italy, Ben, my other brother, rang with his news. He wanted me to know that he had broken with our long-standing family tradition of passive comedy appreciation. He had decided to become a comedian.

It turns out that becoming a comedian is an act of instantaneous self-creation. There are no intermediaries blocking your way, no gallerists, publishers or distributors. Social class is a nonissue; you do not have to pass your eleven-plus. In a sense, it would have been a good career for our father, a creative man whose frequent attempts at advancement were forever thwarted, or so he felt, by his accent and his background, his lack of education, connections, luck. Of course, Harvey wasn't, in himself, *funny*—but you don't always have to be. In the world of comedy, if you are absolutely determined to stand on a stage for five minutes with a mike in your hand, someone in London will let you do it, if only once. Ben was determined: he'd given up the after-school youth group he had, till then, managed; he'd written material; he had tickets for me, my mother, my aunt. It was my private opinion that he'd had a minor nervous breakdown of some kind, a delayed reaction to his bereavement. I acted pleased, bought a plane ticket, flew over. Though tight as thieves as children, I'd barely seen him since Harvey died, and I sensed us settling into the attenuated relations of adult siblings, a new formal distance, always slightly abashed, for there seems no clear way, in adult life, to do justice to the intimacy of childhood. I remember being scandalized, as a child, at how rarely our parents spoke to *their* siblings. How was it possible? How did it happen? Then it happens to you. Thinking of him standing up there alone with a microphone, though, trying to be *funny*, I felt a renewed, Siamese-twin closeness: fearing

for him was like fearing for me. I've never been able to bear watching anyone
die onstage, never mind a blood relative. If he'd told me that it was major heart
surgery he was about to have, on this makeshift stage in the tiny, dark base-
ment of a London pub, I couldn't have been more sick about it.

It was a mixed bill. Before Ben, two men and two women performed a
mildewed sketch show of unmistakable Oxbridge vintage, circa 1994. A certain brittle poshness informed their exaggerated portraits of high-strung
secretaries, neurotic piano teachers, absentminded professors. They put on
mustaches and wigs and walked in and out of imaginary scenarios where
fewer and fewer funny things occurred. It was the comedy of things past. The
girls, though dressed as girls, were no longer girls, and the boys had paunches
and bald spots; the faintest trace of ancient intracomedy-troupe love affairs
clung to them sadly; all the promising meetings with the BBC had come and
gone. This was being done out of pure friendship now, or the memory of
friendship. As I watched the unspooling horror of it, a repressed, traumatic
memory resurfaced, of an audition, one that must have taken place around
the time this comedy troupe was formed, very likely in the same town. This
audition took the form of a breakfast meeting, a "chat about comedy" with
two young men, then members of the Cambridge Footlights, now a popular
British TV double act. I don't remember what it was that I said. I remember
only strained smiles, the silent consumption of scrambled eggs, a feeling of
human free fall. And the conclusion, which was obvious to us all. Despite
having spent years at the grindstone of comedy appreciation, I wasn't funny.
Not even slightly.

And now the compere was calling my brother's name. He stepped out. I
felt a great wash of East Anglian fatalism, my father's trademark, pass over
to me, its new custodian. Ben was dressed in his usual urban street wear, the
only black man in the room. I began peeling the label off my beer bottle. I
sensed at once the way he was going to play it, the same way we had played
it throughout our childhood—a few degrees off whatever it was that people
expected of us, when they looked at us. This evening, that strategy took the
form of an opening song about the Olympics, with particular attention paid to
equestrian dressage. It was funny! He was getting laughs. He pushed steadily

forward, a slow, gloomy delivery that owed something to Harvey's seemingly infinite pessimism. *No good can come of this.* This had been Harvey's reaction to all news, no matter how objectively good that news might be, from the historic entrance of a Smith child into an actual university to the birthing of babies and the winning of prizes. When he became ill, he took a perversely British satisfaction in the diagnosis of cancer: absolutely nothing good could come of this, and the certainty of it seemed almost to calm him.

I waited, like my father, for the slipup, the flat joke. It didn't come. Ben did a minute on hip-hop, a minute on his baby daughter, a minute on his freshly minted stand-up career. Another song. I was still laughing, and so was everyone else. Finally, I felt able to look up from the beer mats to the stage. Up there I saw my brother, who is not eight, as I forever expect him to be, but thirty, and who appeared completely relaxed, as if born with mike in hand. And then it was over—no one had died.

The next time I saw Ben do stand-up was about ten gigs later, at the 2008 Edinburgh Festival Fringe. He didn't exactly die the night I turned up, but he was badly wounded. It was a shock to him, because it was the first time. In comedy terms, his cherry got popped. At first, he couldn't see why: it was the same type of venue he'd been doing in London—intimate, drunken—and, by and large, it was the same material. Why, this time, were the laughs smaller? Why, for one good joke in particular, did they not occur at all? We repaired to the bar to regroup, with all the other comedians doing the same. In comedy, the analysis of death, or near-death, experiences is a clear, unsentimental process. The discussion is technical, closer to a musician's self-analysis than to a writer's: this note was off; you missed the beat there. I knew I could say to Ben, honestly, and without fear of hurting him, "It was the pause—you went too slowly on the punch line," and he could say, "Yep," and the next night the pause would be shortened, the punch line would hit its mark. We ordered more beer. "The thing I don't understand—I don't understand what happened with the new material. I thought it was good, but . . ." Another comedian, who was also ordering beer, chipped in, "Did you do it first?" "Yes."

"Don't do the new stuff first. Do it last. Just because you're excited by it doesn't mean it should go first. It's not ready yet."

We drank a lot, with a lot of very drunk comedians, until very late. Trying to keep up with the wisecracks and the complaints, I felt as if I'd arrived late to a battleground that had seen bloody action. The comedians had the aura of survivors, speaking the language of mutual, hard experience: venues too hot and too small, the horror of empty seats, who got nominated for what, who'd been reviewed well or badly, and, of course, the financial pain. (Some Edinburgh performers break even, most incur debts and almost no one makes a profit.) It was strange to see my brother, previously a member of my family, becoming a member of *this* family, all his previous concerns and principles subsumed, like theirs, into one simple but demanding question: *Is it funny?* And that's another reason to envy comedians: when they look at a blank page, they always know, at least, the question they need to ask themselves. I think the clarity of their aim accounts for a striking phenomenon, peculiar to comedy: the possibility of extremely rapid improvement. Comedy is a Lazarus art; you can die onstage and then rise again. It's not unusual to see a mediocre young standup in January and, seeing him again in December, discover a comedian who's found his groove, a transformed artist, a death defier.

●

Russell Kane, a relatively new British comic, is a death defier, the sort of comedian who won't let a moment pass without filling it with laughter. I went to see him on the last night of his Edinburgh run. His show was called *Gaping Flaws*, a phrase lifted from a negative online review of his 2007 Edinburgh show, which, in turn, was called *Easy Cliché and Tired Stereotype*, a phrase lifted from a negative review of his debut 2006 show, *Russell Kane's Theory of Pretension*. All these reviews came from the same man, Steve Bennett, a prominent British comedy critic who writes for the Web site Chortle. The problem with Kane was class—the British problem. A self-defined working-class "Essex boy" (though, physically, his look is more indie Americana than English suburbia; he's a dead ringer for the singer Anthony Kiedis), he centers his act on the tricky business of being the alien in the family, the wannabe intellectual son of a working-class, bigoted father. To his father, Kane's passion for reading is deeply suspicious, his interest in the arts tantamount to an admission of sexual deviancy. Kane's dilemma has a natural flip side, a typically British ressentiment for those very people his sensibilities have moved him toward. The middle classes, the Guardianistas (readers of the left-leaning liberal newspaper *The Guardian*), the smug elites who have made him feel his class in the first place. *Can't go home, can't leave home:* a subject close to my heart.

In 2006, Kane played this material too broadly, overexploiting a natural gift for grotesque physical comedy: his father was a hulking deformed monster, the Guardianistas fey fools, skipping across the stage. In 2007, the chip on his shoulder was still there, but the ideas were better, the portraits more detailed, more refined; he began to find his balance, which is a rare mixture of inspired verbal sparring and effective physical comedy. Third time's the charm: *Gaping Flaws* had almost none. It was still all about class, but some magical integration had occurred. I couldn't help being struck by the sense that what it might take a novelist a lifetime to achieve a bright comedian can resolve in three seasons. (How to present a working-class experience to the middle classes without diluting it. How to stay angry without letting anger distort your work. How to be funny about the most serious things.)

Audiences love death defiers like Kane. It's what they pay their money for, after all: laughs per minute. They tend to be less fond of those comedians who have themselves tired of the nonstop laughter and pine for a little silence. I want to call it "comedy nausea." Comedy nausea is the extreme incarnation of what my father felt: not only is joke telling a cheap art; *the whole business of stand-up* is, in some sense, a shameful cheat. For a comedian of this kind, I imagine it feels like a love affair gone wrong. You start out wanting people to laugh in exactly the places you mean them to laugh, then they *always* laugh where you want them to laugh—then you start to hate them for it. Sometimes the feeling is temporary. The comedian returns to stand-up and finds new joy in, and respect for, the art of death defying. Sometimes, as with Peter Cook (voted, by his fellow comedians, in a British poll, the greatest comedian of all time), comedy nausea turns terminal, and only the most difficult laugh in the world will satisfy. Toward the end of his life, when his professional comedy output was practically nil, Cook made a series of phone calls to a radio call-in show, using the pseudonym Sven from Swiss Cottage (an area of northwest London), during which he discussed melancholy Norwegian matters in a thick Norwegian accent, some of the funniest and bleakest "work" he ever did.

At the extreme end of this sensibility lies the anticomedian. An anticomedian not only allows death onstage; he invites death up. Andy Kaufman was an anticomedian. So was Lenny Bruce. Tommy Cooper is the great British example. His comedy persona was "inept magician." He did intentionally bad magic tricks and told surreal jokes that played like Zen koans. He *actually* died onstage, collapsing from a heart attack during a 1984 live TV broadcast. I was nine, watching it on telly with Harvey. When Cooper fell over, we laughed and laughed, along with the rest of Britain, realizing only when the show cut to the commercial break that he wasn't kidding.

●

There was an anticomedian at Edinburgh this year. His name was Edward Aczel. You will not have heard of him—neither had I; neither has practically anyone. This was only his second Edinburgh appearance. Maybe it was the fortuitous meeting of my mournful mood and his morbid material, but I thought his show, *Do I Really Have to Communicate with You?*, was one of the strangest, and finest, hours of live comedy I'd ever seen. It started with neither a bang nor a whimper. It didn't really start. We, the audience, sat in nervous silence in a tiny, dark room, and waited. Some fumbling with a cassette recorder was heard, faint music, someone mumbling backstage: "Welcome to the stage . . . Edward Aczel." Said without enthusiasm. A man wandered out. Going bald, early forties, schlubby, entirely nondescript. He said, "All right?" in a hopeless sort of way, and then decided that he wanted to do the introduction again. He went offstage and came on again. He did this several times. Despair settled over the room. Finally, he fixed himself in front of the microphone. "I think you'll all recall," he muttered, barely audible, "the words of Wittgenstein, the great twentieth-century philosopher, who said, 'If indeed mankind came to earth for a specific reason, it certainly wasn't to enjoy ourselves.'" A long, almost unbearable pause. "If you could bear that in mind while I'm on, I'd certainly appreciate it." Then, on a large flip chart, the kind of thing an account manager in an Aylesbury marketing agency might swipe from his office (Aczel is, in real life, an account manager for an Aylesbury marketing agency), he began to write with a Magic Marker. It was a list of what not to expect from his show. He went through it with us. There was to be

No nudity.

No juggling.

No impressions of any well-known people.

No reference to crop circles during the show.

No one will be conceived during the show.

No tackling head-on of any controversial issues . . .

And finally, and I think most important—

No refunds.

I recognized my father's spirit in this list: *No good can come of this.* He then told us that he had a box of jigsaw puzzles backstage, for anyone who became dangerously bored. Later, he drew a graph made up of an x-axis, which stood for "TIME," and a y-axis, for "GOODWILL," on which he tracked the show's progress. Point one, low down: *"Let's all go and get a drink—this is pointless."* Point two, slightly higher up: *"O.K., carry on, whatever."* Point three, still only halfway up: *"We could all be here forever. We think this is great."* He looked at his shoes, then, with mild aggression, at the audience. "We'll never get to that point," he said. "It's just . . . it'll never happen." By this time, everyone was laughing, but the laughter was a little crazy, disjointed. It's a reckless thing, for a comedian, to be this honest with an audience. To say, in effect, "Whatever I do, whatever you do, we're *all* going to die." When it finally came to jokes ("Now we go into the section of the show routinely called 'material,' for obvious reasons"), Aczel had a dozen written on his hand, and they were very funny, but by now he had already convinced us that jokes were the least of what could be done here. It was an easy and wonderful thing to believe this show a genuine shambles, saved only by our attention and by chance. (We were mistaken, of course. Every stumble, every murmur, is identical, every night.) In the lobby afterward, calendars were on sale, each month illustrated by impossibly banal photographs of Aczel in bed, washing his face, walking into work, standing in the road. Mine sits on my desk, next to my father in his Tupperware sandwich box. On the cover, Aczel is pictured in a supermarket aisle. The subtitle reads, "Life is endless, until you die"—Edith Piaf. Each month has a message for me. November: "Winter is coming—Yes!" April: "Who cares." June: "This is not the life I was promised." *There is plenty of hope, an infinite amount of hope—but not for us!*

On the last night of the Edinburgh festival, in another small, dark, drunken venue, I waited for my brother to go on. It was about two in the morning. Only comedians were left at the festival; the audiences had all gone home. I feared for him, again—but he did his set, and he killed. He was relaxed. There was nothing riding on his performance; the pause had been fixed. Then a young Australian dude came on and spoke a lot about bottle openers, and he killed, too. Maybe everybody kills at two in the morning. Then the end of the end: one last comedian took the bar stage. This was Andy Zaltzman, a great, tall man with an electrified Einstein hairdo and a cutting, political-satirical act that got its laughs per minute. He set to work, confident, funny, and instantly got heckled, a heckle that was followed by a collective audience intake of breath, for the heckler was Daniel Kitson, a rather shy, whimsical young comedian from Yorkshire who looks like a beardy cross between a fisherman and a geography teacher. Kitson won the Perrier Comedy Award in 2002, at the age of twenty-five, and his gift is for the crafting of exquisite narratives, shows shaped like Alice Munro stories, bathetic and beautiful. A comedy-snob thrill passed through the room. It was a bit like Nick Drake turning up at a James Taylor gig. Kitson good-humoredly heckled Zaltzman, and Zaltzman heckled back. Their ideas went spiraling down nonsensical paths, collided, did battle and separated. Kitson busied himself handing out fliers for "Our joint show, tomorrow!"—a show that couldn't exist, because the festival was over. We all took one. Zaltzman and Kitson got loose; the jokes were everywhere, with everyone, the whole room becoming comedy. There was a kind of hysteria abroad. I looked over at my brother and could see that he'd got this abdominal pain, too, and we were both doubled over, crying, and I wished Harvey were there, and at the same moment I felt something come free in me.

I have to confess to an earlier comic embellishment: my father is no longer in a Tupperware sandwich box. He was, for a year, but then I bought a pretty Italian art deco vase for him, completely see-through, so I can see through to him. The vase is posh, and not funny like the sandwich box, but I decided that what Harvey didn't have much of in life he would get in death. In life, he found Britain hard. It was a nation divided by postcodes and accents, schools and last names. The humor of its people helped make it bearable. *You don't have to be funny to live here, but it helps.* Hancock, Fawlty, Partridge, Brent: in my mind, they're all clinging to the middle rungs of England's class ladder. That, in large part, is the comedy of their situations.

For eighty-one years, my father was up to the same game, though his situation wasn't so comical; at least, the living of it wasn't. *Listen, I'll tell you a joke:* his mother had been in service, his father worked on the buses; he passed the grammar-school exam, but the cost of the uniform for the secondary school was outside the family's budget. *No, wait, it gets better:* at thirteen, he left school to fill the inkwells in a lawyer's office, to set the fire in the grate. At seventeen, he went to fight in the Second World War. In the fifties, he got married, started a family and, finding that he had a good eye, tried commercial photography. His pictures were good, he set up a little studio, but then his business partner stiffed him in some dark plot of which he would never speak. His marriage ended. *And here's the kicker:* in the sixties, he had to start all over again, as a salesman. In the seventies, he married for the second time. A new lot of children arrived. The high point was the late eighties, a senior salesman now at a direct-mail company—selling paper, just like David Brent. Finally, the (lower) middle rung! A maisonette, half a garden, a sweet deal with a local piano teacher who taught Ben and me together, two bums squeezed onto the piano stool. But it didn't last, and the second marriage didn't last, and he ended up with little more than he had started with. Listening to my first novel on tape, and hearing the rough arc of his life in the character Archie Jones, he took it well, seeing the parallels but also the difference: "He had better luck than me!" The novel was billed as comic fiction. To Harvey, it sat firmly in the laugh-or-you'll-cry genre. And when that *Fawlty Towers* boxed set came back to me as my only inheritance (along with a cardigan, several atlases, and a photograph of Venice), I did a little of both.

REMEMBERING

Seventeen

BRIEF INTERVIEWS WITH HIDEOUS MEN: THE DIFFICULT GIFTS OF DAVID FOSTER WALLACE

I had a teacher I liked who used to say good fiction's job was to comfort the disturbed and disturb the comfortable. I guess a big part of serious fiction's purpose is to give the reader, who like all of us is sort of marooned in her own skull, to give her imaginative access to other selves. Since an ineluctable part of being a human self is suffering, part of what we humans come to art for is an experience of suffering, necessarily a vicarious experience, more like a sort of "generalization" of suffering. Does this make sense? We all suffer alone in the real world; true empathy's impossible. But if a piece of fiction can allow us imaginatively to identify with a character's pain, we might then also more easily conceive of others identifying with our own. This is nourishing, redemptive; we become less alone inside. It might just be that simple. But now realize that TV and popular film and most kinds of "low" art— which just means art whose primary aim is to make money—is lucrative precisely because it recognizes that audiences prefer 100 percent pleasure to the reality that tends to be 49 percent pleasure and 51 percent pain. Whereas "serious" art, which is not primarily about getting money out of you, is more apt to make you uncomfortable, or to force you to work hard to access its pleasures, the same way that in real life true pleasure is usually a by-product of hard work and discomfort. So it's hard for an art audience, especially a young one that's been raised to expect art to be 100 percent pleasurable and to make that pleasure effortless, to read and appreciate serious fiction. That's not good. The problem isn't that today's readership is "dumb," I don't think. Just that TV and the commercial-art culture's trained it to be sort of lazy and childish in its expectations. But it makes trying to engage today's readers both imaginatively and intellectually unprecedentedly hard.

—David Foster Wallace[1]

0. DIFFICULT GIFTS

David Foster Wallace was clever about gifts: our inability to give freely or to accept what is freely given. A farmer can't give away an old tiller for free; he has to charge five bucks before someone will come and take it. A depressed person wants to receive attention but can't bring herself to give it. Normal social relations are only preserved because "one never knew, after all, now did one now did one now did one." In these stories, the act of giving is in crisis; the logic of the market seeps into every aspect of life.

These tales are found in *Brief Interviews with Hideous Men*, a collection that was itself the response to two enormous gifts. The first was practical: the awarding of the MacArthur.[2] A gift on that scale frees a writer from the harsh logic of the literary market, and maybe also from that bind Wallace himself defined as postindustrial: *the need always to be liked*. The second gift was more difficult; it was Wallace's own talent, the bedrock of which was a formidable intellect. That he ended up a fiction writer at all speaks to the radical way Wallace saw his own gifts—not as a natural resource to be exploited but as a suspicious facility to be

---

1. From Larry McCaffery's Dalkey Archive Press 1993 interview with Wallace, conducted during the composition of *Brief Interviews*. The great majority of Wallace quotes in this piece come from that interview.
2. Each year, the MacArthur Fellows Program gives out awards of several hundred thousand dollars (nicknamed genius grants) to individuals working in any field who "show exceptional merit and promise for continued and enhanced creative work." Wallace received his in 1997. *Brief Interviews* was published in 1999.

interrogated. Certainly that unusual triune skill set—encyclopedic knowledge, mathematical prowess, complex dialectical thought—would have had an easier passage to approval within the academic world from which he hailed than in the literary world he joined. Instead, in his twenties, Wallace chose the path of most resistance. He turned from a career in math and philosophy to pursue a vocation in what he called "morally passionate, passionately moral fiction." For the next twenty years, the two sides of that chiasmus would be in constant tension. On the one side, his writing sought the emotive force of fiction; on the other, its formal, philosophical possibilities. These elements attracted him equally but his virtuosity (and his training) was in the latter, and there was always the risk that the philosophy would overwhelm the passion. But Wallace was clever enough to realize that cleverness alone wasn't enough ("I'll catch myself thinking up gags or trying formal stunt-pilotry and see that none of this stuff is really in the service of the story itself; it's serving the rather darker purpose of communicating to the reader 'Hey! Look at me! Have a look at what a good writer I am! Like me!' ") He battled to share his gifts rather than simply display them, seeming to seek the solution in a principle of self-mortification. What do you do with a great gift? You give it away:

> I've gotten convinced that there's something kind of timelessly vital and sacred about good writing. This thing doesn't have that much to do with talent, even glittering talent . . . .Talent's just an instrument. It's like having a pen that works instead of one that doesn't. I'm not saying I'm able to work consistently out of the premise, but it seems like the big distinction between good art and so-so art lies somewhere in the art's heart's purpose, the agenda of the consciousness behind the text. It's got something to do with love. With having the discipline to talk out of the part of yourself that can love instead of the part that just wants to be loved. I know this doesn't sound hip at all. . . . But it seems like one of the things really great fiction-writers do—from Carver to Chekhov to Flannery O'Connor, or like the Tolstoy of "The Death of Ivan Ilych" or the Pynchon of *Gravity's Rainbow*—is "give" the reader something. The reader walks away from the real art heavier than she came into it. Fuller. All the attention and

engagement and work you need to get from the reader can't be for your benefit; it's got to be for hers. What's poisonous about the cultural environment today is that it makes this so scary to try to carry out.

When Wallace wrote he offered everything he had to his readers, including the kitchen sink. His cultish fans were always ready and willing to come away from his work a little heavier—it was his complexity that they loved. For many of us, though, what Wallace had to give looked simply *too* heavy, too much like hard work. And while *Brief Interviews* had its passionate defenders, I remember that the pair of reviews it received in the *New York Times* were bad (in both senses), opening with paragraphs of nervous ridicule:

> How to describe David Foster Wallace's new collection of stories? You might say it's like being a therapist and being forced to listen to one narcissistic patient after the next prattle on—and on and on—about their neuroses and their explanations for those neuroses and the rationalizations behind the explanations for those neuroses. Or you might say it's like being locked in a room with a bunch of speed freaks babbling to themselves nonstop on a Benzedrine-fueled high as they clip their toenails or cut the split ends out of their hair.

> You know the old story about how if you set a billion monkeys to work on a billion typewriters, one of them would eventually compose the complete works of Shakespeare? David Foster Wallace often writes the way I imagine that billionth monkey would: in mad cadenzas of simian gibberish that break suddenly into glorious soliloquies, then plunge again into nonsense.

Perhaps it was easy, when you read Wallace, to distrust "the agenda of the consciousness behind the text." Did he truly want to give you a gift? Or only to demonstrate his own? For why should we be expected to tease out references to De Chirico and logotherapy, or know what happens during an eclipse, or what polymerase does, or the many nuances of the word *prone*? Why go through the pain if this is to be all we get in return: "Discursive portraits of relentlessly self-absorbed whiners, set down in an unappetizing mix of psychobabble, scholarly jargon and stream-of-consciousness riffs"? It's my recollection that this sort of thing had become, in the early noughties, the common "line" on Wallace, especially in England; something to say whether you'd actually read him or not. *Postmodern type? Swallowed a dictionary?* Bad reviews serve many purposes, not least of which is the gift of freedom: they release you from the obligation of having to read the book.

At the time of writing, *Brief Interviews* marks its tenth anniversary and its author is no longer with us. Now might be the time to think of the literary gift economy the other way around. To do this we have to recognize that a difficult gift like *Brief Interviews* merits the equally difficult gift of our close attention and effort. For this reason, the newspaper review was never going to be an easy fit for Wallace. He can't be read and understood and enjoyed at that speed any more than I can get the hang of the Goldberg Variations over a weekend. His reader needs to think of herself as a musician, spreading the sheet music—the gift of the work—over the music stand, electing to play. First there is practice, then competency at the instrument, then spending time with the sheet music, then playing it over and over.

Of course, the arguments that might be employed w/r/t reading in this way are deeply unreasonable, entirely experiential, and impossible to objectively defend.[3] In the end, all that can be said is that the difficult gift is its own defense, the deep rewarding pleasure of which is something you can only know by undergoing it. To appreciate Wallace, you need to *really* read

---

3. Wallace's most attentive mainstream critic, Wyatt Mason, made this point in his 2004 review "You Don't Like It? You Don't Have to Play." There he asks and answers the question—"Why should [the reader] grant Wallace any of his demands . . . when the reader feels, not unreasonably, that Wallace is making unreasonable demands?"—with the only honest response available, that is, an account of Mason's own pleasure: "having read the eight stories in *Oblivion*; having found some hard to read and, because they were hard and the hardness made me miss things, reread them; having reread them and seen how they work, how well they work, how tightly they withhold their working, hiding on high shelves the keys that unlock their treasures; having, in some measure, found those keys; and having, in the solitary place where one reads, found a bright array of sad and moving and funny and fascinating human objects of undeniable, unusual value." But to those readers who find even Wallace's habit of abbreviating the phrase *with regard to* (w/r/t) an unreasonable demand, no counterargument will suffice.

him—and then you need to *reread* him. For this reason—among many others—he was my favorite living writer, and I wrote this piece to remember him by, which, in my case, is best done by reading him once again.

1. BREAKING THE RHYTHM THAT EXCLUDES THINKING

The story "Forever Overhead" is *Brief Interviews* at its most open, and for many readers, its most beautiful. Wallace disliked it, thinking it juvenilia—maybe it was its very openness he suspected. So many of the dense themes of the book are here laid out with an unexpected directness. At first glance, it's simple: a boy on his thirteenth birthday in an "old public pool on the western edge of Tucson," resolving to try the diving tank for the first time. The voice is as blank as a video game, as an instruction manual,[4] and yet, within it, Wallace finds something tender: "Get out now and go past your parents, who are sunning and reading, not looking up. Forget your towel. Stopping for the towel means talking and talking means thinking. You have decided being scared is caused mostly by thinking. Go right by, toward the tank at the deep end." To this he then adds a layer of complication: a sparsely punctuated, synesthetic compression, like a painter placing another shade atop his base. A remembered wet dream does not yet know its own name, it is "spasms of a deep sweet hurt"; the pool is "five-o'clock warm," its distinctive odor "a flower with chemical petals." The noise of the radio overhead is "jangle flat and tinny thin," and a dive is "a white that plumes and falls" until once more "blue clean comes up in the middle of the white." Throughout, the expected verb—*is*—is generally omitted: sensations present themselves directly on the page, as they present themselves to the boy. The unmediated sensory overload of puberty overlaps here with a dream of language: that words might become things, that there would exist no false gap between the verbal representation of something and the something itself.[5]

---

4. The second person present tense imperative—a fashionable conceit of the '90s.
5. Maybe writers have this dream more than most.

Then, with the base coat down, and the wash laid on top, comes another layer. Concrete details so finely rendered they seem to have been drawn from the well of our own memories: your sister's swim cap with the "raised rubber flowers . . . limp old pink petals" and the "thin cruel hint of very dark Pepsi in paper cups"; that SN CK BAR with the letter missing and the concrete deck "rough and hot against your bleached feet." Isn't everything just as you remember it? The big lady in front of you on the ladder: "Her suit is full of her. The backs of her thighs are squeezed by the suit and look like cheese. The legs have abrupt little squiggles of cold blue shattered vein under the white skin." The ladder itself: "The rungs are very thin. It's unexpected. Thin round iron rungs laced in slick wet Safe-T felt." And now, fueled by nostalgia, by the pressing in of times past, the concrete seems to mix with the existential: "Each of your footprints is thinner and fainter. Each shrinks behind you on the hot stone and disappears." And again, on that ladder: "You have real weight. . . . The ground wants you back." Haven't you been in this terrible queue? Aren't you in it now? A queue from which there is no exit, in which everyone looks bored and "seems by himself," in which all dive freely and yet have no real freedom, for "it is a machine that moves only forward."

The difference is awareness (this is always the difference in Wallace). The boy seems to see clearly what we, all those years ago, felt only faintly. He sees that "the pool is a system of movement," in which all experience is systematized ("There is a rhythm to it. Like breathing. Like a machine.") and into which, as the woman in front of him dives, he must now insert himself:

Listen. It does not seem good, the way she disappears into a time that passes before she sounds. Like a stone down a well. But you think she did not think so. She was part of a rhythm that excludes thinking. And now you have made yourself part of it, too. The rhythm seems blind. Like ants. Like a machine.

You decide this needs to be thought about. It may, after all, be all right to do something scary without thinking, but not when the scariness is the not thinking itself. Not when not thinking turns out to be wrong. At some point the wrongnesses have piled up blind: pretend-boredom, weight, thin rungs, hurt feet, space cut into laddered parts that melt together only in a disappearance that takes time. The wind on the ladder not what anyone would have expected. The way the board protrudes from shadow into light and you can't see past the end. When it all turns out to be different you should get to think. It should be required.

Now we see what the board is and feel our own predicament: sentient beings encased in these flesh envelopes, moving always in one inexorable direction (the end of which we cannot see). Bound by time. *Freedom is what you do with what's been done to you.* This, Sartre's dictum, hangs over these passive people who "let their legs take them to the end" before coming down "heavy on the edge of the board and mak[ing] it throw them up and out." Thrown into the world, condemned to be free—and hideously responsible for that freedom.

It strikes me when I reread this beautiful story how poor we are at tracing literary antecedents, how often we assume too much and miss obvious echoes. Lazily we gather writers by nations, decades and fashions; we imagine Wallace the only son of DeLillo and Pynchon. In fact, Wallace had catholic tastes, and it shouldn't surprise us to find, along with Sartre, traces of Philip Larkin, a great favorite of his.[6] Wallace's fear of automatism is acutely Larkinesque ("a style/ Our lives bring with them: habit for a while/Suddenly they harden into all we've got"[7]), as is his attention to that singular point in our lives when we realize we are closer to our end than our beginning. When Wallace writes, "At some point there has gotten to be more line behind you than in front of you," he lends an indelible image to an existential fear, as Larkin did memorably in "The Old Fools:" "The peak that stays in view wherever we go / For them is rising ground." Then there's the title itself, "Forever Overhead": a perfectly accurate description, when you think about it, of how the poems "High Windows" and "Water" close.[8] That mix of the concrete and the existential, of air and water, of the

---

6. I once asked Wallace, in a letter, for a list of favorite writers. Larkin was the only poet mentioned.
7. From "Dockery and Son."
8. The end of "High Windows": "The sun-comprehending glass,/And beyond it, the deep blue air, that shows/Nothing, and is nowhere, and is endless." The end of "Water": "And I should raise in the east/A glass of water/Where any-angled light/Would congregate endlessly."

eternal submerged in the banal. And boredom was the great theme of both. But in the great theme there is a great difference. Wallace wanted to interrogate boredom as a deadly postmodern attitude, an attempt to bypass experience on the part of a people who have become habituated to a mediated reality. "It seems impossible," the boy thinks, arranging his face in fake boredom to match the rest, "that everybody could really be this bored." In this story, the counter-weight to automatism is sensation, expressed here as human reality in its most direct and redemptive form: "Your feet are hurt from the thin rungs and have a great ability to feel." It's no accident that we are in a swimming pool, at fiery sunset, with a high wind blowing and the ground hot enough to remind of us of its solidity. The four elements are intended to work upon "you"; for no mat-ter how many times this queue has formed, no matter how many people have dived before, or have watched other people dive, in life or on TV, *this is you*, diving now, and it should be thought about, and there should be a wonder in it. For Larkin, on the other hand, boredom was *real* ("Life is first boredom, then fear./Whether or not we use it, it goes"[9]), and the inexorability of time made all human effort faintly ludicrous. There is some of this despair in Wallace, too (whatever splash the divers make, the tank "heals itself" each time, as if each dive had never been), but much less than is popularly ascribed to him. Time has its horrors in Wallace but it's also the thing that binds us most closely to the real and to one another: without it we would lose ourselves in solipsism (which, for him, was the *true* horror.) When the boy, in a meditative state, dares to hope that "no time is passing outside," he is soon proven wrong:

Hey kid. They want to know. Do your plans up here involve the whole day or what exactly is the story. Hey kid are you okay.

There's been time this whole time. You can't kill time with your heart. Everything takes time. Bees have to move very fast to stay still.

Yet this is not experienced as a negative revelation. Indeed, the greatness of Wallace's story lies in its indeterminacy, for the boy never quite resolves

---

9. From "Dockery and Son."

which part of his experience is the real one, the hardware of the world or the software of his consciousness:

> So which is the lie? Hard or soft? Silence or time? The lie is that it's one or the other. A still, floating bee is moving faster than it can think. From overhead the sweetness drives it crazy.

What is he jumping into, in the end? Is the tank death, experience, manhood, a baptism, the beginning, the end? Whatever it is, the boy is able to approach it without dread. He pauses to examine the "two vague black ovals" at the end of the board, over which his literary creator has taken such wonderful care:

> From all the people who've gone before you. Your feet as you stand here are tender and dented, hurt by the rough wet surface, and you see that the two dark spots are from people's skin. They are skin abraded from feet by the violence of the disappearance of people with real weight. More people than you can count without losing track. The weight and abrasion of their disappearance leaves little bits of soft tender feet behind, bits and shard and curls of skin that dirty and darken and tan as they lie tiny and smeared in the sun at the end of the board.

But this examination does not result in paralysis. He still dives. Where Larkin was transfixed by the accumulation of human futility, Wallace was as interested in communication as he was in finitude (the last word of the story, as the boy dives, is *Hello*). He was, in the broadest sense, a moralist: what mattered to him most was not the end but the quality of our communal human experience *before* the end, while we're still here. What passes between us in that queue *before* we dive.

In 2005, Wallace gave a commencement speech at Kenyon College that begins this way:

> There are these two young fish swimming along and they happen to meet an older fish swimming the other way, who nods at them and says,

"Morning, boys. How's the water?" And the two young fish swim on for
a bit, and then eventually one of them looks over at the other and goes,
"What the hell is water?"

And ends like this:

The capital-T Truth is about life BEFORE death. It is about the real value
of a real education, which has almost nothing to do with knowledge, and
everything to do with simple awareness; awareness of what is so real and
essential, so hidden in plain sight all around us, all the time, that we have
to keep reminding ourselves over and over: "This is water. This is water."
It is unimaginably hard to do this, to stay conscious and alive in the adult
world day in and day out.

This short piece appeared in many newspapers when he died and has
recently been repackaged as a *Chicken Soup for the Soul*-style toilet book (sentences artificially separated from one another and left, like Zen koans, alone
on the page) to be sold next to the cash register. If you believe the publicity
flack, it is here that Wallace attempted to collect "all he believed about life,
human nature, and lasting fulfillment into a brief talk." Hard to think of a less
appropriate portrait of this writer than as the dispenser of convenient pearls
of wisdom, placed in your palm, so that you needn't go through any struggle yourself. Wallace was the opposite of an aphorist. And the real worth of
that speech (which he never published, which existed only as a transcript on
the Internet) is as a diving board into his fiction, his fiction being his truest
response to the difficulty of staying conscious and alive, day in and day out.

The ends of great fiction do not change, much. But the means do. A hundred years earlier, another great American writer, Henry James, wanted his
readers "finely aware so as to become richly responsible."[10] His syntactically
tortuous sentences, like Wallace's, are intended to make you aware, to break

10. This, and later James quotes, are from the 1908 preface to *The Princess Casamassima*. This
section of the preface has been used before, in the context of the connection between fiction
and philosophy, by Martha Nussbaum in *Love's Knowledge*.

the rhythm that excludes thinking. Wallace was from that same tradition—
but, a hundred years on, the ante had been raised. In 1999, it felt harder to be
alive and conscious than ever. *Brief Interviews* pitched itself as a counterweight
to the narcotic qualities of contemporary life, and then went a step further. It
questioned the Jamesian notion that fine awareness leads a priori to responsibility. It suggested that too much awareness—particularly self-awareness—has
allowed us to be less responsible than ever. It was meant for readers of my
generation, born under the star of four interlocking revolutions, undreamed
of in James's philosophy: the ubiquity of television, the voraciousness of late
capitalism, the triumph of therapeutic discourse, and philosophy's demotion
into a branch of linguistics. How to be finely aware when you are trained in
passivity? How to detect real value when everything has its price? How to be
responsible when you are, by definition, always the child-victim? How to be in
the world when the world has collapsed into language?

2. IT'S NOT WHAT YOU THINK I'M AFRAID OF

If Wallace insists on awareness, his particular creed is—to use a Wallac-
erian word—*extrorse*; awareness must move always in an outward direction,
away from the self. Self-awareness and self-investigation are to be treated with
suspicion, even horror. In part, this was Wallace's way of critiquing the previous literary generation's emphasis on self-reflexive narrative personae. In interview, he recognized his debt to the great metafictionists, but he also took care
to express his own separation from them, and from their pale descendants:[11]

> Metafiction . . . helps reveal fiction as a mediated experience. Plus it
> reminds us that there's always a recursive component to utterance. This was
> important, because language's self-consciousness had always been there,

---

11. Whom he called crank turners: "When you talk about Nabokov and Coover, you're
talking about real geniuses, the writers who weathered real shock and invented this stuff in
contemporary fiction. But after the pioneers always come the crank turners, the little gray
people who take the machines others have built and just turn the crank, and little pellets of
metafiction come out the other end."

but neither writers nor critics nor readers wanted to be reminded of it. But we ended up seeing why recursion's dangerous, and maybe why everybody wanted to keep linguistic self-consciousness out of the show. It gets empty and solipsistic real fast. It spirals in on itself. By the mid-seventies, I think, everything useful about the mode had been exhausted. . . . By the eighties it'd become a god-awful trap.

Solipsism here means more than hipster vanity: Wallace has both its Latin roots (*solus*, "alone"; *ipse*, "self") and philosophical history in mind (the theory that only the self really exists or can be known). The "linguistic turn" of twentieth-century philosophy concerned and fascinated him—that wholesale swallowing of the transcendental by the analytical that left us as "selves alone" in language, with no necessary link to the world of phenomena beyond. In Wallace's view, too many practitioners of metafiction enthusiastically embraced the big Derridean idea—"There is nothing outside the text"—without truly undergoing the melancholy consequences. For inspiration he looked instead to Wittgenstein, both as "the real architect of the postmodern trap" and the writer who best understood its tragic implications for the self:

There's a kind of tragic fall Wittgenstein's obsessed with all the way from the "Tractatus Logico-Philosophicus" in 1922 to the "Philosophical Investigations" in his last years. I mean a real Book-of-Genesis type tragic fall. The loss of the whole external world.

The "Tractatus"'s picture theory of meaning presumes that the only possible relation between language and the world is denotative, referential. In order for language both to be meaningful and to have some connection to reality, words like "tree" and "house" have to be like little pictures, representations of little trees and houses. Mimesis. But nothing more. Which means we can know and speak of nothing more than little mimetic pictures. Which divides us, metaphysically and forever, from the external world. If you buy such a metaphysical schism, you're left with only two options. One is that the individual person with her language is trapped in here, with the world out there, and never the twain shall meet.

Which, even if you think language's pictures really are mimetic, is an awful lonely proposition. And there's no iron guarantee the pictures truly "are" mimetic, which means you're looking at solipsism. One of the things that makes Wittgenstein a real artist to me is that he realized that no conclusion could be more horrible than solipsism.

This, the first option,[12] is where Wallace's hideous men live. Trapped alone in language. The questions in those interviews (represented by the letter Q) are not only formally "missing" from the conversations, *their respondents have internalized them.* These men anticipate all questions and also their own expected answers and also the responses they have already concluded these answers will receive. In fact, *all* exterior referents have been swallowed up by language and loop back into the self. In this spiral, other people simply can't exist. "You" has become just another word, encased in quote marks, and the results are hideous indeed.

Take the control freak in B.I. #48, whose only possible relationship between self and other is a verbal contract, in which you never hear from the second party. This is a man who likes to say to a woman, after a third date, and "without any discernable context or lead-in that you could point to as such"—*How would you feel about my tying you up?* But the casual tone is a deception, the question not even really a question:

It is important to understand that, for there even to be a third date, there must exist some sort of palpable affinity between us, something by which I can sense that they will go along. Perhaps *go along* {flexion of upraised fingers to signify tone quotes} is not a fortuitous phrase for it. I mean, perhaps, {flexion of upraised fingers to signify tone quotes} *play.* Meaning to join me in the contract and subsequent activity.

From the prim specificity of the vocabulary and syntax to this habit of encasing in "quote marks" any ambiguous moment—he's unbearably controlling. And

12. We'll come to the second.

whatever he claims, there's never any real sense of "play," because there is never any way to look past the referents to the other players. Despite all his verbal prowess, we learn nothing of the women; they remain faceless, nameless, featureless, their sole distinction whether they are "hens" or "cocks"—that is, whether they will submit or not. This strange terminology (he calls it "the aptest analogy") is borrowed from the "Australian profession known as {flexion of upraised fingers} *chicken-sexing*," by which the gender of a bird is ascertained merely by looking at it and naming it: *hen, hen, cock, cock, hen.* Naturally, he has a gift for it: he can identify a "hen" or "cock" before they are aware of what they are themselves. But then, he has the words for everything. He understands that he is compelled to "propose and negotiate contracted rituals where power is freely given and taken and submission ritualized and control ceded and then returned of my own free will." He controls both the meaning of the act itself ("I know what the contract is about, and it is not about seduction, conquest, intercourse, or algolgagnia") and its psychological root cause. ("My own mother was . . . erratic in her dealings with, of her two twin children, most specifically me. This has bequeathed me certain psychological complexes having to do with power and, perhaps, trust.") Not only this: he is sufficiently self-aware to know his language (another legacy of his mother, a psychiatric case worker, natch) is "annoying, pedantic jargon." He can "read" both the women's words and their silences ("You are, of course, aware that social silences have varied textures, and these textures communicate a great deal.") He can even tell real shock from false:

> Hence the fascinating irony that body language intended to convey shock does indeed convey shock but a very different sort of shock indeed. Namely the abreactive shock of repressed wishes bursting their strictures and penetrating consciousness, but from an external source. . . .
>
> This interval of shocked silence is one during which entire psychological maps are being redrawn and during this interval any gesture or affect on the subject's part will reveal a great deal more about her than any amount of banal conversation or even clinical experimentation ever would. Reveal.
>
> Q.
>
> I meant woman or young woman, not {f.f} *subject* per se.

The little slip is telling, and the word *abreactive*, too.[13] Here therapy has become the monster it once wished to tame, the talking cure mere talk. And the talk turns outward; we feel *we* are the ones being interrogated, and that the questions are disturbing. When we relive repressed emotions as therapeutic, are we healing ourselves or tunneling deeper into the self? How do abreaction and solipsism interrelate? Does one feed the other? Is one the *function* of the other?

It's tempting to read the interviews as an attack on therapy per se, but "therapy is a false religion" is rather a dull drum to beat,[14] and if it were only this, why not hear from the therapists themselves, instead of the patients? It's not therapy's fundamental principles that find themselves interrogated here (after all, the self-diagnosis of Hideous Man #48 is not incorrect: it's right to say he ties up women because his mother's idea of punishment was physical restraint). More significant is this idea of a looped discourse, of a language meant to *heal* the self that ends up referring only *to* the self. In *Brief Interviews*, the language of therapy is not alone in doing this: in Wallace's world there exists a whole *bunch* of ways to get lost in the self. In the bleak joke of B.I. #2, we listen in as a serial monogamist wields the intimate language of "relationships" against his own girlfriend, precisely to protect himself against a "relationship":

> Can you believe that I'm honestly trying to *respect* you by warning you about me, in a way? That I'm trying to be honest instead of dishonest? That I've decided the best way to head off this pattern where you get hurt and feel abandoned and I feel like shit is to try and be honest for once?

13. OED: **abreaction;** *Psychoanalysis*. The relief of anxiety by the expression and release of a previously repressed emotion, through reliving the experience that caused it; an instance of this.

14. And does not sit with Wallace's respect and interest in AA, an organization he researched during the writing of *Infinite Jest*: "I went to a couple of meetings with these guys and thought that it was tremendously powerful. . . . For me there was a real repulsion at the beginning. "One Day at a Time," right? . . . But apparently part of addiction is that you need the substance so bad that when they take it away from you, you want to die. . . . Something as banal and reductive as "one Day at a Time" enabled these people to walk through hell. . . . That struck me."

That AA is by its nature a communal activity, however, which places therapeutic emphasis on a "buddy system," is also worth noting.

Even if I should have done it sooner? Even when I admit it's maybe possible that you might even interpret what I'm saying *now* as dishonest, as trying somehow to maybe freak you out enough so that you'll move back in and I can get out of this? Which I don't *think* I'm doing, but to be totally honest I can't be a hundred percent sure? To risk that with you? Do you understand? That I'm trying as hard as I can to love you? That I'm terrified I can't love? That I'm afraid maybe I'm just constitutionally incapable of doing anything other than pursuing and seducing and then running, plunging in and reversing, never being honest with anybody? That I'll never be a closer? That I might be a psychopath? Can you imagine what it takes to tell you this?

Again interrogation turns outward, toward the reader. What have we become when we "understand" ourselves so well all our questions are rhetorical? What is confession worth if what we want from it is not absolution but admiration for having confessed?

Wallace took a big risk with these free-floating "interviews": by refusing to anchor them in a third-person narrative, he placed their hideousness front and center, and left the reader to navigate her way through alone, without authorial guidance. It's not surprising that many readers conflated the hostility of these men with authorial sadism. But this is where it becomes vital to acknowledge the unity of the book *Brief Interviews*—this is not a random collection of short stories. The "interviews" themselves, dotted throughout the whole, work like words in a longer sentence, all segments of which need to be articulated if the sentence is to make any sense. The story "Think" is a fine example of this kind of counterpoint. Here a potentially hideous man, about to be seduced by "the younger sister of his wife's college roommate" suddenly experiences "a type of revelation." As she comes toward him, half naked, with "a slight smile, slight and smoky, media-taught," he feels the sudden urge to kneel. He looks at her: "Her expression is from page 18 of the Victoria's Secret catalogue." He puts his hands together. She crosses her arms and utters "a three word question"—which we will assume is *What the fuck?* "It's not what you think I'm afraid of," he replies. But we are not told what he thinks, or what she thinks he thinks, or what he thinks she thinks he thinks. The narrator only comments thus: "She could try, for just a moment to imagine what is happening in his head. . . . Even for an instant to try putting herself in his place." This task, though, is left to us. So here goes: the girl thinks he's afraid of the sin, of the marital betrayal, because that's the kind of thing it usually is on TV. He thinks she thinks this—and he's right. But the man himself is afraid of something else; of this "media-taught" situation, of the falsity, of living a cliché, and he has a sudden urge to feel like a human being, which is to say, humbled, and really connected, both to the person standing naked before him and to the world. ("And what if she joined him on the floor," read the final lines, "just like this, clasped in supplication: just this way.") Solipsism is here countered with humility; the "self alone" prays for a relation.

The popular view of Wallace was of a coolly cerebral writer who feared fiction's emotional connection. But that's not what he was afraid of. His stories have it the other way around: they are terrified of the *possibility of no emotional connection.* This is what his men truly have in common, far more than misogyny: *they know the words for everything and the meaning of nothing.* Which is a strange idea for fiction to explore, given that fiction has a vocational commitment to the idea that language is where we find truth. For Wallace, though, the most profound truths existed in a different realm: "I think that God has particular languages," he said once, "and one of them is music and one of them is mathematics." Certainly in *Brief Interviews* our everyday human language always falls short, even in its apparent clarity, *especially* in its clarity. The curious thing about these men is how they use their verbosity as a kind of armor, an elaborate screen to be placed between the world and the self. In B.I. #42, a man tries to come to terms with the fact his father was a lifelong toilet attendant in a public bathroom. Speaking of his case, he utilizes dozens of fancy words for excretions (*flatus, egestion, extrusion, feculence, lientery, transnudation*) yet his own basic emotions are not available to him:

"Yes and do I admire the fortitude of this humblest of working men? The stoicism? The Old World grit? To stand there all those years, never one sick day, serving? Or do I despise him, you're wondering, feel disgust, con-

tempt for any man who'd stand effaced in that miasma and dispense tow-
els for coins?"

Q.

" . . . "

Q.

"What were the two choices again?"

In B.I. #59, a boy, inspired by the TV show *Bewitched* has a masturbatory
fantasy of "freezing" real life with a wave of his hand so that he might have
sex in public while all around him are "paused." But with a mania for the
consistency of propositions, he is forced to expand upon the fantasy's "first
premise or *aksioma*" in an infinite direction. First he needs only to freeze the
room he's in, but then what of the building? So then the building, and then
the country, and then the continent, and then the planet, each stage neces-
sitating the next until:

> In order not to betray the fantasy's First Premise through causing incon-
> gruities in the scientifically catalogued measurements of the Solar Day and
> the Synodic Period, the earth's elliptical orbit around the sun must itself
> be halted by my supernatural hand's gesture, an orbit whose plane . . .

But I'll stop there. There are times when reading Wallace feels unbearable, and the weight of things stacked against the reader insurmountable:
missing context, rhetorical complication, awful people, grotesque or absurd
subject matter, language that is—at the same time!—childishly scatological
and annoyingly obscure. And if one is used to the consolation of "character,"
well then Wallace is truly a dead end. His stories simply don't investigate
character; they don't intend to. Instead they're turned outward, toward us.
It's *our* character that's being investigated. But this is not quite metafiction.
The metafictionist used recursion to highlight the mediating narrative voice;
to say essentially "I am water, and you are swimming through *me*." *Recursion*,
for the metafictionist, means: looping back, recurring, in infinite regressions.
This is not neutral, it is being written, I am writing it, but who am 'I'? Et cetera.

What's "recursive" about Wallace's short stories is not Wallace's narrative voice but the way these stories *run*, like verbal versions of mathematical procedures, in which at least one of the steps of the procedure involves rerunning the whole procedure. And it's *we* who run them. Wallace places us *inside* the process of recursion, and this is why reading him is so often emotionally and intellectually exhausting.

The apotheosis of this technique is "The Depressed Person." It's not that the depressed person is an unforgettable character. She's banal, typical. It's that when you're reading "The Depressed Person" you're forced to run her recursive thought processes through your own head, to pursue her self-serving self-hatreds through those endless footnotes, to speak with her that absurd therapy-speak, to live with her in the suffocating solipsism of her mind. Many readers will object to this. And there are other problems, besides: sometimes in the attempt to capture a brain from the inside, Wallace aims too low, and patronizes. Much of the therapy terminology in "The Depressed Person" amounts to cheap laughs, gotten too cheaply. ("I have a grossly sentimental affection for gags," he admitted.) *Support System, Blame Game, Inner-Child-Focused Experiential Therapy Retreat Weekend . . .* The idea that specialized language represents the fall within the tragic fall is not news and was territory already extensively covered by a slew of American writers: Thomas Pynchon, Bret Easton Ellis, A. M Homes, Douglas Coupland, et cetera. Wallace's *real* innovation was his virtuosic use of the recursive sentence, a weird and wonderful beast that needs quoting at length to be appreciated:

> As a schoolgirl, the depressed person had never spoken of the incident of the boy's telephone call and the mendacious pantomime with that particular roommate—a roommate with whom the depressed person hadn't clicked or connected at all, and whom she had resented in a bitter, cringing way that had made the depressed person despise herself, and had not made any attempt to stay in touch with after that endless sophomore second semester was finished—but she (i.e., the depressed person) had shared her agonizing memory of the incident with many of the friends in her Support System, and had also shared how bottomlessly horrible

and pathetic she had felt it would have been to have been that nameless, unknown boy at the other end of the telephone, a boy trying in good faith to take an emotional risk and to reach out and try to connect with the confident roommate, unaware that he was an unwelcome burden, pathetically unaware of the silent pantomimed boredom and contempt at the telephone's other end, and how the depressed person dreaded more than almost anything ever being in the position of being someone you had to appeal silently to someone else in the room to help you contrive an excuse to get off the telephone with.

Two simple syntactic units ("The depressed person had never spoken of the incident of the boy's telephone call" and "The boy was pathetically unaware of the incident") have been inserted into a third ("The depressed person dreaded being like the boy") to make a recursive sentence in which prepositional phrases lie inside one another like Russian dolls: *The depressed person, who had never spoken of the incident of the boy's phone call of which the boy was pathetically unaware, dreaded being like the boy.* (And that's not even including the further recursion of the roommate.) In the process, the embedded "incident" is rerun in its entirety, here, and elsewhere in "The Depressed Person," as the poor girl reflects on her "dread" and thus sets the procedure off again, running the whole story through once more. This is *linguistic* recursion—defined as the capacity to embed sentences in other sentences. For many linguists, notably Noam Chomsky, this form of recursion is fundamental to language; it's recursion that permits extension without limitation and makes language a system characterized by "discrete infinity."[15] Infinity was of course a fruitful subject for Wallace (besides *Infinite Jest*, in 2003 he wrote a nonfiction book about it: *Everything and More: A Compact History of Infinity*). He had a gift for articulating our conflicted response to this

---

15. An argument recently challenged by the American professor of linguistics Dan Everett, whose paper "Cultural Constraints on Grammar and Cognition in Pirahã," caused an almighty brouhaha among the sort of people who get all brouhaha-ed about linguistics. In the paper he claimed to have found a tribe in the rainforest of northwestern Brazil—the Pirahã—whose language does not use recursion and is, in fact, finite. *The New Yorker* had an interesting article about all this, "The Interpreter," in the April 16, 2007 issue.

strangest of ideas. For if we feel a certain horror before infinity—because it transcends human scale and is unthinkable—we also hear in it the suggestion of the sacred. As a concept, infinity seems to bear the trace of God's language, of Larkin's "deep blue air, that shows/Nothing, and is nowhere, and is endless." Forever, overhead. In "The Depressed Person," though, infinity is horrific: it has been turned inward and burrows wormholes in the self. The effect on the reader is powerful, unpleasant. Quite apart from being forced to share one's own mental space with the depressed person's infinitely dismal consciousness, to read those spiral sentences is to experience that dread of circularity embedded in the old joke about recursion (*to understand recursion you must first understand recursion*), as well as the existential vertigo we feel when we stand between two mirrors. One suffers to read it, but suffering is part of the point:

> There's always been a strong and distinctive American distaste for frustration and suffering. . . . It seems distinctly Western-industrial, anyway. In most other cultures, if you hurt, if you have a symptom that's causing you to suffer, they view this as basically healthy and natural, a sign that your nervous system knows something's wrong. For these cultures, getting rid of the pain without addressing the deeper cause would be like shutting off a fire alarm while the fire's still going. But if you just look at the number of ways that we try like hell to alleviate mere symptoms in this country—from fast-fast-fast-relief antacids to the popularity of lighthearted musicals during the Depression—you can see an almost compulsive tendency to regard pain itself as the problem.

For the depressed person pain has certainly been fetishized, pathologized: she can't feel simple sadness, only "agony"; she's not merely depressed, she is "in terrible and unceasing emotional pain." Meanwhile, another kind of pain—the kind one feels for other people in *their* suffering—is inaccessible to her. When one of her Support System becomes terminally ill, the only pain this causes her (i.e., the depressed person) is the realization *that she doesn't really care at all*, which in turn sparks in her mind the dreaded possibility that she might in fact be "a solipsistic, self-consumed, endless emotional vacuum and sponge." She is disgusted by herself, and the disgust causes her yet more pain and pica-gnawed[16] hands, and on it goes in its terrible cycle. The last lines of the story put the snake's tongue in its own mouth: "How was she to decide and describe—even to herself, looking inward and facing herself—what all she'd so painfully learned said about her?"

The spiral sentences, the looping syntax, the repetition, the invasion of clinical vocabulary—none of this is mere "formal stunt-pilotry." Nor does it add up to nonsense, or "stream of consciousness" if sloppiness and incomprehensibility is meant by that term: however long they are, Wallace's procedures are always grammatically immaculate. The point is to run a procedure—the procedure of another person's thoughts!—through your own mind. This way you don't merely "have" the verbal explanation. You feel it and know it:

> Fiction's about what it is to be a fucking human being. If you operate . . . from the premise that there are things about the contemporary U.S. that make it distinctively hard to be a real human being, then maybe half of fiction's job is to dramatize what it is that makes it tough. The other half is to dramatize the fact that we still "are" human beings, now.

A lot of *Brief Interviews* is tough and painful: it's doing the first half of that job. The rest of *Brief Interviews* is doing the other.

3. SIGNIFYING NOTHING

We've all got this "literary" fiction that simply monotones that we're all becoming less and less human, that presents characters without souls or love, characters who really are exhaustively describable in terms of what brands of stuff they wear, and we all buy the books and go like "Golly, what a mordantly effective commentary on contemporary materialism!" But we already "know" U.S. culture is materialistic. This diagnosis can be done in

---

16. From the *OED*: "Pica—A tendency or craving to eat substances other than normal food, occurring during childhood or pregnancy, or as a symptom of disease." This is Wallace's way of describing someone chewing her own fingernails.

about two lines. It doesn't engage anybody. What's engaging and artistically real is, taking it as axiomatic that the present is grotesquely materialistic, how is it that we as human beings still have the capacity for joy, charity, genuine connections, for stuff that doesn't have a price? And can these capacities be made to thrive? And if so, how, and if not, why not?

One way out of this bind is to present, on the page, complex human beings. Sensitive souls, able to plumb their own emotional depths, capable of interesting thoughts despite the deadening times. How many of Roth's and Bellow's protagonists are academics, psychiatrists, intellectuals, or just motormouths? And when Henry James spoke of "fine awareness," it was his contention that only characters in possession of this quality could elicit the same quality in their readers:

> Their being finely aware—as Hamlet and Lear, say, are finely aware—
> *makes* absolutely the intensity of their adventure, gives the maximum of
> sense to what befalls them. We care, our curiosity and our sympathy care,
> comparatively little for what happens to the stupid, the coarse and the
> blind; care for it, and for the effects of it, at the most as helping to precipi-
> tate what happens to the more deeply wondering, to the really sentient.

But Wallace's fiction cares what happens to the stupid, the coarse, and the blind. In fact, it is preoccupied by the stupid, the coarse, and the blind to a peculiar degree, as if the necessary counterpoint to the overintellectualized self is the ingenuous self. He seemed to spy in such characters—so unlike himself!—an escape from the "postmodern trap." Take the simple fellow in "Signifying Nothing," a young man whose very coarseness is the apparent key to his salvation. The story opens like this:

> Here is a weird one for you. It was a couple of years ago, and I was 19, and
> getting ready to move out of my folks' house, and get out on my own, and
> one day as I was getting ready, I suddenly get this memory of my father
> waggling his dick in my face one time when I was a little kid.

As pure event, this feels no more or less traumatic than the depressed person's original complaint.[17] But in the young man's case it is a wound he doesn't even know how to worry: "I kept trying to think about why my father would do something like that, and what he could have been thinking of, like, what it could have meant." He is without answers. In his confusion he becomes angry, but when he finally confronts his father with the memory, his form of interrogation is amusingly direct: "What the fuck was up with *that?*" In response his father gives him only a silent look of "total disbelief, and total disgust," and the silence grows; an estrangement occurs; for a year the young man does not see his family. Then something strange. Without extensive analysis, without endless debate, without indulging in bouts of self-interrogation, he heals himself:

> As time passed, I, little by little, got over the whole thing. I still knew that the memory of my father waggling his dick at me in the rec room was real, but, little by little, I started to realize, just because *I* remembered the incident, that did not mean, necessarily, my *father* did. . . . Little by little, it seemed like the moral of a memory of any incident that weird is, anything is possible.

Generally, we refuse to be each other. Our own experiences feel necessarily more real than other people's, skewed by our sense of our own absolute centrality. But this young man in his simplicity does the difficult thing: he makes a leap into otherness. This empathic imaginative leap—into his own father's head—miraculously bypasses the depressed person's equivalent recursive maze. This simple thought—that his father's (non)experience of the memory might be as real to his father as the young man's own *positive* memory of it is real—turns out to be revelatory. It's another recursive sentence, but this time, instead of tunneling inward, it leads out—to the infinite unknowability of other people.

---

17. When still a child, the depressed person's divorced parents had battled each other over who was to pay for her (i.e., the depressed person's) orthodontics. The writer Mary Karr informs me that this detail wasn't accidental; it was lifted from Elizabeth Wurtzel's memoir, *Prozac Nation.*

Maybe the incident is, after all, the kind of narrative Macbeth described: "A tale/Told by an idiot, full of sound and fury,/Signifying nothing."

You don't hear the word *parable* much in connection with Wallace, but I don't know why not—he wrote a lot of them. What else do you call a story like "Yet Another Example of the Porousness of Certain Borders (XI)?" A man has a dream that he is blind, and then, the next day:

> I'm incredibly conscious of my eyesight and my eyes and how good it is to be able to see colors and people's faces and to know exactly where I am, and of how fragile it all is, the human eye mechanism and the ability to see, how easily it could be lost, how I'm always seeing blind people around with canes and strange-looking faces and am always just thinking of them as interesting to spend a couple seconds looking at and never thinking they had anything to do with me or my eyes, and it's really just a lucky coincidence that I can see instead of being one of those blind people I see on the subway.

Here "other-blindness" has been actualized. A simple route to a great revelation. And again, in "The Devil Is a Busy Man," a country hick who can't get anyone to take, for free, an "Old Harrow With Some Teeth A Little Rusted," attracts avid consumers as soon as he lists it in the classifieds for five dollars:

> I asked Daddy about what lesson to draw here and he said he figured it's you don't try and teach a pig to sing and told me to go on and rake the drive's gravel back out of the ditch before it fucked up the drainage.

Another lesson might be: value in capitalism is measured not by real worth but by lack.

The coarse, the blind, the stupid. As effective as these parables are, there is something sentimental about them—albeit a sentiment as old as fiction itself. As city dwellers yearn for Virgil's pastoral, so intellectuals will tend to romanticize the pure relations they imagine exist between simple people. Wallace was on guard against this as he was against everything ("Yes and do I admire the fortitude of this humblest of working men? The stoicism? The

Old World grit?"), and yet still it slips through, here, as well as in the nonfiction, where we find instinctive sportsmen, service-industry workers, farmers, and all kinds of down-home folks (usually from his home state of Illinois) receiving that warmness Wallace could never quite muster for hyperreflexive intellectuals more or less like himself.[18]

But in their defense it should be said that the philosophical significance of these tales is not really that the selves involved are purer than the rest of us in their stupidity, coarseness, and blindness. It's that they have sought—even momentarily—relationships that look outward, away from self. When the young man in "Signifying Nothing" finally reconnects with his father, it is at the birthday of his sister, in his family's "special restaurant," and the ice is broken not by anguished discussion or a sudden moment of personal insight but by a lame family joke shared by all. Which brings us finally to Wittgenstein's second option, the way out of solipsism into communality:

And so he trashed everything he'd been lauded for in the "Tractatus" and wrote the "Investigations," which is the single most comprehensive and beautiful argument against solipsism that's ever been made. Wittgenstein argues that for language even to be possible, it must always be a *function of relationships between persons* (that's why he spends so much time arguing against the possibility of a "private language"). [My italics]

The moralist in Wallace—that part of him that wanted not only to describe the wound but to heal it—invested much in this idea. He was always trying to place "relationships between persons" as the light at the end of his narrative dark tunnels; he took special care to re-create and respect the (often simple) language shared by people who feel some connection with each other. ("Get the fuck outta here" is the sentence that occasions the rapprochement in "Signifying Nothing.") "In the day-to-day trenches of adult existence," Wallace once claimed, "banal platitudes can have a life-or-death

18. In the acknowledgments of *Brief Interviews* Wallace thanks the MacArthur and Lannan foundations, *The Paris Review*, and "The Staff and Management of Denny's 24-Hour Family Restaurant, Bloomington IL."

importance."[19] Among his many gifts was this knack for truly *animating* platitudes, in much the same way that moral philosophers through the ages have
animated abstract moral ideas through "dialogues" or narrative examples.

"Some things are best left unsaid."
"Walk a mile in someone else's shoes."
"You only want what you can't have."

What else are those three stories but complex enactments of platitudes
we would otherwise ignore?

Still, there is something not quite convincing in their optimism. They
seem to me to offer more of a willed solution than an instinctive or deeply felt
one. This isn't a bad thing: it contributes to their compelling ambivalence.
And it's an ambivalence that finds a mirror in Wallace's own doubts w/r/t the
optimism any of us should draw from Wittgenstein's "second option":

So he makes language dependent on human community, but unfortunately
we're still stuck with the idea that there is this world of referents out there
that we can never really join or know because we're stuck in here, in language, even if we're at least all in here together. This eliminated solipsism,
but not the horror. Because we're still stuck. The "Investigation"'s line is
that the fundamental problem of language is, quote, "I don't know my way
about." If I were separate from language, if I could somehow detach from
it and climb up and look down on it, get the lay of the land so to speak, I
could study it "objectively," take it apart, deconstruct it, know its opera-

19. He makes the same point, at greater length, in an interview with Salon: "It seems to me
that the intellectualization and aestheticizing of principles and values in this country is one
of the things that's gutted our generation. All the things that my parents said to me, like 'It's
really important not to lie.' OK, check, got it. I nod at that but I really don't feel it. Until I get
to be about 30 and I realize that if I lie to you, I also can't trust you. I feel that I'm in pain,
I'm nervous, I'm lonely and I can't figure out why. Then I realize, 'Oh, perhaps the way to deal
with this is really not to lie.' The idea that something so simple and, really, so aesthetically
uninteresting—which for me meant you pass over it for the interesting, complex stuff—can
actually be nourishing in a way that arch, meta, ironic, pomo stuff can't, that seems to me to
be important. That seems to me like something our generation needs to feel."

tions and boundaries and deficiencies. But that's not how things are. I'm "in" it. We're "in" language. Wittgenstein's not Heidegger. It's not that language "is" us, but we're still "in" it, inescapably, the same way we're in like Kant's space-time. Wittgenstein's conclusions seem completely sound to me, always have. And if there's one thing that consistently bugs me writing-wise, it's that I don't feel I really "do" know my way around inside language—I never seem to get the kind of clarity and concision I want.

One way, though, of knowing your "way about" would be to focus on the specialized islands of language *within* the system, and when Wallace does this he achieves the clarity and concision he wanted. It's a little perverse, in fact, how profoundly he was attracted, as a fiction writer, to exactly those forms of linguistic specialization he philosophically abhorred. Stories that attend to the language of computers, the language of therapists, the language of carpet salesmen, the language of corporate life, the language of academics—Wallace truly dazzles when he lands on a discourse and masters all its permutations.[20] In "Datum Centurio," a six-page marvel of linguistic fantasy, we meet with *Leckie & Webster's Connotationally Gender-Specific Lexicon of Contemporary Usage*, which, if we pay close attention to the small type of the fake copyright page, we gather to be a futuristic dictionary from the year 2096. It is a dictionary that comes with "11.2gb of Contextual, Etymological, Historical, Usage and Gender-Specific Connotational notes," which is "Hot Text Keyed" and available on DVD (this last being the one detail that makes me smile in the wrong way, and think fondly of 1993). There is even the suggestion of a plug-in one plugs into one's body ("Available Also with Lavish Illustrative Support in All 5 Major Sense-Media"). Wallace has opened this dictionary for us at the Ds. We are defining the word *date*, in its romantic sense:

date³ (*dat*) *n*. {20C English, from Middle English, from Old French, from Medieval Latin *data*, feminine past participle of *dare*, to give.}

---

20. We now know that his last, unfinished novel, *The Pale King*, attends to the specialized language of IRS tax inspectors.

1. *Informal.* (see also **soft date**) **a.** Consequent to the successful application for a License to Parent (KEY at PROCREATIVITY; at BREED/(v); at PARENT/ (v); at OFFSPRING, SOFT), the process of voluntarily submitting one's nucleotide configurations and other Procreativity Designators to an agency empowered by law to identify an optimal female neurogenetic complement for the purposes of Procreative Genital Interface.

This being quite different from a "hard date," which involves the use of a Virtual Female Sensory Array (slang term: "telediddler") for the purposes of Simulated Genital Interface. The fun Wallace has with all this is the fun of a man who loved words and *adored* dictionaries, those sacred sites where his beloved words could be kept pristine and each given their deserved attention. As it was with Borges, a dictionary was, for Wallace, a universe: every etymological root, every usage note, every obsolete meaning was of interest to him. And for good reason: if you believe that what we are able to *say* marks the limit of what we are able to *think* and *be*, the dictionary is our most important human document. The usage note he invents for the word *date* in the year 2096 is a case in point:

date31.a USAGE/CONTEXTUAL NOTE: "You are too old by far to be the type of man who checks his replicase levels before breakfast and has high-baud macros for places like Fruitful Union P.G.I Coding or SoftSci Deoxyribonucleic Intercode Systems in his Mo.Sys deck, and yet here you are, parking the heads on your VFSA telediddler and checking your replicase levels and padding your gen-resume like a randy freshman, preparing for what appears to all the world like an attempt at a soft date." (McInerney et seq {via OmniLit TRF Matrix}2068).

A Polaroid of a society—a miniaturized sci-fi novel! To enjoy it, though, you have to unpack it, and to do this most readers will need their own *OED* and a medical dictionary. Here goes: You're too old to be checking your supply of the enzymes-that-catalyze-the-synthesis-of-ribonucleic-molecules (which molecules carry instructions from your DNA which in turn control the synthesis of your proteins); *way* too old to have, in your possession, high data-per-second programming instructions for such imaginary futuristic genetic reproduction companies as "Fruitful Union" and "SoftSci" sitting there in your "desktop" (or whatever interface they're using in 2068), and yet *still* you're leaving your virtual sex toy alone and instead checking that you're in tip top genetic condition and padding out your "genetic résumé" as if you were about to go and try and have *actual procreative sex with someone*! (And can we assume that in the future "J. McInerney" has become a fictional brand—*et seq*; "and what follows"—made possible by a frightening omnivorous literary computer program that takes literary styles and reproduces them long after the authors are in their graves?)

Look: that language fantasias of this kind are übergeeky and laborious can't seriously be denied. The other story of this type, "Tri-Stan: I Sold Sissee Nar to Ecko," retells the Tristan and Iseult story in the corporate entertainment offices of a futuristic/classical L.A. in futuristic-classical language—

Awakening this in fugues and paroxysms, Agon M. Nar did there upon consult mediated Oracles, offer leveraged tribute to images of Nielsen & Stasis, & sacrifice two whole humidors of Davidoff 9 Deluxes upon the offering-pyre of Emmé, Winged Goddess of Victory. There was much market research.

—and has been known to try the patience of even the hardiest howling fantod.[21] But what they signify, these stories—that words are worlds, that no language is neutral—is also serious and beautiful. Using extreme linguistic specialization to create little worlds was another, far more complicated way of saying THIS IS WATER, of reminding us that wherever we have language, we have the artificial conditions, limits, and possibilities of our existence. Of course, there is a writing that ignores this; that thinks of its own language

---

21. Hard-core Wallace nerds call themselves howling fantods.

as classical and universal and nonspecific; that experiences any trace of the contemporary as a kind of stain (no brand names, no modern words) and calls itself realism even if its characters speak no differently from those in a novel thirty years ago, or sixty. Wallace felt he couldn't ignore the ambient noise of the contemporary, for the simple reason that it is everywhere. It *is* the water we swim in:

> I've always thought of myself as a realist. I can remember fighting with my professors about it in grad school. The world that I live in consists of 250 advertisements a day and any number of unbelievably entertaining options, most of which are subsidized by corporations that want to sell me things. The whole way that the world acts on my nerve endings is bound up with stuff that the guys with leather patches on their elbows would consider pop or trivial or ephemeral. I use a fair amount of pop stuff in my fiction, but what I mean by it is nothing different than what other people mean in writing about trees and parks and having to walk to the river to get water 100 years ago. It's just the texture of the world I live in.

You had to fight to make this case in the 1990s, and writers like Wallace fought it in the face of a certain amount of critical ridicule and the general sense that it couldn't be literature with a capital *L* if it let the trashy language of the contemporary in. Ten years later, few writers feel the need to defend this use of contemporary "texture," and for the generation who grew up on Wallace, specialized language use amounts to realism of the first order: it's the water they grew up swimming in.

But you can also think about water too much. You can forget how to swim. You can develop an extreme self-consciousness w/r/t form, and when this happens in Wallace's work, we can clearly watch metafiction reclaiming him, almost eating him alive. In the story "Adult World," a tale of extreme self-consciousness (a paranoid wife fears that the way she makes love with her husband is "somehow hard on his thingie") devolves into an acute case of *narrative* self-consciousness, which concludes with the story falling apart.

One half is written, but the other half is entirely deconstructed, offered only in the form of a writer's schematic notes, unfinished, unfilled in. I remember how thrilled I was when I first read it—I thought it delicious that such a pyrotechnical stylist would be sufficiently honest to reveal the mechanical levers behind the *Wizard of Oz* facade. Ten years later I reread it and feel that the shock of the backstage glimpse is just that, a shock, and that it wears off and does not satisfy as the full story might have. "Octet," an attempted "cycle of very short belletristic pieces" that are "supposed to compose a certain sort of '*interrogation*' of the person reading them," is another piece that suddenly falls apart (he only manages four of the eight), though in a far more astonishing fashion. As Wallace abandons his story cycle he tells us why: they "don't interrogate or palpate" the reader as he'd wanted them to. What follows is an extremely manipulative breaking of the fourth wall, which, at the same time, claims to come from a place of urgent sincerity. Just like one of his own hideous men, Wallace assumes our consciousness; he parrots all our responses before we have them (he *knows* it looks manipulative, he *knows* this sounds like metafiction, and yes, *he knows we know he knows*.) He won't stop, he hounds us relentlessly even through the footnotes, trying desperately to convince his readers that it's not what we think he's afraid of (which is failure). He knows, too, that "this 100%-honest-naked-interrogation-of-reader tactic" is an incredibly costly one, for him, for you, for your relationship with this book—hell, with David Foster Wallace, period. It's my guess that how you feel about "Octet" will make or break you as a reader of Wallace, because what he's really asking is for you to have faith in something he cannot possibly ever finally determine in language: "the agenda of the consciousness behind the text." His urgency, his sincerity, his apparent desperation to "connect" with his reader in a genuine way—these are things you either believe in or don't. Some writers want sympathetic readers; some want readers with a sense of humor; some want their readers at the political barricades, fired up and ready to go. Strange to say it, but Wallace wanted *faithful* readers. The last line of "Octet"?

"So decide."

4. CHURCH NOT MADE WITH HANDS

It's worth having faith in "Octet." You miss something important if you throw
it across the room unfinished, as I did when I first read it. Buried in the middle
of it there is a sort of confession. Or as close to a nakedly honest statement as
Wallace ever made w/r/t his literary intentions. He is ostensibly talking about the
"semiworkable pieces" of "Octet," but what he has to say applies to all his work:

> [A]ll seem to be trying to demonstrate some sort of weird ambient *same-*
> *ness* in different kinds of human relationships, some nameless but ines-
> capable *"price"* that all human beings are faced with having to pay at some
> point if they ever truly want "to be with" another person instead of just
> using that person somehow (like for example using the person just as an
> audience, or as an instrument of their own selfish ends, or as some piece
> of moral gymnastics equipment on which they can demonstrate their
> virtuous character (as in people who are generous to other people only
> because they want to be seen as generous, and so actually secretly like it
> when people around them go broke or get into trouble, because it means
> they can rush generously in and act all helpful—everybody's seen people
> like this), or as a narcissistically cathected projection of themselves, etc.),
> a weird and nameless but apparently unavoidable "price" that can actu-
> ally sometimes equal death itself, or at least usually equals your giving
> up something (either a thing or a person or a precious long-held "feel-
> ing" or some certain idea of yourself and your own virtue/worth/identity)
> whose loss will feel, in a true and urgent way, like a kind of death, and to
> say that the fact that there could be (you feel) such an overwhelming and
> elemental *sameness* to such totally different situations and *mise en scenes*
> and conundra. . . .—seems to you urgent, truly urgent, something almost
> worth shimmying up chimneys and shouting from roofs about.[22]

22. I have omitted, for the sake of brevity,[23] six footnotes Wallace includes in this paragraph.
23. (Though at this point, who am I kidding?)

There is a weird ambient sameness to Wallace's work. He was always asking essentially the same question. *How do I recognize that other people are real, as I am?* And the strange, quasi-mystical answer was always the same, too. *You may have to give up your attachment to the "self."* I don't mean that Wallace "preached" this moral in his work; when I think of a moralist I don't think of a preacher. On the contrary, he was a writer who placed himself "in the hazard" of his own terms, undergoing them as real problems, both in life and on the page. For this reason, I suspect he will remain a writer who appeals, above all, to the young. It's young people who best understand his sense of urgency, and who tend to take abstract existential questions like these seriously, as interrogations that relate directly to themselves. The struggle with ego, the struggle with the self, the struggle to allow other people to exist in their genuine "otherness"—these were aspects of Wallace's own struggle. One way to read *Brief Interviews* is as a series of intimate confessions of "other blindness." Confessions of solipsism, of misogyny, of ego, of control freakery, of cruelty, of snobbery, of sadism. Of that old Christian double bind: *the wish to be seen to be good.* Speaking of "The Depressed Person" he said: "That was the most painful thing I have ever done. . . . [T]hat character is a part of me I hardly ever write about. There is a part of me that is just like that person." And then there's the moderately overweight careerist poet in "Death Is Not the End." It's about as far from an autobiographical portrait of Wallace as one can imagine, but it's fueled with a disgust that feels somehow personal. Wallace was constitutionally hard on himself, apparently compelled to confess not only to who he was but to who he dreaded being or becoming. "The fifty-six-year-old American poet, a Nobel Laureate," recipient of basically every award and grant literary America has to offer (except the Guggenheim[24] a fact which seems to plague him, and pops up in a footnote apropos of nothing, as if it had thrust itself to the surface of the story in subconscious fury), is "known in American literary circles as 'the poet's poet' or sometimes simply 'the Poet,'" and he is truly selfhood experienced in its unbearable fullness.

---

24. The Guggehein Fellowships are grants awarded anually to those "who have demonstrated exceptional capacity for productive scholarship or exceptional creative ability in the arts."

We get a meticulous description of his self, the exact spot in which he sits (in a lounger, by a pool, in a garden), as well as his exact coordinate in relation to the sun (as if it revolved around him). In short (well, in two gigantic recursive sentences), Wallace annihilates him. God help the man who has chosen to worship himself! Whose self really *is* no more than the awards he has won, the prestige he has earned, the wealth he has amassed. In our last glimpse of the Poet he is surrounded by his expensive shrubbery, which is "motionless green vivid and inescapable and not like anything else in the world in either appearance and suggestion." A footnote adds: "That is not wholly true." Green, vivid, motionless, inescapable? Sounds like money to me.

In *The Gift*, a book that meant a lot to Wallace, the cultural anthropologist Lewis Hyde examines the different modes in which cultures and individuals deal with the concept of gifts and giving. He offers a fine description of the kind of swollen self we find in "Death Is Not the End": "The narcissist feels his gifts come from himself. He works to display himself, not to suffer change." The father in "On His Deathbed, Holding Your Hand" makes a similar judgment about his Pulitzer Prize–winning playwright son: he is appalled by his (i.e., the son's) sense of his own "*limitless gifts* unquote" and the admiration they arouse in everyone:

> As if he actually *deserved* this sort of—as if it were the most natural thing in the world. . . .—as if this sort of love were *due* him, itself of nature, inevitable as the sunrise, never a thought, never a moment's doubt that he deserves it all and more. The very thought of it chokes me. How many years he took from us. Our Gift. Genitive, ablative, nominative—the accidence of "gift."

To Wallace, a gift truly was an accident; a chance, a fortuitous circumstance. Born intelligent, born with perfect pitch, with mathematical ability, with a talent for tennis—in what sense are we ever the proprietors of these blessings? What rights accrue to us because of them? How could we ever claim to truly own them?

It's very interesting to me that this attitude toward gifts should have within it a current that is strongly anti-American, being both contra "rights" and contra "ownership." I've always had the sense, philosophically speaking, that Wallace's ethical ideas were profoundly un-American: he had more in common with the philosophical current that runs from Kant's "realm of ends" through Simone Weils "sacred humans" and on to John Rawls's "veil of ignorance,"[25] than the Hobbes/Smith/Locke waters from which the idea of America was drawn. Wallace's work rejects "goal-directed" philosophies of human happiness, both because they isolate the self (the pursuit of happiness is a pursuit we undertake alone) and because this Western obsession with happiness as a goal makes people childishly "pain-averse," allergic to the one quality that is, in Wallace's view, the true constant of human life: "Look at utilitarianism . . . and you see a whole teleology predicated on the idea that the best human life is one that maximizes the pleasure-to-pain ratio. God, I know this sounds priggish of me. All I'm saying is that it's shortsighted to blame TV. It's simply another symptom. TV didn't invent our aesthetic child-ishness here any more than the Manhattan Project invented aggression . . . " His stories repel the idea that a just society can come from the contract made between self-interested or egoistic individuals, or that it is one's "personhood" that guarantees one a bigger slice of the pie. (The fat poet's talents or per-sonal merits can't make him more worthy than anyone else.)

And in a few extreme cases, Wallace's stories go further, lining up behind a quasi-mystic such as Weil, who, like the Buddhists, abandons "Personhood" entirely: "What is sacred in a human being is the impersonal in him. . . . Our personality is the part of us which belongs to error and sin. The whole effort of the mystic has always been to become such that there is no part left in his

25. All three having in common the idea that the business of ethics properly concerns good relations *between* people rather than the individual's relation toward some ultimate goal, or end. For Kant, all people are ends in themselves; for Weil they are sacred in themselves. For Rawls they are communal individuals whose differences are to be respected and yet not counted as relevant when it comes to justice, which must concern itself with fairness. In Rawls's view, if we were to choose the principles of a just society, we would have to be placed under a "veil of ignorance" in which we knew nothing of one another's (or our own) personal qualities, that is, race, talents, religion, wealth, class, gender—an awesome idea that reminds me of Wallace at his most parabolic. Let's say it's your job to choose the "role of women" in this society, a society in which you're going to live. But as you make the decision you don't know if you yourself are to be a woman or not. So decide!

soul to say 'I'."[26] Consequently, the statement *You have no right to hurt me* is to Weil meaningless, for rights are a concept that attaches to "personhood" and one person can always feel their "rights" to be more rightful that another's. *What you are doing to me is not just*—this, for Weil, is the correct and sacred phrase. "The spirit of justice and truth is nothing else," she writes, "but a certain kind of attention, which is pure love."

Isn't it exactly *this* "certain kind of attention" that Wallace explores in B.I. #20 (sometimes known as The Granola Cruncher)? It is the darkest story in the collection,[27] and it has an extreme setup, even by Wallace's standards: a hippie girl, viciously raped by a psychopath, decides to create, in the middle of the act, a "soul connection" with her rapist because she "believes that sufficient love and focus can penetrate even psychosis and evil." In the process she is able to forget herself, and focus on *his* misery—even to feel pity for him. But this all happened some time ago: when the story opens we are being retold it as an anecdote by a man who has himself heard it as anecdote:

B.I. #20 12-96

NEW HAVEN CT

"And yet I did not fall in love with her until she had related the story of the unbelievably horrifying incident in which she was brutally accosted and held captive and very nearly killed."

New Haven? A recently graduated Yalie, perhaps. Definitely overeducated, supercilious, and full, initially, of bombastic opinions about the girl, whom he picked up at a festival as a "strictly one night objective," because she had a sexy body ("Her face was a bit strange") and because he thought it would be easy. She's an open book to him—he feels he can read her easily:

What one might call a quote Granola Cruncher, or post-Hippie, New Ager, what have you . . . comprising the prototypical sandals, unrefined fibers,

---

26. From Weil's essay "Human Personality."
27. But it won Wallace his sole literary prize: the Aga Khan Prize for Fiction from *The Paris Review*.

daffy arcane, emotional incontinence, flamboyantly long hair, extreme liberality on social issues . . . and using the, well the quote L-word itself several times without irony or even any evident awareness that the word has through tactical over-deployment become trite and requires invisible quotes around it now at the very least.

She is an object on which to exert his superiority. A body from which his own body will take its pleasure. In the event, though, her strange postcoital anecdote unnerves and destabilizes him: she tells her story of extraordinary focus *with* extraordinary focus and he (like one of Henry James's ideal readers) finds his own fine awareness stimulated by hers:

> I found myself hearing expressions like *fear gripping her soul*, unquote, less as televisual clichés or melodrama but as sincere if not particularly artful attempts to describe what it must have felt like, the feelings of shock and unreality alternating with waves of pure terror.

But there is something chilling in both his modes of processing her experience. First it is "televisual cliché"; then something so unexpectedly real he becomes desirous of her precisely *because* of it, seeing, perhaps, in her realness, a way of becoming real himself. But when did the real become unexpected? When did we become so inured to the real that it gathered around it this strange *aura*? In the age of mechanical reproduction, prophesized Walter Benjamin, a painting such as the *Mona Lisa* will lose its aura: the more cheap postcards we make of her, the more she will disappear. But he was wrong—it turned out the erotic logic of capital worked the other way around. Her authentic aura increased. So what happens to the authentic aura of, say, "fear" when you've seen a thousand women scream on TV? Wallace's answer is frightening: we're so deadened by the flat televisual repetition of all our human emotions, we have begun to fetishize "real" feelings, *especially* real pain. It's as if we've stopped believing in reality—only extremity can make us feel again. And here is extremity, and the man suddenly *feels*. He is there with her, in her moment of "soul-connection." So are we. "Have you ever heard of *the couvade*?" he asks his

therapist, and in the usual nonresponse we become aware of this story's tripli-
cate act of empathy: ours for the girl via the man's anecdote, his for the girl via
her anecdote, the girl's for the rapist via the experience itself. In the couvade,
a man feels his wife's pregnancy: a porous border. In this story, several borders
feel porous at once. The man is able to feel the "fathomless sadness" of the
rapist; we, as readers, aggressively challenged by the very setup (a woman *pit-
ies* her rapist?), begin by sharing the skepticism of the Yalie, but as we move
toward him, he moves away from us to a place where he is capable of believing her. The anecdote has created a force field of fine awareness around it.
Through the man's attempts to appropriate it, and our own need to judge it,
Wallace manages to create a sense of its sacred otherness. Evidence of one
woman's capacity for the L word, perhaps, but not something we can turn to
our own devices, not a story we can own.

The Granola Cruncher is one of the few people in *Brief Interviews* not using
another person as an example or as an object or as a piece of "moral gymnastic
equipment." She exists in a quite different moral realm from the manipulator
who uses his deformed arm, his "flipper," as bait to "catch" sympathetic women
who then sleep with him, or the guy who twists Viktor Frankl's holocaust memoir, *Man's Search for Meaning*, into a perverse apologia for destroying another
human being. (Frankl's therapeutic school, logotherapy, explores the idea that
selves in an extreme state of personal degradation or loss are often better able
to comprehend what is really meaningful. But this, of course, does not mean
you create a second holocaust in order to generate meaning.) Most of Wallace's
people refuse, even for a moment, to give up the self. They have been taught
"that a self is something you just have," like you have a car, or a house, or a bank
account. But selves are not consumer items, and the journey to becoming "a
fucking human being" is one that lasts as long as our lives: "The horrific struggle to establish a human self results in a self whose humanity is inseparable from
that horrific struggle. . . . Our endless and impossible journey toward home is
in fact our home." Those quotes are from a talk Wallace gave on Franz Kafka,
another writer for whom he felt a deep affinity. Their connection is not obvious
at the level of sentence but their deep currents run parallel: the attachment to
parables, the horror of the self in its fullness (think of the cipher Georg dash-

ing from his charismatic father in "The Judgment," vaulting over that bridge), the dream of self-less-ness. And despite their attempts to root themselves in "relationships between persons" they both expressed a longing for the infinite, which is nothing and is nowhere and is endless. Throughout this essay, which I began writing when Wallace was alive, I have defined that longing as purely philosophical—events have shown this to be wishful thinking on my part. The story "Suicide as a Sort of Present" now inevitably resonates beyond itself, but it is also same story it always was: a reminder that there exist desperate souls who feel that their nonexistence, in the literal sense, would be a gift to those around them. We must assume that David was one of them.

In the end, the truly sublime and frightening moments in *Brief Interviews* do not involve families joshing each other in Italian restaurants. When he offers his readers generous, healthy interpersonal relations as a route out of "the postmodern trap," well, that's the responsible moral philosopher in him. But the real mystery and magic lies in those quasi-mystical moments, portraits of extreme focus and total relinquishment. We might feel more comfortable calling this "meditation," but I believe the right word is in fact *prayer*. What else is the man in "Think" doing when he falls on his knees and puts his hands together? What is the Granola Cruncher doing as the psychopath moves on top of her? What is the boy in "Forever Overhead" doing just before he dives? It's true that this is prayer unmoored, without its usual object, God, but it is still focused, self-forgetful, and moving in an outward direction toward the unfathomable (which the mystic will argue *is* God). It is the L word, at work in the world. Wallace understood better than most that for the secular among us, art has become our best last hope of undergoing this experience.

"Church Not Made with Hands" is a gift of this kind. It is *about* extreme focus and it *requires* extreme focus. In its climactic scene, a priest kneels praying in front of a picture of himself praying, which feels like the ultimate DFW image, as DeLillo's most-photographed barn holds within it something of the essential DeLillo. "Church Not Made with Hands" is my favorite gift in a book laden with them. I think that must be why I'm loathe to take it apart as I have the others. More than any other story in *Brief Interviews* it seals its doors tightly and the joy for each reader will come in finding the keys that fit the locks—and who's to say your keys you will be the same as mine? Still, here are a few of mine, in case you feel like picking them up.

●

Giorgio de Chirico painted what he called "metaphysical town squares." They are full of exquisite renderings of shadow.

●

The intense colors of a Soutine. In fact, colors generally. Count them.

●

In volume five of *A la recherché du temps perdu*, the novelist Bergotte dies while standing in a gallery, looking at Vermeer's *View of Delft*. These are his last words: "That's how I ought to have written, my last books are too dry, I ought to have gone over them with a few layers of color, made my language precious in itself."

●

Just before a partial eclipse, the wind rises. And another thing happens, too: shadow bands (also known as flying shadows) appear, making the ground look like the bottom of a swimming pool.

●

Solar eclipse. The Nazca Lines in Peru. "Eye in the sky."

●

"The screen breaths mint"? A confessional box. A priest chewing gum.

●

From the *OED*:
Prone
a) ORIGIN. French prône, the grating or railing separating the chancel of a
    church from the nave, where notices were given and addresses delivered.

b) Ecclesiastical history. An exhortation or homily delivered in church. Also, prayers, exhortations, etc., attached to a sermon.

c) Adjective & adverb. Directed or sloping downward. Also loosely, descending steeply or vertically, headlong.

d) Facing downward; bending forward and downward; lying face downward or on the belly; spec. (of the hand or forelimb) with the palm downwards or backwards and the radius and ulna crossed. Later also loosely, lying flat.

●

From the *OED:*

Apse, Apsis

Astronomy: Either of the two points in the elliptical orbit of a planet or other body at which it is respectively nearest to and furthest from the primary about which it revolves. Architecture. A large semicircular or polygonal structure, often roofed with a semi-dome, situated esp. at the end of the choir, nave, or an aisle of a church.

●

A song by The Waterboys
C. S. Lewis. *Shadowlands*
A *Grief Observed*. Death

●

Acts 17:24: *God dwelleth not in temples made with hands.*

●

Acts 7:48: *Howbeit the most High dwelleth not in temples made with hands?*

●

DAVID FOSTER WALLACE 1962–2008

ACKNOWLEDGMENTS

Zora Neale Hurston: What Does *Soulful* Mean?" was originally conceived as an introduction for the Virago edition of *Their Eyes Were Watching God* and appeared subsequently in a revised version in *The Guardian*. "Middlemarch and Everybody" and "Hepburn and Garbo" were first published in *The Guardian*. "E. M. Forster: Middle Manager," "F. Kafka, Everyman" and "Two Directions for the Novel" were published in *The New York Review of Books*. "Speaking in Tongues" was given as the 2008 Robert B. Silvers Lecture at the New York Public Library and published in a revised version by *The New York Review of Books*. "That Crafty Feeling" was given as a lecture at Columbia University, commissioned by Ben Marcus, and later published in *The Believer*. A revised version appears here. "One Week in Liberia" was the fruit of a trip organized and funded by Oxfam. It was published by *The Observer*. "At the Multiplex, 2006" and "Notes on Oscar Weekend" were published by *The Sunday Telegraph*. "Accidental Hero" appeared in a short version in *The Sunday Telegraph* and appears in full here. "Smith Family Christmas" was commissioned by *The New York Times* and "Dead Man Laughing" was published by *The New Yorker*. "Rereading Barthes and Nabokov" began life as a lecture, given at Harvard University, although it has been revised so extensively almost nothing of the original remains.

I am grateful to my editors, Simon Prosser and Ann Godoff, and to my agent, Georgia Garrett, for all their efforts on my behalf over the past ten years. For the help and advice I received on individual essays I thank Devorah Baum, Tom Bissell, Mark Costello, Hadley Freeman, Bret Gladstone, Mary Karr, Lee Klein, Cressida Leyshon, Lee Rourke, Lorin Stein, Martina Testa, Adam Thirlwell and Sunil Yapa. Particular thanks to Bob Silvers for sending interesting books and projects my way, and for so many ingenious edits. Special thanks to Lysbeth Holdaway for her guidance in Liberia.

My greatest debt, as ever, is to Nick Laird, my best reader and fiercest editor. Your work on this book—and support of its author—were essential.

INDEX

death of, 240–42
  fatalism and pessimism of, 244, 245
  in World War II, 230–36, 240, 251
Smith, Luke, 227, 242
Smith, Perry, 199, 200
solipsism, 263, 267, 268, 272, 276, 281
Spielberg, Steven, 186, 187, 188
Spinoza, Baruch, 32, 35–36, 39, 41
Starks, Joe (char.), 5, 8, 11
Stewart, Jimmy, 151, 152, 155, 156, 159, 218,
  228
Stiller, Mauritz, 161, 162
Stop! Or My Mom Will Shoot (film), 185
Suddenly; Last Summer (film), 157
"Suicide as a Sort of Present" (Wallace), 295
Sunday Telegraph, 204
Sylvia Scarlett (film), 154–55
Syriana (film), 201–4
S/Z (Barthes), 49
Szymborska, Wislawa, 72, 91–92

Tapestry (album), 226–27
Taylor, Charles, 112, 121
text:
  codes in, 50
  indeterminacy of, 44, 48–49
  readerly, 49
  writerly, 49–50
Thalberg, Irving, 162
Their Eyes Were Watching God (Hurston), 3–13
Theron, Charlize, 210
"Think" (Wallace), 271
Thirlwell, Adam, 59–60, 61
Tolbert, William, 119, 121, 125
Tolstoy, Leo, 9, 54, 257
"Tractatus Logico-Philosophicus"
  (Wittgenstein), 267, 281
Tracy, Spencer, 154, 156–58
Traffic (film), 202, 203
Transamerica (film), 208–10
Treadwell, Timothy, 191–92
*Tremendous World I Have Inside My Head, The:
  Franz Kafka: A Biographical Essay* (Begley),
  58–59, 60n, 62, 63–64, 65, 66, 67, 68, 69
Trial, The (Kafka), 12n, 60, 62
"Triple Dream, The" (Lermontov), 54
"Tri-Stan: I Sold Sissee Nar to Ecko" (Wallace),
  285
True Whig Party, 119
Tsotsi (film), 207–8
Tubman, William, 119, 127
Turturro, John, 210–11
Two-Faced Woman (film), 164
Two Ronnies, 238

Unity Temple, 52

Valentino, Rudolph, 159
Valéry, Paul, 23

Vallon, Annette, 26
van den Broek, Hans (char.), 73, 74–75, 76–79,
  81–82, 83, 87
van den Broek, Rachel (char.), 73, 77, 78, 79
Van Eyck, Hubert, 54
vdokhnovenie (recapture), 49, 54
V for Vendetta (film), 205–7
Vincy, Fred (char.), 29, 30, 34, 35, 36, 37–38
Vincy, Rosamund (char.), 30, 31, 32, 33,
  35, 36
Virgil, 280
Visconti, Luchino, 168, 171–72, 173, 175, 176
Vitti, Monica, 173
vorstorg (initial rapture), 49, 54
Vyas, Nazrul Ram (char.), 87, 95

Wade, Aubrey, 115, 117, 121, 122, 123, 127, 130
Walker, Alice, 9n
Walk the Line (film), 189–91, 199
Wallace, David Foster, 33, 74, 85, 103, 255–97
  commencement speech of, 264–65
  difficulties of, 257, 258–59
  insistence on awareness in work of, 265,
    266–67
  Larkin's poetry and, 261–63, 264, 276
  linguistic specialization in work of,
    283–86
  MacArthur won by, 256, 281
  parables of, 280
  "self" in work of, 266–68, 270–71, 281,
    289
Wasteland, The (Eliot), 108
Watanabe, Ken, 180
"Water" (Larkin), 262
Waugh, Evelyn, 24–25, 28n, 103
Weil, Simone, 291, 292
Wells, H. G., 24, 25, 27
Werfel, Franz, 61n, 67
West Point, 114, 122, 123–24
"What I Believe" (broadcast), 26
Where Angels Fear to Tread (Forster), 17
White Teeth (Smith), 109
Wide Sargasso Sea (Rhys), 3
Wilcox, Henry (char.), 17, 22
Wilkerson, Mr., 136
Willesden, 133, 238
Wilton, Penelope, 112
Witherspoon, Reese, 190–91, 194
Wittgenstein, Ludwig, 248–49, 267–68, 281,
  282–83
Wodehouse, P. G., 24, 103
Women and Children Development Association
  of Liberia (WOCDAL), 121–22
Women Love Diamonds (film), 163
Woods, Vergible "Tea Cake" (char.), 6, 7, 10,
  12n, 13
Woolf, Virginia, 10, 15, 17, 23, 31, 103
Wordsworth, William, 18, 26–27, 217
World Is Not Enough, The (film), 182

World War II, 230–36, 240, 251
World Wildlife Fund, 123
Wrapped in Rainbows: The Life of Zora Neale Hurston (Boyd), 8n
Wright, Frank Lloyd, 4, 52
writers, writing:
  inspiration of, 49, 54
  pleasures of, 53
Wyllie, David, 71n

Yates, Richard, 93
Yeats, William Butler, 16
Yeoh, Michelle, 180, 181–82

"Yet Another Example of the Porousness of Certain Borders (XI)" (Wallace), 280
"You've Got a Friend" (song), 227, 229

Zaltzman, Andy, 250–51
Zellweger, Renée, 194
Zhang, Ziyi, 181
Zikeh, Nyan P., 125, 126, 127, 128–29
Zischler, Hanns, 187
Žižek, Slavoj, 82
Zora Neale Hurston: A Life Letters, 8n
Zurer, Ayelet, 187

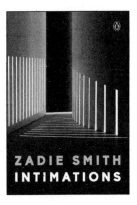

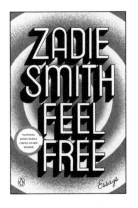

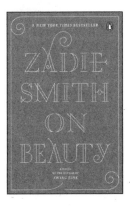
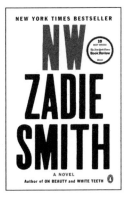
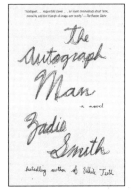
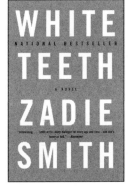